AF564584

E-Commerce
Concepts, Models and Strategies

E-Commerce
Concepts, Models and Strategies

Neha Arora

RANDOM PUBLICATIONS
NEW DELHI (INDIA)

E-Commerce Concepts, Models and Strategies

ISBN 978-93-5111-345-4

Published in 2014 in India by

Reprint 2020

RANDOM PUBLICATIONS
4376-A/4B, Gali Murari Lal, Ansari Road
New Delhi-110 002
Phone : +91-11-43580356, +91-11-23289044
e-mail: randomexports@gmail.com, sales@randompublications.com, info@randompublications.com

Type Setting by : Keystoneprintads, Delhi-110051
Printed at : Mehra Printers, Delhi-110 092

Preface

Electronic commerce or ecommerce is a term for any type of business, or commercial transaction, that involves the transfer of information across the Internet. It covers a range of different types of businesses, from consumer based retail sites, through auction or music sites, to business exchanges trading goods and services between corporations. It is currently one of the most important aspects of the Internet to emerge.

The buying and selling of products and services by businesses and consumers through an electronic medium, without using any paper documents. E-commerce is widely considered the buying and selling of products over the internet, but any transaction that is completed solely through electronic measures can be considered e-commerce. E-commerce is subdivided into three categories: business to business or B2B (Cisco), business to consumer or B2C (Amazon), and consumer to consumer or C2C (eBay). also called electronic commerce.

By definition e-commerce refers to businesses and consumers buying and selling products online. The majority of e-commerce websites on the internet are retail stores selling products directly to the public. However there are also a proportion of online stores dedicated to business-to-business (B2B) sales or wholesale activity. E-commerce does not only refer to the selling of physical products, it can also refer to the selling of services where payments for the services are made online.

Electronic commerce is generally considered to be the sales aspect of e-business. It also consists of the exchange of data to facilitate the financing and payment aspects of business transactions. This is an effective and efficient way of communicating within an organization and one of the most effective and useful ways of conducting business.

The book is of utmost importance to students, teachers, businessmen, traders and general readers.

I thank all members of my team who have helped in the preparation of the book. My special thanks go to "Random Publications" who have published the book.

—Neha Arora

Contents

1

The Nature of E-commerce

INTRODUCTION

Before looking at the legal detail and common pitfalls of e-commerce, we will initially consider the nature of e-commerce — what exactly is it? We will also look at some terminology that is frequently used by e-commerce lawyers and business people, always bearing in mind that what we are dealing with here is not the technology, but rather the way the law applies to the transactions that are undertaken using the technology. E-commerce (or electronic commerce) is the term used to denote a commercial (usually contractual) transaction that takes place between two or more people using the communications infrastructure known as the Internet.

The first thing to note is that there is a range of e-commerce transactions, the following of which are examples:

- The purchase by an individual of a book from a commercial website such as that run by Amazon.com
- The ordering by Company A of office stationery from Company B's website
- The exchange of e-mails between two persons whereby it is agreed that a certain service will be carried out by one party in exchange for a fee from the other.

We do not usually think of the latter type of transaction as falling within the category of e-commerce, but it is just as much an electronically formed contract as the other two examples: an exchange of e-mails can result in a legally binding contract. For example, if anyone send you an e-mail offering to sell you one dozen doughnuts, and you respond accepting my offer, this is just as much an e-commerce transaction as one taking place using the colourful pages and flash technology of the World Wide Web.

Initially it will be important for an e-commerce business to identify whether its e-commerce transactions will be classified as B2B (business-to-business) or B2C (business-to-consumer). This is because the law applies in a different way to each. Of course, it may be that the e-commerce business anticipates engaging in both types of transaction. The differences between these two types of transaction will be referred to throughout this Report. Other terms commonly referred to throughout this Report are as follows:

- World Wide Web — that part of the Internet which uses the Hyper Text Transfer Protocol (HTTP) to display so-called web pages and to allow links between such pages anywhere on the Internet.
- ISP (Internet Service Provider) a provider of Internet connectivity.
- ASP (Applications Service Provider) — an online provider of computer applications, such as software.

E-COMMERCE CONTRACTS

Virtually all commercial transactions are undertaken in the setting of a legally binding contract. Indeed, without the presence of such a contract the parties would generally be unwilling to perform their obligations (such as the delivery of goods, the performance of a service or the payment of money) under the transaction.

Contracts provide certainty as to the obligations of each party and, more importantly, a guarantee of the right to sue the non-performing party for breach. The law of contract dates back centuries, and has equal application to an ecommerce transaction as an offline contract. But the nature of an e-commerce transaction gives rise to some special problems that do not arise offline:

- Formation of the contract — for each party to have confidence that the performance of its obligations will have legal effect, it is of vital importance that the contract has actually been formed at the time of that performance. In the offline world the existence of a contract can be evidenced in many ways — such as a signature on a printed order form or a note of a conversation — that are not available in the online world.
- Incorporation of contractual terms — commercial transactions take place under a set of contractual rules. Usually these rules are set out in written form and will apply to the contract by virtue of being 'incorporated' within it.

  In the offline world terms are included in a contract by agreement. There is a considerable body of caselaw that describes how and why such terms will be incorporated. That caselaw may not, and indeed in some cases cannot, apply to online transactions.
- Non face-to-face transactions — e-commerce transactions, by their definition, take place electronically. The advantage of this is that the parties do not need to be in each other's presence at the time of formation of the contract.

  One disadvantage of this is that the law treats differently those contracts that are entered into between a business and a consumer 'at a distance' — the e-business must comply with a set of rules that do not generally apply to its offline competitors.

Formation of a Contract

It is generally well-known that a legally binding contract will arise where there is an offer to do something that is met by an unconditional acceptance of that offer. By way of example, where X offers to pay £250 for the delivery of a case of champagne to her home and Y agrees to perform that task for that sum of money, a contract is formed. To complicate matters, the law distinguishes an *offer* from an 'invitation to treat'. An *invitation to treat* is something that might appear to be an offer, but in fact is not.

An example is the display of goods in a shop window or on the shelf of a supermarket. It has long been decided that such displays are not offers and that therefore they cannot be 'accepted'. This is the rule that prevents a customer from being able to force a shopkeeper to sell goods to him at the displayed price, even where that price is clearly erroneous.

Whilst in the offline world it is easy to determine when a particular communication is an offer or an invitation to treat, such a distinction is unclear in a virtual transaction. Argos recently felt the effect of this when it mistakenly advertised televisions on its website with a price tag of £2.99 instead of £299. When several people placed orders for the televisions Argos realised its mistake and refused to supply the televisions at the price advertised.

One 'purchaser' sued the company for failure to deliver on the contract that she said had been created. The case was settled before it reached trial so we do not know what the judge would have decided. Although we can speculate that, in English law at least, a website is probably an invitation to treat as opposed to an offer, it would be wise for e-businesses to make clear the status of pricing and other information on their sites.

Incorporation of Terms

Of central importance to the e-commerce transaction are the terms and conditions on which the contract is based and by which it is governed. An e-business will always wish to trade on those terms that are favourable to it. For example, the business may wish to state that it is not to be held liable for late delivery of goods, or that its total liability for defective goods is to be limited to a certain monetary figure.

In most cases this will be done by the insertion of terms and conditions on the website and by making some reference to them during the contracting process. By completing the transaction the customers will effectively be binding themselves to those terms and conditions.

For the reasons mentioned above it is important for the terms and conditions of trade to form part of the contract. Without them we must rely on the 'default position' provided by the law and this is rarely ideal for a seller. The difficulty with e-commerce transactions is incorporating the terms into the contract is rarely a straightforward matter. There are various techniques, such as those listed below:

- Click-through with acceptance — here the customer is required to click on a button which says, 'I accept' or similar. This is the best position for the e-commerce business because the acceptance by the customer is clear and traceable. However, there is a perception that customers may be 'put off' by the need for this formality.
- Click-through without acceptance — the customer is required to scroll through the conditions but there is no acceptance button. Here there will be, at the very least, implied acceptance by the customer if they continue with the transaction after having scrolled through the terms and conditions.
- Reference with link—here the customer is referred to terms and conditions of trade but not forced to scroll through them. However, there is a link that will take the customer to the terms should they wish to see them. This is not ideal but may amount to 'incorporation by reference' under English law — this has not yet been tested by the courts in the context of online transactions.
- Reference without link—there is a reference to terms and conditions of trade but they do not appear on the site. Again this is an attempt at incorporation by reference. It is the least satisfactory method and is unlikely to have the desired effect in an e-commerce transaction as there is no reason why the terms and conditions could not appear somewhere on the website.

The legal formalities for online trading are expected to grow. The European Union, for example, has recently proposed several new laws which will govern e-commerce in the future. With this in mind, businesses would be wise to adopt a policy of requiring those persons they contract with online to click an 'acceptance button' to demonstrate their assent to the terms and conditions displayed on the website.

UNFAIR TERMS

E-businesses must be aware that since 1999 certain terms in their contracts with consumers will be void, i.e. unenforceable and of no legal effect. The Unfair Terms in Consumer Contracts Regulations 1999 apply, by definition, only to B2C contracts. For the purpose of the Regulations a 'consumer' is a person acting privately and not in the course of business. In contracts with such persons any unfair term is void. An 'unfair' term is one which, 'contrary to the requirements of good faith, causes a significant imbalance in the consumer's rights under the contract, to the detriment of the consumer'. Examples of terms that would be regarded as unfair under the Regulations include:

- Allowing the business to change the characteristics of goods or services offered without recourse to the consumer; and
- Allowing the business to terminate the contract without reasonable notice of such termination being given to the consumer.

THE DISTANCE SELLING REGULATIONS

A consumer who purchases goods or services from an e-commerce business is protected to a greater degree than a business purchaser is. It is important therefore, at an early stage, to determine whether the e-business will engage in B2B or B2C transactions.

In many cases of course the e-business will wish to trade with both businesses and individual customers. Where the e-business anticipates that part of its customer base will be individual consumers, the so-called 'Distance Selling Regulations' become relevant.

The Consumer Protection (Distance Selling) Regulations 2000 came into force on 31 October 2000.

They apply to contracts between a business and a consumer that are not 'face-to-face' e.g. contracts concluded by way of coupons in newspapers, 'teleshopping', and of course the Internet. The Regulations impose two main obligations on suppliers of goods or services.

The first is to provide certain information to the consumer. The second is to furnish the consumer with a 'cooling off' period of seven working days during which the consumer is able to return the goods to the e-business for a full refund.

It is interesting to note that a recent survey of all 235 UK websites listed on Yahoo!, offering goods in the publishing, music and computer hardware sectors, found that 92% of the sites gave incomplete or incorrect advice on the right to withdraw. About half contained key contractual information that was not clear or prominent.

Most of those companies would be shocked to be informed that after each online sale has taken place the customer could contact the business at any time within three months and request the business to collect the goods from them. The e-business would then be required to refund the purchase price to the customer, whether or not it decided to collect the goods.

The Information Requirements

In most cases the 'information requirements' in the Distance Selling Regulations can be satisfied by posting the appropriate information online.

The consumer must also be informed of any intention by the supplier to provide substitute goods if the goods ordered are not available, and of the fact that the supplier will meet costs of return of such substitute goods by the consumer to the supplier in the event of cancellation.

THE COOLING-OFF PERIOD

The requirement of a 'cooling-off' period for distance contracts puts e-commerce businesses at a disadvantage when compared with their offline competitors. For a consumer to be legally entitled to return goods purchased in the offline world (for example in a shop) for a full refund, they must prove that there is some defect in the goods or that the goods are not of satisfactory quality. The Regulations however allow an online purchaser to return goods within seven working days for a full refund, without obliging the purchaser to furnish any reason for doing so.

As far as the cooling off period is concerned, consumers must be given a period of seven working days, from the day after *receipt* of the goods, in which to change their mind. During that period the consumer has the right to return the goods to the e-commerce business for a full refund.

Crucially, if consumers are not informed of their right to cancel in this way, then the time period during which they have the right to cancel increases automatically to three months plus seven working days. Businesses should therefore be aware that their failure to inform consumers of the cooling-off period will effectively extend their potential liability to refund the purchase price by three months.

Excluded Contracts

The requirement to provide consumers with the above information, and to give a cooling-off period, does not apply to the following contracts:

- For the sale or other disposition of an interest in land except for a rental agreement
- For the construction of a building
- For financial services
- Contracts concluded by means of an automated vending machine
- Contracts concluded with a telecommunications operator by use of a public payphone
- Contracts concluded at an auction.

It should be remembered that the Distance Selling Regulations apply to contracts with consumers, but not to contracts with corporate and business customers. The information above must be stated clearly and concisely on the website — this may mean some changes to existing sites. Additionally, the cooling-off period does not apply to bespoke or tailor-made products. Any attempt to exclude the operation of the Regulations will have no legal effect.

WEBSITE LINKING AGREEMENTS

To date operators of websites have provided links from their own sites to those of third parties with little thought for the legal consequences. Several legal actions in recent months have shown that this carefree attitude to linking is not good business practice. In one case, involving the website of a Scottish newspaper, an e-business was sued for providing a link to a page within the site of the newspaper.

This practice, known as deep linking, was challenged on the basis that it allowed users access to the site without being required to travel via the homepage — it was the homepage on which revenue-generating advertising appeared. In a case by Stepstone, the recruitment site, an injunction was obtained in early 2001 that forced OFiR, a Danish media company, to remove links to Stepstone's site. Recently a view has emerged that a link from one website to another could infringe the database right in the linked-to site.

In any event, it seems that there is an emerging right for e-commerce businesses to control how users experience their sites, and a growing willingness by the courts to recognise such a right. E-commerce businesses should therefore consider, in appropriate circumstances, putting in place a written contract that sets out the obligations of the parties to a linking agreement. The contract should deal with the following issues:

- The link — consideration should be given as to how the link should be constructed, any technical requirements and where on the relevant web page the link should appear.
  If deep linking is to be allowed then the requirements and specifications for this should be set out. The contract should set out those circumstances in which the parties are able to sever the link.
- Intellectual property — even where a copy of part of the site is not made when the link is used (this would raise copyright issues), there may be use of the linked site's trade mark on the link itself. A licence to use all relevant Intellectual Property Rights should appear in the contract.
- Commission — sometimes the motivation for providing a link will be in receiving revenue as a result of users travelling to a third party site via the link.
  The commission arrangements should be clear in their terms — will commission be paid for example merely upon the site visit by a user or must the user first purchase goods from the site?
  There should be appropriate provisions for monitoring traffic such that commission can be verified and charged.
- Data protection — if there is to be a sharing of customer information between the linked sites then it must be clear that each site is to obtain the data protection consent of its customers for that transfer to be able to take place
- Database right — the contract should make it clear that the links envisaged by the agreement will not constitute infringement of the database right investment.

This book provides the objectives, drivers, and measures of e-commerce success.

From a perspective that we didn't have a few years ago, we can now analyse why certain approaches to e-commerce were destined to fail. The twelve industry cases provide an opportunity to examine both successes and failures and identify specific lessons learned. The guidelines set out here characterize the most successful actions of established e-commerce leaders, providing pertinent advice to senior managers in all segments, industries, and stages of e-commerce.

The dynamic model centered on these guidelines focuses on the key factors for corporate success in e-commerce integration. It includes the critical inputs and processes that lead to success in e-commerce (outputs), as measured by its contribution to overall corporate profitability (outcome). We see how a company that lacks significant e-commerce operations can become a company that uses e-commerce operations to significantly enhance its profitability.

A company's existing strategy, structure, and systems represent important inputs to the model, leading to processes through which a strong leader can transform all three to achieve e-commerce success. This book is grounded both in the latest academic and managerial research and in extensive research on company activities and experiences.

This book is written for the many large corporations that are reexamining the formulation and the implementation of e-commerce strategies and their level of investment in e-commerce. Its target is the large manufacturing, distribution, and service firms that would like to improve their return on e-commerce investments.

The processes begin with leadership in the formulation and implementation of a successful e-commerce initiative. Leadership starts with a commitment by the CEO and other senior managers to consider a significant role for e-commerce in the organization. The CEO should initiate a dialogue within the company on the changes necessary for a full-scale e-commerce effort. The CEO, along with other key executives, must examine the emerging role of e-commerce within the company's industry, ascertain its current position with respect to its competitors, and determine an appropriate level of investment.

Next, proven guidelines for e-commerce strategies permit the company to build on its position and quickly increase its online business activities. Though these strategies do represent some different options, successful e-commerce operations will likely incorporate all of them into its activities.

Senior managers must decide how to organize, finance, manage, and provide IT solutions for e-commerce. We encourage a perspective that looks at the various alternatives and generally propose a structure that leads to full integration of e-commerce throughout the fabric of the organization. The company should avoid the temptation of small benefits in one company segment in favour of the larger benefits of total or near-total integration.

Appropriate systems must also be implemented to ensure the successful integration of e-commerce. Corporate culture, performance and operational measures, and compensation systems must all be considered unique challenges.

Customer data management and demand and supply chain management are vital to maximizing the value of e-commerce. The introduction of changes to these systems may not have any deleterious effect on traditional commerce, but systems designed for traditional commerce may fail to provide proper management control for e-commerce.

DETERMINING E-COMMERCE ROLE AND INVESTMENT

Understanding competitive position is necessary but not sufficient to formulate the e-commerce strategy. Companies must also determine the appropriate role for e-commerce inside the company and the level of investment to be made. Thus, the external positioning must be supplemented with an internal analysis of company fit. The fit may be related to items such as organization structure, product type and mix, customer type and mix, channels, geographical breadth, and financial resources. Thus, every company utilizes e-commerce by directly selling goods or services on the Internet. Some find profitability in supply-chain management, procurement, marketing, and providing general information online.

That decision may become obvious before any significant strategic planning or may be determined after a fuller examination of the facts. But, a full examination of the broad opportunities must be completed and becomes an important input to the investment decision. Among the most important issues is the amount of resources to be committed to e-commerce. As companies examine reports of competitor investments, companies often question whether the size of their commitment is adequate.

Though the late 1990s saw some reckless spending on e-commerce without any justification of an ultimate payoff, current approaches to e-commerce require a carefully determined return on investment, as determined by a methodology. But, the investment must follow a serious commitment to an e-commerce strategy and should not waver with modest changes in either the technology or the business environment. For companies selling online, the geographic scope of sales efforts is also a consideration.

Selling overseas creates numerous challenges, many of which are known to traditional business but are complicated further by e-commerce. Demographics of Internet users, online payment mechanisms, online marketing, and patterns of online buyer behaviour all vary greatly by country and may present too many permutations for a nascent Internet venture to handle. A company may be understandably hesitant to begin global e-commerce immediately, even if its traditional business contains a global component. Some companies have chosen to limit the geographic scope of the venture until it has proven feasible and profitable on a domestic scale. The wisdom of such a limitation has been shown clearly in the case of grocery stores such as Tesco.

Among the geographic considerations for an e-commerce venture are:

- A Web site can be viewed from anywhere around the world. Companies should be equipped to handle such a change in market size, or be prepared to explain the reasons for necessary geographic limitations.
- Product type is a key factor in any geographic consideration. Customers have far different expectations when using the Internet to order computers than when ordering groceries.

PREPARING IMPLEMENTATION AND ALIGNING COMPANY CULTURE

Most laggard companies do not have the luxury of delaying the implementation of e-commerce until the company culture is sufficiently prepared. Instead, company leaders must constantly reinforce the importance of IT in order to build the appropriate culture for e-commerce. As their personal behaviour and attitudes often send the strongest messages, private behaviour must not undermine or contradict public statements about company commitment to e-commerce ventures.

Senior managers must reinforce the message that while technology itself is not a strategy, it remains a tool with strategic implications, and that the introduction of technology does not change the role of every contributor to the success of the company. Leadership must also choose the proper motivational tools, including incentives, coaching, and creating stretch targets.

For an e-commerce venture to be successful in a traditional company, senior managers must also impart a number of clear messages on company strategy and its value proposition. Instead of trying to create a unique culture for units handling the e-commerce venture, the company must create a culture conducive to integrating e-commerce throughout the company. Attitudes of either "the Internet changes everything" or "the Internet changes nothing" should be avoided, and a much more moderate position endorsed. Employees should not feel threatened or overwhelmed by the introduction of e-commerce.

The purpose of the e-commerce venture must also be carefully outlined to all employees, with a focus on the benefits of integration and the notion that e-commerce is typically a new channel for business, not a new business. People in each business unit must be apprised of the way e-commerce interacts with their current work and how best to develop that relationship to maximize integration benefits. At GE, this was achieved in the form of a company-wide initiative called Destroy Your Business, which required business units to analyse the impact and potential pitfalls of e-commerce on their business. Its associated programme, Grow Your Business, required units to formulate solutions to each of these problems.

Belief in the value of IT must be instilled throughout the organization, and resistance to IT generally, and to e-commerce specifically, must be handled through education that emphasizes the functionality of these endeavors and their importance to long-term corporate success. Training programs must ensure that everyone, especially those employees who directly interact with customers, understands basic e-commerce concepts. Senior management is not immune to these requirements and must lead by example in this area with both public statements and behaviour.

Finally, a sense of urgency must be created throughout the organization, and business decisions should reflect that urgency. The pace of e-commerce is faster than that of traditional commerce, and easing into an e-commerce venture is not a promising strategy. In all areas that impact e-commerce, aggressiveness should be rewarded, and the value of speed should often supplant cost considerations.

Many of these considerations must be addressed by specific changes in the company's systems and business processes, but the CEO should be prepared to create this orientation long before strategy implementation begins. Without strong leadership in the early stages, the changes in systems will be too drastic to implement the e-commerce strategy in a timely manner.

Thus, to create a proper culture for e-commerce, companies must recognize that:

- Attitudes are as important as company policies regarding e-commerce. Company leaders must not only work to make an e-commerce venture a success, but show that they actually believe in the venture.
- E-commerce should be treated as a new channel for business, not as a revolution for the company. Employees need to be encouraged to embrace e-commerce instead of fearing it.
- The goals of the e-commerce venture need to be clearly outlined for everyone in the company.
- Aggressiveness in e-commerce should be rewarded.

E-commerce represents a major transformation, and the general principles of organizational change management are as applicable as advice specific to e-commerce. John Kotter's organizational change model provided a general framework for the consideration of how to approach significant change in business. As one can see, it can be easily adapted to the challenge of the changes necessary in the implementation of an e-commerce strategy.

ARCHITECTURE OF E-COMMERCE SYSTEMS

The buying and selling of products and services over the Internet is termed 'online trading'. Online trading or e-Commerce is important to businesses because it provides a flexible source of trading with customers, and with business partners.

To enable online trading, companies need to combine existing computerized transaction processing systems and information systems with Internet and Web technology. Existing computerized systems, databases, and Internet and Web technology are the basic components of online trading and form the architecture of e-Commerce systems. Computer system architecture consists of hardware and software components that are configured in terms of the needs of organizations.

Companies connect computers to a LAN, WAN and the Internet, using TCP/ IP, based on client-server architecture, to share computer software, printers or scanners. Basic Internet tools such as e-mail, browsers, search engines and protocols such as file transfer protocol (FTP) and Telnet are combined to form the system architecture for e-Commerce. The systems architecture for a company will depend on its trading activities. A retail company will have a different architecture from a manufacturing company or a service company. As a company changes and evolves its mission or objectives, its e-Commerce system architecture will need to change too. Alternatively, the stimulus to change may come from competitors who use the most modern e-Commerce technology.

INTERNET, E-COMMERCE SYSTEMS AND INFORMATION SYSTEMS

Some of the terms used to describe a company's involvement with the Internet are that it has 'an online presence' or it has 'a Web site'. Such terms hide the complex IT and IS that form the infrastructure that underpin e-Commerce systems.

An information system is the application of a computer to capture and process data to provide information for managers and executives for the purposes of decision making and management. A company will normally have various information systems, such as an airline reservation system or an inventory control system.

These systems will be linked to a corporate database that stores relevant data, like product or customer details. A company's Web site is connected to such information systems and databases to provide the essential product or service information for customer and employee use.

Companies' existing client-server technology and its IS/IT infrastructure is connected to the Internet to form part of an e-Commerce architecture. The e-Commerce architecture is based on a company's business model, consisting of the basic logic of what it wants to produce or sell, how it will market it, how it defines its customers and other fundamental business issues. IT is combined with Internet technology to enable a company to personalize its service to a customer.

DATABASES

A computer database consists of records on specific items of interest, for example customers' contact details or the products they have bought. It is a collection of data that can be queried for specific purposes such as targeting a particular customer for certain products. Databases are used to market products and services. This is termed *database marketing*. Databases are used to store data on the purchasing habits of customers and enable a company to develop a tailored relationship with its customers.

The data are then processed to provide tailored information on individual customers' preferences that are then sent information about products or services relevant to their current buying habits. Data-mining techniques are used to reprocess existing data in databases to extract previously unrealized information of potential commercial use.

E-COMMERCE SYSTEMS AND THE CUSTOMER

e-Commerce systems that interface with the customer need to be pragmatic. The selection and evaluation of Internet technology need to be appropriate to both the company's needs and the customer's ability to use the system. A good business model will assume that the customer has little interest in technology and avoid the technology trap. *Avoiding the technology trap.*

It is not user-friendly to use over-complex Internet and Web technology in e-Commerce systems. The technology needs to be appropriate to prevent prolonging the time it takes for customers' commands to be executed by the system.

WEB SITE EVALUATION SOFTWARE

It is possible to measure the popularity of a company's Web site using evaluation software that generates log files. Such log files record the number of visitors to the site or page impressions.

They record which parts of the Web site are most popular, the times of the day people visit, record which search engines are being used by visitors and how long they spend on the site, known as the 'stickiness' of the site. These log files can subsequently be used to evaluate the performance of the site from a business perspective and the information can be used to make it easier for customers to make transactions.

INTERNET SERVICE PROVIDERS

A company wanting to trade over the Internet has to agree a contract with an Internet service provider (ISP). ISPs provide communication and hosting services for individuals and companies wanting to access the Internet. ISPs provide access to the Internet and enable Internet commerce by connecting individuals and companies to the Internet.

There are thousands of ISPs that a company can choose from, all of them providing domain name services and electronic mail. The two most popular ISPs are UUNET Technologies and AT&T World Net. Other organizations, like a bank with mainframe computers, may also act as an ISP.

ISPs also provide hosting services for Web sites by installing and operating the server computers and software for a company. The computers and software are located at the ISP's site. Transaction services such as payment systems or order capture and fulfilment are also provided by ISPs.

EXAMPLE OF E-COMMERCE ARCHITECTURE

The important considerations for designing e-Commerce architecture are the customer, the company, the company's existing information systems and how payment will be made. For example, a company with a Web site that includes an order form would need a Web server that can provide a catalogue, whose details would be retrieved from a catalogue database, and order form. It would need to interface with an existing database to collect and record the order details entered by the customer. The payment might be transacted with a credit card whose details would be captured on the order form utilizing standard security features available on the Web.

This example shows that an e-Commerce system is composed of existing information systems, databases and Internet technology. Other sophisticated e-Commerce architectures are possible for companies that need distributed transaction processing. For example, the Open Buying Consortium (OBI) has proposed a system architecture consisting of six fundamental system components split into buy-side, the customer and sell-side activities. These components are: Browse, Request, Approve, Fill, Receive and Pay.

E-COMMERCE SECURITY TECHNOLOGY

The success of e-Commerce depends on the security of data like personal details and credit card numbers transmitted over the Internet. The domain name system Internet protocol that makes IP addresses readable by humans is insecure. Security measures need to be taken in e-Commerce systems to prevent compromising the systems. Some of these measures include building firewalls, incorporating cryptography and authentication, and using secure connections.

Firewall

A firewall is hardware and software that are used to secure a private computer network system from uninvited intruders. A firewall is used to control whether a client is permitted to connect to the private network it protects.

Cryptography

Cryptography is a science that provides secure communication over vulnerable channels. Cryptography is fundamental to the success of the Internet and e-Commerce. Governments regulate cryptographic technology because of its importance to national security. In cryptography a message, like a credit card number, is encrypted using a key and the encrypted message is transmitted. The receiver uses the key to decrypt the message and convert it back to its original form.

The basic elements of a cryptographic system are algorithms, protocols and key management. An example of key management is the secret-key encryption algorithms. These algorithms are 'secret' because only the receiver and sender know the secret key. Cryptography is used to provide secure transmission of data over the Internet. Private data like credit card details or digital signatures are encrypted and then transmitted over the Internet. Cryptography can keep a message secret and act as a gateway for identifying senders and receivers. It provides the secure electronic transaction technology for credit card transactions on the Internet.

Authentication

Authentication procedures are used to establish the identity of an individual or another computer system. Authentication procedures can be hardware-or software-based. Authentication procedures make use of personal items of knowledge or possession such as secret names or birth dates. Good authentication systems make use of two-factor authentication, such as a place name and memorable date known to the user. Some banking systems make use of three-factor authentication before allowing customers to make online account transfers.

Secure Socket Layer

The secure socket layer (SSL) is a layer of security between the application and the transport protocol. The purpose of SSL is to enable secure and reliable data transmission and communication over the Internet. The SSL provides private connection, making use of encryption and secret-key cryptography.

Authentication in SSL is achieved using public-key cryptography, which consists of a private key that is never made public chosen by one participant in the data exchange, and a public key chosen by the other participant in the exchange. Either key may be used for encryption. Reliability of data transmission is achieved by using secure hash functions like SHA or MD5. Secure hash functions check the integrity of a message. SSL is commonly used in e-Commerce systems.

FUTURE DEVELOPMENTS IN E-BUSINESS TECHNOLOGY

THE INTERNET

Just as the internal combustion engine (the motor car) and jet engine (aeroplane) have radically changed our lives, the Internet is beginning to do the same. In the short time of its existence the Internet has greatly affected business and society. The Internet's evolution and future development are set to continue.

The TCP/IP protocol is evolving with the development of IPv6, the next generation of the Internet protocol. The improvements in IPv6 are scalability, security and support for real-time media quality. Companies such as Ciena Corporation are working on improving bandwidth. They have a product called Wave Division Multiplexing (WDM) that moves data at the speed of 100 billion bits per second (100,000,000,000 b.p.s.). This contrasts with the standard modem's 36,600 b.p.s.

THE WORLD WIDE WEB

The Web's HTTP protocol is evolving to encompass better performance and flexible interactions between clients and servers. Companies compete in complex and increasingly competitive markets. They do so by following, for example, competitive strategies of product differentiation or cost reduction. Similarly, *relationships* are becoming increasingly important in business models. Current developments in Web technology are best placed to enable companies to exploit their differences and build personal relationships with customers, suppliers or business partners. For example, the eXtensible Mark-up Language, the Semantic Web and other Internet developments are leading the way to providing tailoring capability in e-Business technology.

Extensible mark-up Language

The extensible mark-up language (XML) is gaining popularity over HTML with companies. XML offers companies the ability to define tags that uniquely describe their products, services or customer service culture. Companies can design XML tags to display price or product or service descriptions that cannot be done in HTML. In short, XML allows a company to tailor the feel and look of its Web site and order forms to its needs.

The Semantic Web

Semantic Web is the name given to developments in Web technology by the World Wide Web Consortium (W3C), headed by Tim Berners-Lee, who invented the Web. The Semantic Web enables communication of contextual data and information. Information makes sense to humans only when it is used in context. The Semantic Web enables such context to be captured in Web applications. The primary contribution of the Internet, the Web and associated technologies is to enable collaboration and sharing of information and knowledge among people.

The types of collaboration are numerous, ranging from intra-organizational to inter-organizational and across the boundary of the organization with the customer. Future technology development will focus on this collaborative aspect of e-Commerce and will lead to radically different organizational structures and patterns of interaction among and between businesses and their customers.

E-MAIL MARKETING CAMPAIGN

- Acquire e-mail addresses (e.g. of people who have registered to receive information)
- Obtain permission to use the e-mail address for marketing. This is best done at the time of collection, e.g. registration or free samples may only be possible if the respondent checks the 'yes' box
- Select the addresses to target for the particular message
- Execute the campaign (possibly in conjunction with other communications channels)
- Respond to customer replies
- Correct and clean the e-mail list
- Track and measure the campaign performance.

Short Message Systems (SMSs) and Multimedia Messaging Services (MMSs)

While mobile phones and other mobile devices can be useful for 'distress' purchases such as paying a congestion charge (to drive into a city), the growth of m-commerce has been slow, even since the introduction of 3G. Nevertheless, even though it represents a small proportion of marketing budgets, advertising via *short message systems (SMSs)* and *multimedia messaging services (MMSs)* achieves high response rates.

Because of this, spending on mobile advertising has been predicted to rocket to £6 billion over the next year or two. Mobile advertising is growing in popularity not just because of the high response, but also because mobile Web users represent an attractive demographic, with the majority being males aged 20-39 with incomes over £30,000. They are well segmented as a target for games, gambling and travel services - currently the biggest mobile advertising categories.

For example, in the US, the marketing agency Mobliss has launched Snow Report (www.mysnowreport.com). Customers who have registered their interests can receive text messages detailing snow conditions at winter sports resorts. Recipients of the message can follow a link for a travel package to the resort. As with e-mail, the key to success is opt-in, with customers giving permission for these marketing activities when they register for the information service.

Viral Marketing

Viral marketing is growing as more companies use it to promote and brand their products and services. For example, the low-budget horror movie *The Blair Witch Project* owed worldwide success to a vast volume of 'word of mouse' recommendations passed around Internet chat rooms. These campaigns are becoming more sophisticated with tracking of open, click-through and success rates.

A potential problem with viral marketing campaigns is that the company is reliant on each individual in the chain to have permission to send such messages to each recipient. In many cases this is not done: viral marketing spreads much spam. The responsible marketer will be using tracking systems that can be used for follow-up of sample recipients to ensure that they do not object to such communications.

As an example of *opt-out* viral marketing, consider the hypothetical way that this book could be promoted. Prospects may initially receive an information-only message, for example an invitation to a marketing conference, ending with something along the lines of: Please forward this message to anyone else who may be interested. In the future we may want to inform you of other services and products in which we think you may be interested. If you do not wish to receive such messages, please contact the sender to be removed from the list.

Banners, pop-ups and Interstitials *

Online advertising expenditure on media such as banners and pop-ups is growing and has reached well over £150 million per year (£30 million more than cinema advertising, for example). The interstitial a pop-up that interrupts browsing to show an ad - is a much more active form of advertising than banners. Some people using the Web for a specific purpose find these irritating, though. Online advertising company RealMedia (www.uk.realmedia.com) is using a less-intrusive system called adPointer. This generates an ad when the cursor has not moved for a specific time.

Schemes that incentivize users to look at advertisements have been around for some years, but in the UK Bananalotto.com (www.bananalotto.com) has raised the stakes by offering the chance to win one million pounds as you click the banner ad. KPE, the media and entertainment consultancy, has developed around ten games for their clients. Managing Director Paul Zwillberg says:

This section is summarized and adapted from Marketing Business e-business supplement So much of the Internet has been characterised by repurposing things that worked well in print or TV. 'Advergaming' is... a new combination that's made for the medium.... You take one of the most popular uses of interactive content and marry it with tried and tested advertising models like brand association, trial or data capture and you get something really wonderful.

Customer Relationships

The direct mail and e-mail activities described above are part of the management of customer relationships. Building on these basic communication tools, the most successful e-retailers such as Amazon (www.amazon.com) and Tesco (www.tesco.com) use various techniques of data mining, personalization and customization. For example, Amazon customizes the web page, making offers for new books, music or movies that are likely to be of interest based on past purchase patterns. Tesco likewise personalizes its communi-cations and special offers almost down to the level of the individual. These e-retailers are thus able to satisfy customers more specifically and therefore are better using the customer relationship and data mining tools.

Web Atmospherics

Web atmospherics is too important and complex a topic for this single section, in greater depth. Briefly, atmospherics includes *visual* (e.g. text, design, colour management, video clips, 3-D), *aural* (e.g. music or sound effects) and *olfactory* (e.g. perfume and samples) stimuli. The Edmunds (www.edmunds.com) car sales site is a good example of the use of exciting downloads of video and sound effects to illustrate cars in action. With effects like this, there is a need to avoid long download times (e.g. by having a separate 'click here for broadband' version for the larger memory effects). Perfume is available by e-retail, although most suppliers rely on description and well-known brands, rather than offering samples, for example Perfumania (www.mydesign erperfume.com): 'Contains citron, rose, jasmine and is accented with honeysuckle, vanilla and oakmoss making Allure by Chanel perfect for romantic use'. Atmospherics, even when fairly low-tech, have much to offer in communications mix design.

Link Popularity

Search engines use 'link popularity' in locating and ranking sites. Improving link popularity by persuading other sites to link to yours raises a site in search-engine rankings and is therefore a critical aspect of the communications mix.

Case Study: EBAY.CO.UK

The eBay site was founded in the US in 1995, originally under the name Auctionweb. The UK site was launched in 1999, growing after a slow start to become the UK's top e-commerce site measured by monthly audience numbers, with 6.8 million people (compared with Amazon's 6.1 million and Tesco's 2.7 million). In the year to March 2003, eBay's audience increased by 160 per cent, compared to Amazon's 28 per cent. Internet growth overall was only 7 per cent.

The figures are 'a significant sign of the potential of [the most profitable and successful Internet players] to sell to consumers', according to Nielsen/ NetRatings (www.nielsen-netratings.com), who supplied the figures. Cheap though most individual products may be, eBay still sells over £1 billion of them per year.

If eBay were considered to be an e-retailer, this would make them number one in UK market share. While many dot.coms are mainly hype, eBay is profitable, making a quarter of a billion dollars on worldwide operations in 2001. It survived the dot.com crash relatively unscathed and the share price rose from US$18 in 1998 to US$110 by 2003.Visitors to eBay spend an average of 1 hour and 11 minutes per month on the site - one of the longest of any UK site.

Visitors return to the site to check the status of items they are bidding for or selling and ebay.co.uk is one of very few e-retailers to achieve over a billion pages views per month. Many UK users are earning a healthy living as 'power sellers', taking advantage of the worldwide market to offer everything from sports utility vehicles (SUVs) to comics, records and oddments like garden gnomes, T-shirts and kettles. In the same way as the major bricks retailers are suffering increasing competition from charity shops and car-boot sales, so the established e-retailers face growing competition from online auctions. Most sellers are private individuals.

For example, Pat Austin makes £30,000 per year selling an assortment of bric-a-brac that she finds in charity shops, car-boot sales and physical auctions. She sells 1,000+ items per year and 99.9 per cent of her transactions have been positive. It is a full-time job, though, with correspondence and despatch taking up the mornings and sourcing goods the afternoons. Rosie English has a turnover of £100,000+ selling high-class women's fashion for prices of £100 to £1,000+.

She reads the fashion press to identify what editors recommend and what celebrities are wearing, then buys from sample and factory sales or direct from designers. However, eBay is not all one-person businesses, as the 'big boys' are seeing the opportunities and joining in with companies like Dell, Dixons and Sears using eBay to shift excess stock. It's a case of 'buyer beware', as auction sites do not take responsibility for deals that go wrong and offer only low insurance cover for losses. The way for buyers to identify the most reliable sellers is from feedback ratings - many regular sellers have hundreds of positive ratings.

PAYMENTS THROUGH M-COMMERCE

Using a mobile network device to make a payment is often referred to as a *micro-payment*. Depending upon the mobile device and available networks in the geographic region, a consumer has the option of making a micropayment in one or all of these modes:

- *Short Message Service (SMS) charges* The consumer keys in the SMS number that is assigned to the merchandise to be purchased and a charge appears on the billing consumer's account where SMS charges are normally listed. For example, some Coca-Cola beverage vending machines accept traditional coin payments and also display the SMS number for the particular machine. The beverage buyers call the SMS number from their own mobile device and, once the vending machine receives the SMS signal, the consumer may select the beverage to be dispensed. The charge for the beverage appears on the consumer's next SMS bill.
- *Direct charge billing to the account linked to the consumer's mobile device* Mobile network devices today are fitted with facilities to transmit data to another computerized device in close proximity without making a telephone call. These data transmission facilities range from inferred (IR) beams, Bluetooth and Wi-Fi transmissions. The owner of the mobile device transacts the purchase sequence as they would do traditionally, that is, select the merchandise to be purchased and take it to the sales counter/ checkout for payment. The only difference is that, instead of payment by cash, EFTPoS (Electronic Funds Transfer Point of Sale) or credit card, the mobile device owner transmits the account details using one of the data transmission facilities noted above.

Similar to the already described Coca-Cola SMS purchases, India's BPL mobile customer may send a message to 2233, which will be displayed on the LCD panel of the vending machine.

The vending machine confirms the customer's mobile number, then asks for the choice of chocolate and, once selected, dispenses the chocolate. Finally, the customer receives an SMS confirming the transaction. The vending transaction cost is debited from a pre-paid card or added to the monthly bill of a post-paid customer.

- *Using a clearing house service* Intermediaries allow for payment authorities on behalf of the customer to pay for merchandise. One group, the Mobile Payment Services Association, is a coalition between Spain's Telefonica Moviles SA, Germany's T-Mobile AG and Britain's Orange SA and Vodafone Group PLC. The system of making payments through a mobile communications device is often referred to as a micropayment.

Micropayments

M-shopping-enabled technology permits the shopper to make payments in a variety of situations that may be grouped as:

- *Unmanned point of sale equipment,* i.e. food and beverage vending machines, parking meters, public transport ticketing systems.
- *Manned shopping counters,* i.e. fast food and beverage providers.
- *Full-time cellular phone merchant connections,* i.e. SMS and WAP sites that automatically take payments by way of a cellular phone account rather than needing to enter credit card details.

The benefits of micropayment to retailers include:

- Billing the accounts linked to the mobile devices, e.g. the cellular phone does not carry the charges associated with the transfer of credit card funds.
- Reduced need to provide customers with change for vending machines.
- Bill fraud is reduced. When a mobile device is stolen, the communications carrier usually disables network access for that device and so it cannot be used to make further micropayments.
- Extends the frequency of impulse purchases for items of small value.

The benefits of micropayment to the mobile consumer include:

- Reduced dependence upon carrying cash and credit cards.
- Record of purchase appears on the account attached to the micropayment, e.g. cellular phone account.

PROFILING THE M-SHOPPER

The mobile shopping environment is still in its emergent stage of retailer development and shopper adoption. For retailers to tailor their market offering to the needs of the mobile shoppers, we should profile the current and intended adopters of m-shopping. As a contributor to this profiling we have incorporated the wireless shopping research of Fenech (2002, 2003). *Buying behaviour* Such individuals are frugal, enjoy shopping and take up new shopping facilities when they become available.

In summary they are:

- Buying impulsive;
- Highly desirous of shopping convenience;
- Innovative in shopping;
- Positive in their attitude towards non-store marketing;
- Positive in their attitude towards shopping;
- Price conscious;
- Seekers of variety.

Use of mobile communication technology This individual already uses the functionality of their mobile technology; this is demonstrated by:

- Frequently Sending SMSs.

Shopping and communication environment This shopper is confident in the parties that contribute to the shopping process and desires the convenience of m-shopping. In summary they:

- Desire the convenience of mobile phone shopping;
- Enjoy mobile phone shopping;
- Have a low concern of financial risk from visited Web retailer;
- Have a low concern of privacy risk from ISP;
- Are satisfied with mobile phone carrier.

As surprising as the concept of Web-based e-retailing was in 1996, the concept of mobile shopping far from a phone jack or retailer must also be surprising in the beginning of this new millennium. Fortunately, we have already seen the benefits of e-retailing and this should significantly shorten the adoption rate of m-shopping.

THE WORLD OF E-RETAILING E-RETAIL

The business of *e-retail* has been defined as the sale of goods and services via Internet or other electronic channels, for personal or household use by consumers. This definition includes all e-commerce activities that result in transactions with end consumers (rather than business customers), i.e. *B2C* rather than *B2B*. Some e-marketing activities that do not directly involve transactions, such as providing (free) information or promoting brands and image, are considered to be part of B2C but are not normally considered as being within the scope of e-retail.

Despite the *dot.com crash* of 2000, e-retailing has been growing, particularly for the 'top eight' categories that account for three-quarters of all European sales. These major growth areas comprise: books, music and *DVD* movies, groceries, sex products, games and software, electronic and computer equipment, travel, and clothes.

DISADVANTAGES OF E-RETAILING FOR RETAILERS

Retailers have been slow to take up e-retailing. This is to some extent understandable in the light of many disadvantages and problems. Retailers, for example, may lack the technical know-how, the substantial investment required or the order fulfilment capabilities. Set-up costs start from around £20,000 for a small site and up to £500,000 for a large operation ($A53,000 to $A1.4 million).

And set-up costs are only the start - Datamonitor estimates that high street retailers are spending more on ongoing costs than on setting up new sites. A continuous cost will be fulfilment and logistics. Successful e-retailers such as Next and Land's End have had the advantage of already operating profitable mail-order catalogues.

There can be legal problems. For example, if purchaser and supplier are in different countries, there may be conflict between the laws and taxation of the two countries. In Europe, the *VAT (Value Added Tax)* position is still unclear, but Richard Branson's Virgin group's e-retail operation is registered in Madeira, the country with the lowest VAT rate in the European Union (EU).

A further disadvantage is that e-selling is less powerful than face-to-face selling (it is easier to say 'no' to a computer). This viewpoint is linked to a concern of traditional high street retailers that e-retailing offers a diminished role for their expertise. For example, there are obvious difficulties with products sold by 'atmosphere' - touch, feel, smell - and impulse purchases.

In addition, consumers have a perception of lower prices online. This puts pressure on margins for e-retailing, and can lead to shoppers expecting consistent low prices in-store. Finally, aftercare can be difficult, especially if the shopper is overseas.

DISADVANTAGES OF E-RETAILING FOR RETAILERS

- May lack know-how and technology
- Substantial set-up, investment and ongoing costs
- Complex logistics of fulfilment
- e-Selling less powerful than face-to-face - uptake slow for goods selected by taste or smell
- Fewer impulse purchases
- Legal problems
- Lesser role for traditional high street retail expertise
- Pressure on margins and prices in-store
- After-sales care difficulties

ADVANTAGES OF E-RETAILING FOR RETAILERS

On the other hand, there are a number of advantages for retailers. First, location is unimportant. According to some textbooks, adapting an old saying, the three most important elements in *retail* are 'location, location and location'. The best high street locations are therefore expensive. The e-retailer, though, can sell equally well to anywhere in the country and even overseas. Second, size does not matter - small e-retailers can compete on equal terms to large ones, can reach a larger audience than the high street and can be open 24 hours a day. For example, the independent, northern UK-based Botham's of Whitby has been a pioneer of e-retailing.

There are many other advantages. The socio-demographic profile of e-shoppers is attractive to many retailers, with higher-than-average education, employment and disposable income levels. In theory at least, online selling saves on the wages costs of face-to-face sales people and the costs of premises. The savings may be less than expected, though, as there are still costs in Internet customer contact, and packaging and delivery can be more expensive to provide.

Perhaps a more substantial advantage is the ease with which e-retailing integrates with *customer relationship management (CRM)* and micro-marketing systems - identifying and treating the customer as an individual. This, together with the easier provision of product information, leads to greater opportunities for cross-selling and selling up. Finally, the late entrants into e-retailing are largely being driven by 'if we don't, our competitors will'.

ADVANTAGES OF E-RETAILING FOR RETAILERS

- Location is unimportant
- Size does not matter
- Saves on the wages and premises costs
- Reaches a larger audience
- Higher disposable income profile than average
- Accepts orders 24 hours a day
- More opportunities for CRM, micro-marketing, cross- and up-selling
- If we don't, our competitors will

Other retailers, though, are put off e-retailing by what they perceive as consumer resistance. According to e-research company Forrester, nearly 40 per cent of UK homes are now connected to the Internet, but estimates vary from only 12 per cent (Verdict) up to 20 percent (Forrester) of UK adults shopping online. This contrasts with the faster take-up of e-business for B2B, with 25 per cent of businesses ordering online.

THE (E-)RETAIL MIX: SALE THE 7CS

The (e-)retail mix is a shorthand term for the blend of tools and techniques that (e-)retailers use to provide value for customers. It is a development of the well-known marketing mix, more specific to retail and e-retail. As far back as the first half of the twentieth century, the job of the marketer was described as a 'mixer of ingredients'. Marketers devise strategies and tactics aimed at providing satisfaction and adding value for customers. The various elements are blended into a 'marketing mix' - a phrase first coined by Neil Borden (1964) of Harvard Business School.

The marketing mix is most widely known as E. Jerome McCarthy's (1960) '4Ps': Place, Product, Price and Promotion. 'Place' is not quite self-explanatory, but refers to the routes that organizations take to get the benefits of the product or service to the intended customers - channels of distribution. Product' means both tangible product and also 'service', and all the ways that an organization adds value. 'Price' means not just the price charged, but also all aspects of pricing policy, including, for example, distributor margins. 'Promotion' is not just the more specialized 'sales promotion', but also every way that a product is promoted to customers - from print advertising to websites.

In recent decades there have been numerous attempts to update and revise the marketing mix. One development is particularly descriptive of the way that marketers think about the customer. The '4Cs' imply more emphasis on customer wants and concerns than do the 4Ps. The 4Cs (in the same order as the equivalent 4Ps listed above) are: Convenience for the customer; Customer value and benefits; Cost to the customer; and Communication. Reflecting the emphasis of 'new' marketing on long-term relationships with customers, we include 'Customer relationships' within the umbrella of the 'Communication' C.

C1 Convenience for the Customer

'Place' (from the 4Ps), rather than implying management's methods of placing products where they want them to be, can be thought of as 'Convenience for the customer', recognizing customers' choices for buying in ways that are convenient to them. For the retailer, 'Place' incorporates what can be the most critical decisions concerning 'location'. For the e-retailer, this is also important, as many customers prefer a multi-channel approach: browse on the Web, buy in-store or vice versa - or buy on the Web, return to the store for a refund! This perhaps goes some way towards explaining the success of *high street* and *multi-channel retailers* in e-retail, as compared to the 'pureplays'.

Physical location can also be important for the e-retailer as many customers prefer to buy from, or are more likely to trust, an e-retailer based at least in the same country, where carriage costs and maybe taxes are cheaper. Location' for the e-retailer also means virtual location and the ease of finding the website. This entails registration with search engines, location in e-malls and links from associates. Convenience also includes key aspects of website design, such as navigation, layout and ease of purchase. For the '*bricks*' retailer, convenience decisions include shelf space allocation and layout. The equivalent in 'clicks' e-retail is site design and page layout - for example, whether layout follows the 'free-flow' or 'grid' type of layout, or indeed a combination such as 'free-grid'.

C2 Customer Value and Benefits

'Product', rather than being something that a company has to sell, can be thought of as 'Customer value and benefits' - meaning the bundle of service and satisfactions wanted by customers. People do not buy 'products' as such, but rather solutions to problems or good feelings. Retailers and e-retailers now specify (and sometimes design) products to a much greater extent than previously, reflecting closeness to the customer and appreciation of benefits that customers want.

An essential task of retail and e-retail is selecting the range of products offered for sale - assembled for target markets from diverse sources. The wide and deep range that can be offered is one of the areas where the clicks e-retailer can score relative to the bricks retailer.

When buying online, customers are far less likely to request help than they are in the store. Rather, e-shoppers who need help in understanding a product are more likely to abandon the transaction and find an alternative supplier or even buy through a different channel. Therefore, e-businesses need to be particularly careful about describing products clearly in customer value and benefits terms.

C3 Cost to the Customer

'Price' may be what companies decide to charge for their products, but 'Cost to the customer' represents the real cost that customers will pay, including, for example, in the case of bricks retail, their own transport costs. For clicks e-retail, there are also the costs of carriage and perhaps taxes to be added to the quoted prices. High carriage charges may be one reason for the high rate of carts abandoned at the checkout. Customers also need to consider the costs of Internet and telephone access.

Consumers have a perception that prices should be lower online than in-store, and this can cause problems when customers buying via other channels realise that they are paying more than online customers. For example, Screwfix, a well-known supplier of tradesperson's supplies via paper catalogue and telesales, has a number of attractive special offers available only online.

Customers who have looked up what they want online, then telephone to order, can be irritated to learn that the extra discounts are not available when ordering by phone.

C4 Communication and Customer Relationships

'Communication' is equivalent to the final 'P' in the 4Ps: 'Promotion'. Promotion suggests ways in which companies persuade people to buy, whereas communication is a two-way process also involving feedback from customers to suppliers. Reflecting an increasing control of elements of the retail mix by retailers rather than manufacturers, retailers spend more on advertising than manufacturers do (assisted by advertising allowances from manufacturers). Retailers are closer to the customer than are manufacturers and have more access to customer feedback. Communication is not just advertising, though, but all the ways in which retailers communicate with their customers, including, for example, marketing research surveys, public relations (PR), direct mail, *e-mail*, Internet, marketing database and loyalty schemes. Successful e-retailers often use offline advertising such as magazines and 'click here' sections of newspapers integrated with online marketing communications. Online methods include banner ads and pop-ups (often incentivized); paid-for listings in search engines and directories; and affiliate programmes.

In addition to solving problems, there is another reason for customers buying products - to get good feelings. This is a particularly difficult area for e-retailers. The bricks retail store and the face-to-face salesperson are often much better at identifying and satisfying customers' emotional needs and wants. The physical store uses *atmospherics* in the attempt to change mood and give shoppers a pleasant emotional experience when buying. Emotional cues may be visual (decor), olfactory (perfume), tactile (smooth and cool or soft and cuddly) and aural (music).

e-Retailers can create a 'web atmosphere' using, for example, music and visuals such as 3-D displays and downloadable video clips. Such enhancements must always be a compromise, on account of the need to avoid long download times.

One way of tackling the problem is to provide a 'click here for *broadband*' 'Customer relationships' is an area that successful bricks retailers such as Tesco have used to gain a major lead over competitors.

The importance of the emotional aspects of selling has already been mentioned. The sales representative selling face-to-face in the bricks retail store can use verbal and non-verbal (body language) communication to build personal relationships with customers, enhancing the emotional value of products. In trying to replicate the physical buying experience, the e-retailer is at a disadvantage.

On the other hand, with transaction data ready-digitized, the e-retailer is well placed to enhance product value using CRM techniques. For example, data mining can be used to build a picture of products most likely to be wanted by individual customers. Products tailored specifically can be offered pro-actively. Amazon, for instance, uses such a system to match new books to existing customers who are likely to be interested in them.

There has been a number of suggestions for structuring a 'retail mix', equivalent to the 4Ps or 4Cs of the marketing mix, adding other aspects that may be key to retailer success. For example, McGoldrick (2002) uses a nine-element mix. In addition to those that can be incorporated into the 4Cs framework above, McGoldrick also includes factors such as 'brand image', 'logistics' and 'information'. Most versions of the retail mix are not as 'catchy' as the 4Ps or 4Cs of the marketing mix.

Therefore we propose a simplified '7Cs' for the *e-retail mix*, adding Computing and category management issues; *Customer franchise*; and Customer care and service.

C5 Computing and Category Management Issues

The success of retailers has been founded on supplying the products that customers want, in the right sizes and quantities, at the right time and in the right place. With the growth in consumer choice has come a proliferation of products. Superstores carry 20,000-plus branded products and department stores from 100,000, and even up to one million or more. Efficient control of this degree of complexity needs effective computer and logistics systems.

Retail logistics have been changing rapidly over recent decades. First, the growth of retailer power has involved major retailers taking more control of their supply chains. The involvement of wholesalers has been reduced, tending to give way to contract logistics (under retailer control). At the same time, supply chains have become more efficient with computer network links between suppliers and retailers - many still based on *electronic data interchange (EDI)*.

Pre-dating the Web, EDI is based on privately owned third-party computer networks. Stock levels have been reduced using techniques such as *efficient customer response* (*ECR* -the retailers' equivalent of *Just in Time* or *JIT*). EDI networks are expensive to install, costing at least hundreds of thousands of pounds. There is a growing trend towards the use of the Internet, particularly for smaller businesses (suppliers and customers) and smaller order quantities. Increasingly, retailers such as Tesco are allowing Internet access to their suppliers for realtime *Electronic Point of Sale (EPoS)* data. Trusted supplier partners can thus respond more quickly to changes in customer demand.Cooperation between suppliers and retailers has been key to improving the efficiency of satisfying customers while minimizing stocks and costs.

On the larger scale, this cooperative process is known as *category management (CM)*, the retailer/ supplier process of managing categories as strategic business units.

High efficiency of the computer-controlled logistics systems is largely behind the success of 'bricks and clicks' retailers such as Tesco. Ironically, deficiencies in this area have been a major factor in the failure of a number of pureplay dot.coms that have concentrated on advertising and promotion at the expense of other areas of the e-retail mix. One exception is Amazon, which is founded on efficient logistics systems and customer care and service.In the UK, Amazon is using its logistics expertise to carry out distribution services on contract for bricks retailers such as WHSmith and Toys R Us.

Apart from Amazon and the major bricks and clicks retailers, many of the e-retailers with the most efficient computer and logistics efficiency are established direct-selling businesses. For example, Quill and Screwfix, office supplies and tradesperson supplies respectively, operate established mail businesses via a paper catalogue. Dell have been pioneers in telemarketing and direct selling since the late 1980s, demonstrating that a complex product like a computer could be sold without face-to-face contact. Much of the success has been due to investment in computer-based *mass customization* systems, along with excellent customer care and service. The company was one of the first e-retailers and is the market leader worldwide for computer hardware.

SCREWFIX

Screwfix started out as a UK trade wholesale supplier, but also now sells extensively for DIY. Screwfix.com earned *Retail Week's* 'Retailer of the Year' award for 2002. Screwfix is an example of the successful niche e-retailer and one of few to gain favourable mentions in the *Sunday Times* (UK) survey. Screwfix is owned by Kingfisher, i.e. in the same stable as the B&Q UK DIY stores.

Although the branding, ordering and fulfilment are completely separate, the supply chains are integrated, resulting in economies of scale and buying power. Screwfix has 0.5 per cent of the UK repairs, maintenance and home improvement market, but a massive 20 per cent of the *direct* market for those products. Web sales are over £20 million per year (15 per cent and growing of Screwfix's total business). The (e-)retail mix is summarized below.

Convenience for the Customer

Express shopping: if you have the catalogue, simply type in the quantities and catalogue number, or alternatively use 'search' to find what you want. A freephone telephone number is available 24 hours a day, plus fax and e-mail options, offering improved personal interaction.

Customer Value and Benefits

Products include not only screws, bolts and nails, but also fixings, adhesives, tools, hardware, lighting, plumbing and cleaning products - the claim is 'Everything for the trade and DIY - next day', and 100 per cent stock availability of 6,000 products.

Cost to the Customer

A number of special offers are always available. Most prices are significantly cheaper than in DIY retail sheds.

Communication and Customer Relationships

The homepage has many examples of good practice, for example: Recommend a Friend - get a reward when they order for the first time; Open a Business Account; Testimonials - 'I have just received my order and felt I must congratulate you on an excellent service. Your site is well designed. The products are well laid out and the order processing excellent.' ... 'Your website is brilliant, the designer needs a big pat on the back. Well laid out, and to order online is so easy.'; and Register/Login - optional registration makes ordering quicker and easier. There are regular communications by mail with catalogues, 'What's new' and special offers for registered customers.

Computing and Category Management Issues

Winner of best use of Supply Chain Management at the 2001 Internet Business Awards.

Customer Franchise

Without the need for heavy advertising, Screwfix has quickly built up a reputation for cheap prices, with quick and reliable delivery based on actual performance.

IMPORTANCE OF GOING GLOBAL

Globalization involves the transfer of an existing business system to other countries or the management of another business system in other countries. The terms 'international', 'multinational', 'global' and 'transnational' have been used to describe different stages in the globalization ladder of business development.

The decision of nationally based e-Commerce to go global will depend on factors such as demography, entry modes, socio-cultural diversity, as well as the approach and management style to be used when entering new markets. The United States today represents the largest national market in the world, with roughly 25 per cent of the total world market for all products and services. The fact that 75 per cent of the world market potential is outside their national territory has been the force driving many US companies to 'go international' and even to extend further and 'go global'.

With three-quarters of its revenue generated by its soft drink business outside the United States, Coca-Cola, acknowledged as the most successful global company, has driven the message of globalization further than anybody else. For non-US companies the incentive is even stronger. The two wealthiest countries after the United States, Japan and Germany, have 85 per cent and 94 per cent respectively of the world market potential.

Today there are only seven countries where English is the primary language spoken, by about half a billion people or 8 per cent of the total population, their combined economies representing only 30 per cent of the total world economy. e-Commerce companies that will continue to target this small percentage of the world market will miss out on capturing a much larger potential market. The total global e-Commerce market is forecast to reach $1.6 trillion by 2003, a very powerful incentive for companies entering this arena.

If present e-businesses have been able to achieve year-upon-year growth in visitors, sales or members using only domestic focused Web sites, then in order to sustain or increase this growth it will be almost impossible to do so without entering and servicing new markets. Almost 10 per cent of the world's population has access to the Internet. The global Internet audience had grown to 580.78 million people by the end of May 2002.

The survey indicated that, for the first time ever, Europe has the highest number of Internet users in the world, with 185.83 million Europeans online, compared with 182.83 million in the United States and Canada, and 167.86 million in Asia-Pacific. The survey's findings also indicate that the digital divide between developed and developing nations is as wide as ever.

While Europeans account for 32 per cent of global Internet users, only 6 per cent of the world's Net users are based in Latin America. The Middle East and Africa combined account for just 2 per cent of global Internet users; the lack of telecommunications infrastructures in those regions means that most citizens remain unconnected.

Methods of Entry

Until recently a traditional business has had the options of entering new geographical markets through direct or indirect exporting, new start-ups, franchising, joint ventures, acquisitions, concessions or licensing, depending on the degrees of risk and the level of involvement they were prepared to accept.

To these alternatives can be added now the virtual business via the Internet. The nationally based business will start with cautious testing of new markets, often selected with a similar culture, having a focus that is culturally and managerially 'ethnocentric' or centred around the home market. A multinational business will have a 'polycentric' orientation, i.e. a focus based on the understanding and appreciation of different operating contexts.

The global or transnational business will have a fully global strategy, focusing on maximizing the benefits obtained from economies of scale in sourcing, product standardization and marketing. Typical of global operators is their adaptable, geocentric approach, which allows them to 'think globally but act locally'.

Opportunities and Threat

The Internet has already made a big difference in the way business operates globally, offering substantial advantages to both buyers and sellers, because it can cope with a rapidly changing environment. Many industries have further motives for embracing the Web, as it offers huge savings on their marketing and distribution costs, which in certain cases, for example the airlines, can make up about a quarter of their total operating expenses. The Internet has made a big difference to aviation, with portable computers becoming essential in the process of booking and buying air travel. Simplifying booking and cutting out the cumbersome process of issuing card tickets can be very attractive to customers. Since 2000, an increasing number of airlines, such as Northwest and Swissair, have been offering online facilities for seat selection and check-in, as well as for booking and paying for flights. e-Commerce will also allow businesses to learn more about their Web customers, so they can package offers tailored to their individual needs. This is what in marketing terms is called 'customer of one' and it applies to airlines, just as it does to cars or computers.

Continuing with the same example, there are distinguishing characteristics between the different levels of airline Web sites. The most basic are 'brochure sites' which offer simple static information, not much different from the printed brochures found in the bricks-and-mortar travel agents. At the next level are the constantly updated versions of the 'brochure sites'.

The third level contains sites that obtain information from the customer as he logs on and builds a profile of his travel needs and preferences. It can answer requests for information, take bookings and issue e-mail confirmation of bookings.

This sort of e-Commerce transaction is now quite common, especially for the no-frills, low-cost airlines. The next generation Web site will recognize and greet the customer by his or her name when s/he logs on and will know that s/he is a valuable customer. It will be able to analyse his travel history and suggest alternative itineraries that might suit him better.

Niche Marketing

No-frills, low-fare carriers such as EasyJet and Ryanair have been using this low-cost, high service strategy to carve out successful niches. The emergence of these new companies has increased the level of competition in the industry, putting established carriers under increasing threat of loss of business on their traditional routes and ultimately bankruptcy. One notable example is Swissair, and even British Airways has felt the pinch with the threat of its shares losing their blue-chip status.

Other examples of industries that have made good use of the trend towards personalization through the Internet are the perfume and fashion industries. Custom fragrance marketers have been established, usually family-run businesses where the Internet has radically changed the direction of this niche market. In 2001 a number of new entrants have included Procter & Gamble with Reflect.com, Ashford.com, RomanceHer.com, Eleuria.com and Creativescent.com.

The Internet is about to turn this niche market into a major profit-making category of prestige fragrance and force the major perfume companies to create custom divisions. Nevertheless these new ways of doing business are at risk for being untested and vulnerable to sudden market downturns or fashion changes.

Small and medium-size enterprises are the main beneficiaries of the low-cost marketing possibilities offered by the Internet, which can turn them from small niche players into global ones. A fundamental change is happening in the world of Asian marketing that could prove a bonanza for struggling companies. The Internet is providing low-cost ways for small to medium-size businesses to get their advertising message across, focusing on specific audiences. Asia has been experiencing a phenomenal growth in Internet advertising, whose potential demand has been recognized by US Internet advertising agencies.

DoubleClick Asia, a joint venture between New York-based Double Click and Hong Kong Web portal builder Asiacontent.com, has been able to track Internet users' movements by collecting 'cookies' or files embedded in users' Web browsers that log the pages they visit and for how long. This information allows marketing solution providers such as DotMedia China or Next Media to help their customers, which are local companies, to target their own local audience in a far more efficient way by posting relevant ads on their Web sites.

Another interesting SME example is Charles Tyrwhitt, a UK manufacturer of mainly shirts, but also ties and other accessories, to the exclusive ABC1 men market. The company has adopted a 'clicks and mortar' strategy, which hopefully will turn this British niche player into a global one. It will also reduce its brochure and marketing costs.

The company's strong customer service culture is being translated on to the Net, where this is so important. The firm's success lies in its ability to carry more than 3,000 lines of stock at any one time, with each shirt being offered in up to forty-eight combinations of size, cuff and sleeve. The company is able to maximize sales by targeting groups of people more effectively than could ever be done through mail order.

The key to the success of niche e-businesses is first and foremost brand awareness. Second, expanding the customer base geographically is leading to the need for a greater product range to meet strong local preferences in style and fashion.

The Internet has proved to be the perfect messenger for niche interests, serving individual tastes and diverse geographical demands. In certain industries, such as national media, which were previously dedicated to mass markets, the Internet is offering for the first time the possibility of meeting specialist demands. As successful online newspapers in the United States reach less than 25 per cent of their local Net users, some have tried to add an interest-based niche to their regional focus.

For example, the *San Jose Mercury* is concentrating its online energies to SiliconValley.com, a specialist site for technology news. The objective is to have a network of loyal users by meeting specialist demand with detailed information. In the United Kingdom the commercial site Fish4, which is backed by local newspaper publishers, owned by the Guardian Media Group, is claiming to have reached the necessary critical mass of information to make a niche product. BBC News online is another example where the battle between general and niche is being fought. The way it uses its huge breadth of content, both broad-brush and localized, demonstrates the diversity of its users and their demands. In just one day 98,450 different stories were read, amounting to a staggering 20 per cent of all the stories the site has ever produced.

Understanding the Global Environment

For the e-Commerce organization shaping the direction of its global expansion it is vitally important to understand the external environment as a means of identification of opportunities and threats. An analysis of the variety of factors and environmental influences is necessary in order to allow a balance of internal capabilities and resources with the opportunities offered externally that ultimately would affect business planning and implementation within the organization. The elements of the external environment connected with the organization can be divided into four distinct groupings, known by the acronym STEP.

2

Management Systems in E-Commerce

INTRODUCTION

Over the past five years, e-commerce has rapidly evolved from an experiment for trend-conscious businesses to a vital channel in the business world that no company can afford to ignore. In response to this change, there has been a plethora of studies on the subject of e-commerce, most of which have focused on the formulation of e-commerce strategies. More recently, the importance of structure has come to the forefront, as the dot.com bust caused a reexamination of failed e-commerce structures and as a trend toward integration has spread throughout business.

The importance of management control systems in e-commerce, however, has often been overlooked by both managers and observers of managerial practices. Although studies of traditional business readily acknowledge the importance of various systems, studies of e-commerce have given rather scant attention to systems, in part because the early e-commerce environment embraced two opposing positions on systems.

One view was that e-commerce changes everything and that traditional systems were obsolete. Many e-commerce startups reveled in their rejection of traditional business systems, embraced creativity as the ultimate virtue, and ran companies that barely resembled traditional businesses. At the most trivial level, this meant behavioral changes, such as the rejection of dress codes and cubicles in the work environment.

More important, it comprised the rejection of traditional business models and operating procedures and traditional measures of success. In the stock market, these changes were reflected in huge market capitalizations that had no relation to company profitability. Many traditional companies strived to imitate the startup model and gave their spin-offs similar operating rules.

The second position, held by many traditional companies less convinced of the validity of the e-commerce model, was that e-commerce changed nothing. To many corporate boards, e-commerce was derided as "just technology, " and this condescension was reflected in the type of systems that were set up for e-commerce ventures.

Spending was tightly controlled from above, budgeting had to conform to outdated corporate standards, innovation was discouraged, and few incentives were created for employees working in e-commerce. Often, e-commerce would be a part-time project or diversion for both employees and the executives charged with overseeing it.

We now know that neither of these visions is appropriate for the creation of an e-commerce business or for e-commerce systems. The values that underlie those two visions are certain to doom any e-commerce venture, regardless of the specific strategy or structure. With our new understanding of the proper role of e-commerce, it is necessary to articulate how proper management control systems are critical for a successful e-commerce venture.

As with strategy and structure, the relationship between e-commerce systems and the traditional business is dynamic. There is an ever-changing dynamic relationship between corporate strategy, structure, and systems and e-commerce strategy, structure, and systems.

The systems used to implement an e-commerce strategy will have implications throughout the company and its traditional business, and the effects of changed policies and regulations will not be limited to e-commerce. Our general e-commerce business model highlights the importance of e-commerce systems and the relation of these systems to corporate and e-commerce strategy and structure and to organizational systems.

Owing to this dynamism, commenting on e-commerce systems requires two separate but equally important perspectives. One is the extent to which traditional systems must be altered, augmented, or eliminated to create a business environment in which e-commerce success is possible. The second perspective examines how a focus on the success of e-commerce can bring greater effectiveness to the governance of the traditional business.

These e-commerce systems decisions fall into four broad areas: information practices, human resources, measurement processes, and customer service. First, a company's information practices can become the bridge from appropriate corporate culture to successful individual and organizational behaviour. Though strong leadership and resource commitment can help to create a culture in which IT knowledge and stature are sufficient for starting e-commerce, long-term e-commerce success requires more.

The company must categorically promote information sharing and information transparency, instill a sense of urgency, and enable real-time and flexible decision-making processes. The company can also benefit from e-commerce by putting these information practices to use throughout the value chain. E-commerce provides opportunities for cost savings and speed improvements at every stage of the value chain.

Human resources policy and practices is the second area of systems that needs to be carefully managed for e-commerce success. Because e-commerce is characterized by speed, risk-taking, and new business models, a company must create the proper incentives for those overseeing e-commerce. For the CIO and for all IT and e-commerce personnel, employees must sometimes be rewarded outside the traditional compensation structure.

Managing incentives and rewards to give organizations equity and the appropriate incentives for creativity, flexibility, and innovation is often a significant challenge. E-commerce can benefit the traditional business in the hiring practices of HR. Using the Internet to stimulate job applications can bring both efficiency and a more IT-knowledgeable applicant base.

Measurement is another area in which the nature of e-commerce demands rethinking traditional systems. E-commerce facilitates improvement in measurement systems throughout the organization, allowing a better flow of timely information to decision makers and an aggregation and disaggregation of data never before possible. It permits an analysis of causal relationships and the business model to better understand the payoffs of various corporate actions.

Finally, the systems that govern customer relationships must adjust to implement the important customer service aspects of an e-commerce strategy. Providing service at all times and across channels makes unique demands on the parts of the company closest to the customer. But e-commerce also provides unprecedented capabilities to learn about customers, their behaviour, and their interaction with offerings. Mining this customer data is an area that is still maturing and offers new competitive advantages.

HUMAN RESOURCES IN E-COMMERCE

Management of personnel is also central to the implementation of e-commerce strategy. Even in the aftermath of the fallout of the dot.com bust in the stock market, e-commerce is still inexorably linked to the notions of large performance bonuses, stock options, Silicon Valley whiz kids, and new-wave office environments.

It is still necessary to find ways to develop and retain employees who are creative, flexible, and innovative—in addition to competent and diligent. In this light, a company must endeavor to put systems in place that retain key personnel and make strategic new hires throughout the course of an e-commerce venture.

Designing appropriate compensation systems is instrumental both in attaining initial e-commerce success and in retaining the leaders and employees who made that success possible. Above all, compensation systems must be properly aligned with strategy and structure.

Symbolically, the CIO's compensation is one of the more important decisions a company dedicated to implementing e-commerce will encounter. CIO compensation should be in line with that of other members of senior management to signal respect for the IT function as a creator of value. Failure to fully and explicitly acknowledge the value of IT and e-commerce contradicts the other messages that must be communicated for e-commerce to succeed.

At lower levels of the company, compensation systems have more practical consequences for alignment. Some companies believe that compensating e-commerce managers the same as managers in traditional commerce fails to create proper incentives for e-commerce and value creation. Differential compensation sometimes creates an incentive to cannibalize from the company's traditional channels as well as more effectively and more quickly to execute an e-commerce strategy.

But, e-commerce compensation should be tied to the overall success of the venture company-wide, rather than rewarding performance within an individual unit. This is particularly true when the company is seeking full integration, because it helps ensure cooperation between departments.

Companies must be prepared to manage the channel conflict that often arises when e-commerce begins to cannibalize the traditional business. Cannibalization is necessary to optimize the use of each channel, and an integration strategy cannot succeed if traditional business units do not accept it.

Companies must design compensation systems that gradually shift compensation toward the creation of value, particularly in businesses heavily dependent on salespersons who work on a commission basis. Traditional business units must be placated not by compensating inefficiencies, but by carving out new roles that optimize the use of each channel and produce a successfully integrated and profitable multi-channel coordinated effort.

At aviation parts distributor Aviall Inc., a few weeks after an upper-management shakeup brought in a new CEO in 1996, a new Web-based order-entry system was introduced. In response, Aviall's 300 sales reps feared their jobs were at stake and told customers not to use it. Despite the benefits to the consumer that were realized through the Web-based system, the role of the sales reps had not been modified to permit them to survive such a drastic change in company strategy.

As companies develop and implement e-commerce strategies, the Internet must be examined and the pre-existing channels must be modified in a way that complements the e-commerce initiative. While compensation systems must often be reevaluated and reconstructed in e-commerce implementations, hiring practices can be improved simply by using the same Web site that showcases other e-commerce activities. Hiring online can significantly reduce advertising costs associated with print and other listings.

It can also ensure that potential applicants possess at least some skills in using the Internet and implies a confidence and understanding of the importance of e-commerce. Cisco is one company that greatly improved its hiring process by advertising openings online. Further, special attention should be paid to HR policies covering to those who work in e-commerce and IT.

Companies should recognize the fluidity of the IT labour market and must often create more flexible labour policies than for other employees.

To ensure that proper human resources practices are employed in an e-commerce implementation;

- Compensation systems for traditional and e-commerce personnel should be properly aligned with the company's new e-commerce strategy.
- Companies must be prepared for channel conflict due to cannibalization of traditional company segments into an e-commerce venture.
- Hiring practices must fully take advantage of the exposure opportunity and cost savings made available by Internet hiring.

INFORMATION PRACTICES IN E-COMMERCE

For e-commerce to be successful, it is necessary but not sufficient that members of the organization are competent and confident in their use of IT. Strong leadership and investment can bring an organization to that stage, but systems must be created to harness the power of IT for organizational integration. It has recently been emphasized that interactive control systems in traditional business must focus on constantly changing information.

These systems provide the sensing and monitoring that is necessary whenever strategic uncertainties are high. In most businesses today, more interactive control systems are needed as strategic uncertainties have been increasing. In e-commerce, these systems become increasingly central to the successful implementation of strategy.

A new policy on information practices must become a central component of the company's systems. Information should be transparent and the sharing of information facilitated. Organizational boundaries must not impede the flow of information. An integration strategy cannot be properly implemented if information about e-commerce stalls within the e-commerce unit and is not disseminated widely.

Ideally, internal processes are developed in-house with substantial consultation and communication; obstacles are easily recognized, understood, and dealt with, internally and quickly. Companies such as Amazon and Office Depot not only have garnered more efficient business practices because of their internal development, but also have been able to expand into other markets such as technology consulting and Web design because of their in-house expertise.

Companies can also use the implementation of an e-commerce strategy as a starting point for proper information practices. Prior to moving online, 3M had a fragmented information system that made it difficult to cross-sell to existing customers. Even having the same customer listed in different systems had additional costs. After moving online, the company created a $20 million data warehouse to store all information, as part of a larger restructuring of information systems. Senior management must set the example of open information practices and transparency, even when the information is bad news for the company or reflects negatively on an individual or business unit. Problems should be discussed openly, without fear of repercussions. As appropriate, information on the company's goals, measures, and progress should be made available to all employees and the public through the company's Web site.

This information is increasingly available to interested parties, and by making it transparent, a company may build trust with its constituent groups. In addition, it is often beneficial to increase the information flow to the public to ensure that accurate information is communicated, rather than to risk inaccurate information being made public by a third party.Further, many organizational processes should be restructured to fully take advantage of e-commerce.

In particular, e-commerce should encourage and facilitate companies to move away from strict hierarchical reporting in some areas and move toward the use of cross-functional remote teams. By collaborating with other business functions and units, the e-commerce initiative is likely to encounter less resistance in the traditional business. Processes should also be adaptable and flexible enough to respond to changes in real-time information.

Numerous virtual organization techniques serve these purposes, including:

- Cross-functional teams that form themselves
- Teams that may go into and out of existence regularly
- Use of both in-person and remote meetings
- Teams that span organizational boundaries
- Encouragement of innovation through mutual trust
- Self-governance
- Harnessing global resources to solve local problems

An organization that utilizes these processes should then be able to assemble teams to innovate or to resolve challenges associated with e-commerce. Most important, all these techniques should be fully consistent with an integration strategy, eliminating any need for moving e-commerce outside the organization.

By upgrading these information practices, a company positions itself to make significant improvements throughout the value chain. For many companies, value chain management is an integral part of the e-commerce strategy. But even for those companies that focus primarily on selling online, subtle improvements can be made with minimal extra cost and effort. Thus, improving information practices can create significant benefits for sales, distribution, and procurement, along with various other processes throughout the organization.

Cisco has used its real-time capabilities to create supplier-side processes that vastly improve its supply-chain management. Cisco and its suppliers and manufacturers share extensive information on product quality. This allows Cisco to measure the number of defective products while they are still in the supplier's possession, rather than after they have been delivered. In turn, the supplier can make faster adjustments in its manufacturing process to minimize future quality problems. Dell has mastered the use of e-commerce in limiting the amount of inventory kept on hand. Many component parts such as monitors and peripherals are never kept in inventory by Dell, and their movement and distribution is entirely handled by email communication. But even for parts retained by Dell, real-time ordering forecasts are sent to suppliers to minimize the inventory and buffer stocks on a cycle as short as two hours. This relationship with suppliers, coupled with its information practices, also permits a *negative* cash conversion cycle.

At the delivery end of the supply chain, Tesco spanned traditional organizational boundaries to create the most efficient delivery process. While many in the grocery industry mimicked the Amazon model by attempting to deliver from large, high-tech warehouses, Tesco chose to deliver directly from stock at local physical locations. While this limited the potential delivery zone, it also saved Tesco the effort and resources of building expensive warehouses with uncertain profitability. Delivering from the store meant no separate inventories and no need for entirely new processes.

Nike, Inc. recently implemented a supply-chain system linking the company with its manufacturing partners. Before these system changes, 30 percent of Nike's total volume of shoe orders were based on estimates; now, only 3 percent of the orders are guesswork, because of better forecasting and planning.

Whirlpool Corporation has linked every Whirlpool factory and sales site worldwide through e-business software, allowing factories and sales sites to coordinate with suppliers and key retail partners. This has reduced inventories and increased vital communication.

Krispy Kreme Doughnut is another company that has used e-commerce to its advantage by devising an intranet network linking its stores. The Web system tracks doughnut mix, doles out the right colors of sprinkles, monitors managers' decisions, and permits users to fix errors such as damaged goods, by allowing replacements to be sent. The system allows employees to focus more on customer service, reduce problem orders, and increase productivity.

For proper information practices to improve the success of e-commerce implementations:

- Organizational boundaries should not represent an impediment to the free flow of information in a company.
- Company leadership must set the example of open information practices.
- Companies must be willing to move away from strict hierarchical reporting systems.

MANAGEMENT INFORMATION SYSTEM

Management information systems (MIS) are the most common form of management support systems. They provide managerial end users with information products that support much of their day-to-day decision-making needs. Management information systems provide a variety of reports and displays to management. The contents of these information products are specified in advance by managers so that they contain information that managers need.

Management information systems retrieve information about internal operations from database that have been updated by transaction processing systems. They also obtain data about the business environment from external source. Information products provided to managers include displays and reports that can be furnished (1) on demand, (2) periodically, according to a predetermined schedule.

DECISION SUPPORT SYSTEMS

Decision support systems (DSS) are a natural progression from information reporting systems and transaction processing systems. Decision support systems are interactive, computer-based information systems that use decision models and specialized database to assist the decision making process of managerial end users.

EXECUTIVE INFORMATION SYSTEMS

Executive information systems (EIS) are management information systems tailored to the strategic information needs of top management. Top executives get the information they need from many sources, including letters, memos, periodicals, and reports produced manually as well as by computer systems.

Other sources of executive information are meetings, telephone calls, and social activities. Thus, much of a top executive's information comes from non-computer services. Computer generated information ahs not played a primary role in meeting many top executives' information needs.

TRENDS IN COMPUTER SYSTEMS

Today's computer systems come in a variety of sizes, shapes, and computing capabilities. Rapid hardware and software developments and changing end user needs continue to drive the emergence of new models of computers, from the smallest hand-held personal digital assistant for end users, to the largest multiple-CPU mainframe for the enterprise.

Categories such as mainframes, midrange computers, and microcomputers are still used to help us express the relative processing power and number of end users that can be supported by different types of computers. In addition, experts continue to predict the merging or disappearance of several computer categories. They feel, for example, that many midrange and mainframe systems have been made obsolete by the power and versatility of client/server networks of end user microcomputers and servers.

COMPUTER GENERATIONS

It is important to realize that major changes and trends in computer systems have occurred during the major stages-or generations-of computing, and will continue into the future. The first generation of computers developed in the early 1950s, the second generation blossomed during the late 1960s, the third generation took computing into the 1970s, and the fourth generation has been the computer technology of the 1980s and 1990s. A fifth generation of computers that accelerates the trends of the previous generations is expected to evolve as we enter the 21st century. Notice that computers continue to become smaller, faster, more reliable, less costly to purchase and maintain, and more interconnected within computer networks.

First-generation computing involved massive computers using hundreds or thousands of vacuum tubes for their processing and memory circuitry. These large computers generated enormous amounts of heat; their vacuum tubes had to be replaced frequently. Thus, they had large electrical power, air conditioning, and maintenance requirements. First-generation computers had main memories of only a few thousand characters and millisecond processing speeds. They used magnetic drums or tape for secondary storage and punched cards or paper tape as input and output media.

Second-generation computing used transistors and other solid-state, semiconductor devices that were wired to circuit boards in the computers. Transistorized circuits were much smaller and much more reliable, generated little heat, were less expensive, and required less power than vacuum tubes. Tiny magnetic cores were used for the computer's memory, or internal storage. Many second-generation computers had main memory capacities of less than 100 kilobytes and microsecond processing, speeds.

Removable magnetic disk packs were introduced, and magnetic tape merged as the major input, output, and secondary storage medium for large computer installations. Third-generation computing saw the development of computers that used integrated circuits, in which thousands of transistors and other circuit elements are etched on tiny chips of silicon. Main memory capacities increased to several megabytes and processing speeds jumped to millions of instructions per second (MIPS) as telecommunications capabilities became common.

This made it possible for operating system programs to come into widespread use that automated and supervised the activities of many types of peripheral devices and processing by mainframe computers of several programs at the same time, frequently involving networks of users at remote terminals. Integrated circuit technology also made possible the development and widespread use of small computers called minicomputers in the third computer generation.

Fourth-generation computing relies on the use of LSI (large-scale integration) and VLSI (very-large-scale integration) technologies that cram hundreds of thousands or millions of transistors and other circuit elements on each chip. This enabled the development of microprocessors, in which all of the circuits of a CP are contained on a single chip with processing speeds of millions of instructions per second.

Main memory capacities ranging from a few megabytes to several gigabytes can also be achieved by memory chips that replaced magnetic core memories. Microcomputers, which use microprocessor CPUs and a variety of peripheral devices and easy-to-use software packages to form small personal computer (PC), systems or client/server networks of linked PCs and servers, are a hallmark of the fourth generation of computing, which accelerated the downsizing of computing systems.

Whether we are moving into a fifth generation of computing is a subject of debated since the concept of generations may no longer fit the continual, rapid changes occurring in computer hardware, software, data, and networking technologies. But in any case, we can be sure that progress in computing will continue to accelerate, and that the development of Internet-based technologies and applications will be one of the major forces driving computing into the 21st century.

MICROCOMPUTER SYSTEMS

Microcomputers are the most important category of computer systems for end users. Though usually called a personal computer, or PC, a microcomputer is much more than a small computer for use by an individual. The computing power of microcomputers now exceeds that of the mainframes of previous computer generations at a fraction of their cost. Thus, they have become powerful networked professional work stations for end users in business.

Microcomputers come in a variety of sizes and shapes for a variety of purposes. For example, PCs are available as handhled, notebook, laptop, portable, desktop, and floor-standing models. Or, based on their use, they include home, personal, professional, workstation, and multi-user systems. Most microcomputers are desktops designed to fit on an office desk, or notebooks for those who want a small, portable PC for their work activities.

Some microcomputers are powerful workstation computers (technical work-stations) that support applications with heavy mathematical computing and graphics display demands such as computer-aided design (CAD) in engineering, or investment and portfolio analysis in the securities industry. Other microcomputers are used as network servers. They are usually more powerful microcomputers that coordinate telecommunications and resource sharing in small local area networks (LANs), and Internet and intranet Web sites.

Another important microcomputer category includes handheld microcomputer devices known as personal digital assistants (PDAs), designed for convenient mobile communications and computing. PDAs use touch-screens, pen-based handwriting recognition of keyboards to help mobile workers send and receive E-mail and exchange information such as appointments, to do lists, and scales contacts with their desktop PCs or Web servers.

MULTIMEDIA SYSTEMS

Multimedia PCs are designed to present you with information in a variety of media, including text and graphics displays, voice and other digitized audio, photographs, animation, and video clips. Mention multimedia, and many people think of computer video games, multimedia encyclopedias, educational videos, and multimedia home pages on the World Wide Web. However, multimedia systems are widely used in business for training employees, educating customers, making sales presentations, and adding impact to other business presentations.

The basic hardware and software requirements of a multimedia computer system depend on whether you wish to create as well as enjoy multimedia presentations. Owners of low-cost multimedia PCs marketed for home used do not need authoring software or high-powered hardware capacities in order to enjoy multimedia games and other entertainment and educational multimedia products. These computers come equipped with a CD-ROM drive, stereo speakers, additional memory, a high-performance processor, and other multimedia processing capabilities.

People who want to create their own multimedia production may have to spend several thousand dollars to put together a high-performance multimedia authoring system. This includes a high-resolution color graphics monitor, sound and video capture boards, a high-performance microprocessor with multimedia capabilities, additional megabytes of memory, and several gigabytes of hard disk capacity.

Sound cards and video capture boards are circuit boards that contain digital signal processors (DSPs) and additional megabytes of memory for digital processing of sound and video. A digital camera, digital video camcorder, optical scanner, and software such as authoring tools and programs for image editing and graphics creation can add several thousand dollars to the star-up costs of a multimedia authoring system.

STARTING THE SYSTEMS DEVELOPMENT PROCESS

Do we have business problem (or opportunity)? What is causing the problem? Would a new or improved information system help solve the problem? What would be a feasible information system solution to our problem?

These are the questions that have to be answered in the system investigation stage-the first step in the systems development process. This stage may involve consideration of proposals generated by an information systems planning process.

FEASIBILITY STUDIES

The process of developing a major information system can be costly, the systems investigation stage frequently requires a preliminary study called a feasibility study. A feasibility study is a preliminary study which investigates the information needs of prospective users and determines the resource requirements, costs, benefits, and feasibility of proposed project. You would use the methods of gathering information to collect data for a feasibility study.

Then you might formalize the findings of this study in written report that includes preliminary specifications and a development plan for the proposed system. If management approves the recommendations of the feasibility study, the development process can continue. The goal of feasibility studies is to evaluate alternative systems and to propose the most feasible and desirable systems for development. The feasibility of a proposed system can be evaluated in terms of four major categories.

The focus of organizational feasibility is on how well a proposed information system supports the objectives of the organization and its strategic plan for information systems. For example, projects that do not directly contribute to meeting an organization's strategic objectives are typically not funded. Economic feasibility is concerned with whether expected cost savings, increased revenue, increased profits, reductions in required investment, and other types of benefits will exceed the costs of developing and operating a proposed system. For example, if a project can't cover its development costs, it won't be approved, unless mandated by government regulations or other considerations. Technical feasibility can be demonstrated if reliable hardware and software capable of meeting the needs of a proposed system can be acquired or development by the business in the required time.

Finally, operational feasibility is the willingness and ability of the management, employees, customers, suppliers, and others to operate, use, and support a proposed system. For example, if the software for a new system is too difficult to use, employees may make too many errors and avoid using it. Thus, it would fail to show operational feasibility.

Cost/Benefit Analysis. Feasibility studies typically involve cost/benefit analysis. If costs and benefits can be quantified, they are called tangible costs are the costs of hardware and software, employee salaries, and other quantifiable costs needed to develop and implement an IS solution. Intangible costs are difficult to quantity; they included the loss of customer goodwill or employee morale caused by errors and disruptions arising from the installation of a new system.

Tangible. Benefits are favorable results, such as the decrease in payroll costs caused by a reduction in personnel or a decrease in inventory carrying costs caused by a reduction in inventory. Intangible benefits are harder to estimate. Such benefits as better customer service or faster and more accurate informations for management fall into this category.

DATABASE MANAGEMENT SYSTEMS

A database management system (DBMS) consists of software that operates databases, providing storage, access, security, backup and other facilities. Database management systems can be categorized according to the database model that they support, such as relational or XML, the type(s) of computer they support, such as a server cluster or a mobile phone, the query language(s) that access the database, such as SQL or XQuery, performance trade-offs, such as maximum scale or maximum speed or others.

Some DBMS cover more than one entry in these categories, e.g., supporting multiple query languages. Examples of some commonly used DBMS are MySQL, PostgreSQL, Microsoft Access, SQL Server, FileMaker,Oracle,Sybase, dBASE, Clipper,FoxPro etc. Almost every database software comes with an Open Database Connectivity (ODBC) driver that allows the database to integrate with other databases.

COMPONENTS OF DBMS

Most DBMS as of 2009 implement a relational model. Other DBMS systems, such as Object DBMS, offer specific features for more specialized requirements. Their components are similar, but not identical.

RDBMS Components

- *Sublanguages*: Relational DBMS (RDBMS) include Data Definition Language (DDL) for defining the structure of the database, Data Control Language (DCL) for defining security/access controls, and Data Manipulation Language (DML) for querying and updating data.
- *Interface drivers*: These drivers are code libraries that provide methods to prepare statements, execute statements, fetch results, etc. Examples include ODBC, JDBC, MySQL/PHP, FireBird/Python.
- *SQL engine*: This component interprets and executes the DDL, DCL, and DML statements. It includes three major components (compiler, optimizer, and executor).
- *Transaction engine*: Ensures that multiple SQL statements either succeed or fail as a group, according to application dictates.
- *Relational engine*: Relational objects such as Table, Index, and Referential integrity constraints are implemented in this component.
- *Storage engine*: This component stores and retrieves data from secondary storage, as well as managing transaction commit and rollback, backup and recovery, etc.

ODBMS Components

Object DBMS (ODBMS) has transaction and storage components that are analogous to those in an RDBMS. Some DBMS handle DDL, DML and update tasks differently. Instead of using sublanguages, they provide APIs for these purposes. They typically include a sublanguage and accompanying engine for processing queries with interpretive statements analogous to but not the same as SQL. Example object query languages are OQL, LINQ, JDOQL, JPAQL and others. The query engine returns collections of objects instead of relational rows.

TYPES OF ANALYTICAL DATABASE

Analysts may do their work directly against a data warehouse or create a separate analytic database for *Online Analytical Processing*. For example, a company might extract sales records for analyzing the effectiveness of advertising and other sales promotions at an aggregate level.

Data Warehouse

Data warehouses archive modern data from operational databases and often from external sources such as market research firms. Often operational data undergoes transformation on its way into the warehouse, getting summarized, anonymized, reclassified, etc. The warehouse becomes the central source of data for use by managers and other end-users who may not have access to operational data. For example, sales data might be aggregated to weekly totals and converted from internal product codes to use UPCs so that it can be compared with ACNielsen data.

Some basic and essential components of data warehousing include retrieving and analyzing data, transforming,loading and managing data so as to make it available for further use. Operations in a data warehouse are typically concerned with bulk data manipulation, and as such, it is unusual and inefficient to target individual rows for update, insert or delete. Bulk native loaders for input data and bulk SQL passes for aggregation are the norm.

Hypermedia Databases

The World Wide Web can be thought of as a database, albeit one spread across millions of independent computing systems. Web browsers "process" this data one page at a time, while Web crawlers and other software provide the equivalent of database indexes to support search and other activities.

Distributed Database

These are databases of local work-groups and departments at regional offices, branch offices, manufacturing plants and other work sites. These databases can include segments of both common operational and common user databases, as well as data generated and used only at a user's own site.

End-User Database

These databases consist of data developed by individual end-users. Examples of these are collections of documents in spreadsheets, word processing and downloaded files, even managing their personal baseball card collection.

External Database

These databases contain data collected for use across multiple organizations, either freely or via subscription. The Internet Movie Database is one example.

Operational Database

These databases store detailed data about the operations of an organization. They are typically organized by subject matter, process relatively high volumes of updates using transactions. Essentially every major organization on earth uses such databases.

Examples include customer databases that record contact, credit, and demographic information about a business' customers, personnel databases that hold information such as salary, benefits, skills data about employees, Enterprise resource planning that record details about product components, parts inventory, and financial databases that keep track of the organization's money, accounting and financial dealings.

MODELS JOF OBJECT DATABASE MODELS

In recent years, the object-oriented paradigm has been applied in areas such as engineering and spatial databases, telecommunications and in various scientific domains. The conglomeration of object oriented programming and database technology led to this new kind of database. These databases attempt to bring the database world and the application-programming world closer together, in particular by ensuring that the database uses the same type system as the application programme.

This aims to avoid the overhead (sometimes referred to as the *impedance mismatch*) of converting information between its representation in the database (for example as rows in tables) and its representation in the application programme (typically as objects). At the same time, object databases attempt to introduce key ideas of object programming, such as encapsulation and polymorphism, into the world of databases. A variety of these ways have been tried for storing objects in a database.

Some products have approached the problem from the application-programming side, by making the objects manipulated by the programme persistent. This also typically requires the addition of some kind of query language, since conventional programming languages do not provide language-level functionality for finding objects based on their information content.

Others have attacked the problem from the database end, by defining an object-oriented data model for the database, and defining a database programming language that allows full programming capabilities as well as traditional query facilities..

POST-RELATIONAL DATABASE MODELS

Products offering a more general data model than the relational model are sometimes classified as post-relational. Alternate terms include "hybrid database", "Object-enhanced RDBMS" and others. The data model in such products incorporates relations but is not constrained by E.F. Codd's Information Principle, which requires that all information in the database must be cast explicitly in terms of values in relations and in no other way

Some of these extensions to the relational model integrate concepts from technologies that pre-date the relational model. For example, they allow representation of a directed graph with trees on the nodes. The German company *sones* implements this concept in its GraphDB.

Some post-relational products extend relational systems with non-relational features. Others arrived in much the same place by adding relational features to pre-relational systems. Paradoxically, this allows products that are historically pre-relational, such as PICK and MUMPS, to make a plausible claim to be post-relational.

STORAGE STRUCTURES

Databases may store relational tables/indexes in memory or on hard disk in one of many forms:

- ordered/unordered flat files
- ISAM
- heaps
- hash buckets
- logically-blocked files
- Fractal Tree indexes
- B+ trees.

The most commonly used are B+ trees and ISAM. Object databases use a range of storage mechanisms. Some use virtual memory-mapped files to make the native language (C++, Java etc.) objects persistent. This can be highly efficient but it can make multi-language access more difficult. Others disassemble objects into fixed- and varying-length components that are then clustered in fixed sized blocks on disk and reassembled into the appropriate format on either the client or server address space.

Another popular technique involves storing the objects in tuples (much like a relational database), which the database server then reassembles into objects for the client. Other techniques include clustering by category (such as grouping data by month, or location), storing pre-computed query results, known as materialized views, partitioning data by range (e.g., a data range) or by hash. Memory management and storage topology can be important design choices for database designers as well. Just as normalization is used to reduce storage requirements and improve database designs, conversely denormalization is often used to reduce join complexity and reduce query execution time.

INDEXING

Indexing is a technique for improving database performance. The many types of indexes share the common property that they eliminate the need to examine every entry when running a query. In large databases, this can reduce query time/cost by orders of magnitude. The simplest form of index is a sorted list of values that can be searched using a binary search with an adjacent reference to the location of the entry, analogous to the index in the back of a book.

The same data can have multiple indexes (an employee database could be indexed by last name and hire date.) Indexes affect performance, but not results. Database designers can add or remove indexes without changing application logic, reducing maintenance costs as the database grows and database usage evolves. Given a particular query, the DBMS' query optimizer is responsible for devising the most efficient strategy for finding matching data.

The optimizer decides which index or indexes to use, how to combine data from different parts of the database, how to provide data in the order requested, etc. Indexes can speed up data access, but they consume space in the database, and must be updated each time the data is altered. Indexes therefore can speed data access but slow data maintenance. These two properties determine whether a given index is worth the cost.

TRANSACTIONS

As every software system, a DBMS operates in a faulty computing environment and prone to failures of many kinds. A failure can corrupt the respective database unless special measures are taken to prevent this. A DBMS achieves certain levels of fault tolerance by encapsulating in database transactions units of work (executed programmes) performed upon the respective database.

THE ACID RULES

Most DBMS provide some form of support for transactions, which allow multiple data items to be updated in a consistent fashion, such that updates that are part of a transaction succeed or fail in unison.

The so-called ACID rules, summarized here, characterize this behaviour:

- Atomicity: Either all the data changes in a transaction must happen, or none of them. The transaction must be completed, or else it must be undone (rolled back).
- Consistency: Every transaction must preserve the declared consistency rules for the database.
- Isolation: Two concurrent transactions cannot interfere with one another. Intermediate results within one transaction must remain invisible to other transactions. The most extreme form of isolation

is serializability, meaning that transactions that take place concurrently could instead be performed in some series, without affecting the ultimate result.

- Durability: Completed transactions cannot be aborted later or their results discarded. They must persist through (for instance) DBMS restarts.

In practice, many DBMSs allow the selective relaxation of these rules to balance perfect behaviour with optimum performance.

CONCURRENCY CONTROL AND LOCKING

Concurrency control is essential for the correctness of transactions executed concurrently in a DBMS, which is the common execution mode for performance reasons. The main concern and goal of concurrency control is isolation.

Isolation

Isolation refers to the ability of one transaction to see the results of other transactions. Greater isolation typically reduces performance and/or concurrency, leading DBMSs to provide administrative options to reduce isolation. For example, in a database that analyzes trends rather than looking at low-level detail, increased performance might justify allowing readers to see uncommitted changes ("dirty reads".)

A common way to achieve isolation is by locking. When a transaction modifies a resource, the DBMS stops other transactions from also modifying it, typically by locking it. Locks also provide one method of ensuring that data does not change while a transaction is reading it or even that it does not change until a transaction that once read it has completed.

Lock Types

Locks can be *shared* or *exclusive*, and can lock out *readers* and/or *writers*. Locks can be created *implicitly* by the DBMS when a transaction performs an operation, or *explicitly* at the transaction's request. Shared locks allow multiple transactions to lock the same resource. The lock persists until all such transactions complete. Exclusive locks are held by a single transaction and prevent other transactions from locking the same resource. Read locks are usually shared, and prevent other transactions from modifying the resource. Write locks are exclusive, and prevent other transactions from modifying the resource.

On some systems, write locks also prevent other transactions from reading the resource. The DBMS implicitly locks data when it is updated, and may also do so when it is read. Transactions explicitly lock data to ensure that they can complete without complications. Explicit locks may be useful for some administrative tasks. Locking can significantly affect database performance, especially with large and complex transactions in highly concurrent environments.

Lock Granularity

Locks can be coarse, covering an entire database, fine-grained, covering a single data item, or intermediate covering a collection of data such as all the rows in a RDBMS table.

Deadlocks

Deadlocks occur when two transactions each require data that the other has already locked exclusively. Deadlock detection is performed by the DBMS, which then aborts one of the transactions and allows the other to complete.

REPLICATION

Database replication involves maintaining multiple copies of a database on different computers, to allow more users to access it, or to allow a secondary site to immediately take over, if the primary site stops working. Some DBMS piggyback replication on top of their transaction logging facility, applying the primary's log to the secondary in near real-time. Database clustering is a related concept for handling larger databases and user communities by employing a cluster of multiple computers to host a single database that can use replication as part of its approach.

Security

Database security denotes the system, processes, and procedures that protect a database from unauthorized activity.

DBMSs usually enforce security through access control, auditing, and encryption:

- Access control manages who can connect to the database via authentication and what they can do via authorization.
- Auditing records information about database activity: who, what, when, and possibly where.
- Encryption protects data at the lowest possible level by storing and possibly transmitting data in an unreadable form. The DBMS encrypts data when it is added to the database and decrypts it when returning query results. This process can occur on the client side of a network connection to prevent unauthorized access at the point of use.

Confidentiality

Law and regulation governs the release of information from some databases, protecting medical history, driving records, telephone logs, etc. In the United Kingdom, database privacy regulation falls under the Office of the Information Commissioner. Organizations based in the United Kingdom and holding personal data in digital format such as databases must register with the Office.

MEASURING E-COMMERCE SUCCESS

CIOs often suggest that better measures of the payoffs of e-commerce operational and capital investments are necessary to demonstrate the value creation of e-commerce initiatives and to obtain additional resources for critical e-commerce projects. The measures are essential to monitor the key performance drivers (inputs and processes) and assess whether the e-commerce initiative is achieving its stated objectives (outputs) and thus contributing to the long-term success of the corporation (outcomes).

Companies often waste resources on e-commerce initiatives or do not invest when they should because they cannot effectively evaluate the potential payoffs of e-commerce investments.Measuring returns on e-commerce projects can be a daunting challenge. Predicting customer behaviour is difficult, because using the Web to do business is still relatively new to many businesses and thus forecasting sales and profits is typically imprecise. There is not much historical data and experience for managers to draw upon when developing or applying metrics, and many economic benefits of e-commerce projects are seen as difficult to measure.

Further, the pace of change in e-business and Web-based technologies has been so rapid that precise measurements are often difficult.Many senior managers have come to believe that further investment in new technology and e-commerce is an imperative that is required to maintain or develop a competitive position. They often make expenditures without completing a rigorous analysis. However, today's more stringent economic environment and the widely publicized negative impacts of many e-commerce initiatives has caused many senior managers to question the payoffs of e-commerce investments. As companies assess the choice of appropriate measures to evaluate e-commerce initiatives, numerous potential issues arise.

Since the choices are different for each company, because the strategies, structures, and systems are different, substantial customization is necessary. Senior managers should consider six initial questions that can lead to the development of appropriate measures for e-commerce operations:

- What measurement systems are currently in place and being utilized within the organization?
- What are the important criteria to the company and its constituencies and stakeholders?
- What does the company desire to accomplish with the e-commerce initiative?
- What is the anticipated time frame associated with the e-commerce programme?
- Who are the parties involved in implementing the e-commerce project, and who will be affected by the results?
- What critical processes are associated with the successful execution of the e-commerce project?

To address these questions, it is imperative that companies not only specifically tailor their e-commerce measurement approach but also utilize multiple measures to fully analyse their situations. Different measurement criteria are important for companies that have different strategies or may be in a different stage of their life cycle or their e-commerce development. The multiple measures will typically include both financial and nonfinancial measures that are leading and lagging indicators of performance.

They may be used in a balanced-scorecard, shareholder-value-added, or other approach and can be developed specificallyf or IT or e-commerce or as a part of an overall corporate performance measurement system. Companies can also use a weighted scoring system to evaluate investments related to overall IT, e-commerce, or business strategy.

There are many obstacles to implementing a successful measurement system, whether a lack of focus, a low priority, or just difficulty. It is the responsibility of senior managers to evaluate the e-commerce initiatives and decide on the right measures for their organization and ensure that the measures are captured and responded to properly.

To obtain adequate resources for e-commerce and to effectively manage e-commerce initiatives, the payoffs of e-commerce investments must be calculated and integrated into management decision-making systems.

DEVELOPING APPROPRIATE METRICS

To closely monitor the cause and effect relationships evidenced in the e-commerce causal linkage model, appropriate metrics must be developed. These metrics must be consistent with and support the objectives and drivers and key success factors already defined. The selected metrics will likely include a combination of input, processes, output, and outcome metrics to effectively measure performance.

Senior managers involved in the e-commerce decision-making process should develop metrics appropriate to the strategy and objectives of the e-commerce initiative, the company, and its stakeholders. During the measure selection process, it is useful for the involved individuals to choose just a few measures, to focus those senior managers involved in the e-commerce initiative on the critical performance indicators.

The list of metrics presented here is not meant to be a comprehensive set of e-commerce performance measures. Rather, it is a selection and example of some metrics that may be appropriate. Managers must select those that most closely fit their strategy and adapt or develop others. There is no rule for the right number of metrics to include in a measurement system; however, including too many tends to distract managers from pursuing a focused strategy. Generally, a complete measurement system includes perhaps three to six measures for each element being evaluated and no more than twenty measures in total.

For each key success factor, a specific target should be identified and results should be measured against these targets. These results should be widely communicated among not only those senior managers directly involved in the e-commerce initiative, but also other individuals within the organization upon whom the initiative will have an impact.

One of the important contributions that e-commerce can make to an organization is an expanded communication and informational capability. Any e-commerce measurement system will have little impact if the results are not fully discussed. Results should be monitored regularly and used to identify areas of weakness, address the plans and systems in place, and establish new initiatives to improve deficiencies.

The measures chosen should be quantifiable, in either absolute or percentage terms, as well as complete and controllable. They should be complete in that the measure sums up in one number the contribution of all elements of performance that matter; for example, profitability is a summary measure of revenue generation and cost control. They should be controllable in that employees in the organization can actually influence improvement in the factor measured.

Some of the metrics shown here are evaluations of overall firm performance. Others are indicators of e-commerce performance that are derived through an aggregation of measures of individual business units and functions. It is important to evaluate the performance of both overall e-commerce performance and the specific aspects of e-commerce that lead to revenue enhancement or cost savings to determine the success of various operations and corrective action that can be taken to make improvements.

The measures should be of use to both senior and middle managers in the business units and functions. Thus, they must be disaggregated so each unit can examine its contribution to the achievement of the company's e-commerce strategy.

These analyses ensure that each unit is making a contribution to the e-commerce initiative and improving corporate profitability. Additionally, these metrics can be used to provide a gap analysis that permits managers to determine what other inputs or processes are required to meet the company's e-commerce project objectives. Different tools and techniques are available to measure the different aspects of e-commerce performance.

For example, online surveys and polls are powerful tools to help e-commerce enabled companies to better understand the benefit of Internet usage for increasing revenue or decreasing costs related to their customers, thus providing valuable information regarding opportunities to improve overall profitability. Internally, surveys, focus groups, and other techniques are increasingly being used to measure and monitor employee, personnel, and stakeholder reactions and provide valuable feedback.

Once metrics have been developed, data on these indicators must be collected and statistical analysis, such as multiple regression, should be performed to analyse and test the validity of the customized e-commerce measurement system and causal relationships hypothesized by the company. As companies evaluate the initial measurement system's performance, they will typically add some metrics and drop others because of a lack of evidence of a strong relationship. It is here that a final measurement system emerges, and the focus then shifts to applying the model to support improved decision making.

Outputs and outcomes: Overall-firm and e-commerce-specific performance. If the e-commerce initiatives are well designed and executed and the model of causal relationships properly specified, the identified inputs and processes should lead to improved performance. This should include increasing the success of the e-commerce initiative (outputs) and ultimately to improve corporate performance either through increased revenues or decreased costs (outcomes). To properly evaluate e-commerce performance, input, process, output, and outcome measures are all necessary and should be clearly linked in a causal relationship.

These performance indicators empower senior managers with the information to evaluate whether the e-commerce programme is achieving its stated objectives and contributing to overall corporate profitability. For example, metrics such as the percentage of customer attrition are indicators of the e-commerce customer service provided by the company and the related level of customer satisfaction. Since the goals relate to increasing corporate profits, not just improving customer satisfaction, both output and outcome measures are necessary.

A weak performance on the output metrics should signal a need to examine the inputs and processes and determine whether they have been misspecified or just poorly executed. It also can provide an opportunity to identify potential benefits to organizational effectiveness and profitability from e-commerce that may have been overlooked.

This is an opportunity to examine how well e-commerce programs are contributing to corporate profits and should unveil specific opportunities, directions for improvements, and standards of performance. The e-commerce measurement system should highlight the specific contributions of the e-commerce activities, in addition to providing valuable feedback that can lead to future e-commerce programme and corporate improvements.

Results from the e-commerce evaluation and measurement process should be widely communicated throughout the organization. In a well-executed e-commerce venture, all units of the company will have some involvement in the e-commerce initiative.

The evaluation and measurement of the e-commerce programme will have little impact if the results are not disseminated throughout the organization to the many disparate areas that both affect and are affected by it. Results should be monitored regularly and used to identify areas of weakness, challenge the plans and systems in place, and present new initiatives to improve deficiencies.

MEASUREMENT PRACTICES IN E-COMMERCE

Strong measurement practices form one of the cornerstones of good systems, particularly in e-commerce. Performance measures for e-commerce must overcome the uncertainty and unique dynamics associated with the Internet and must be more frequently adjusted in response to real-time information.

With these considerations, no company should simply extend its existing performance measures to an e-commerce venture. Still, long-term cost differentials must be balanced with other financial and nonfinancial measures and leading and lagging indicators that are particularly useful for successful e-commerce implementations.

The information systems of the 1990s gave CEOs a new method of accessing, analyzing, and reporting on the accountability of their organization. The systems developed during this time of advancement in information technology helped to create a more streamlined capability for centralized accountability. The variety of data made available to a company at that time ranged from corporate-level results to the small-scale measurements of performance that enabled management to recognize advantages and potential problems in real-time. E-Commerce transforms these capabilities.

Like the root system of a massive tree, IT accountability systems helped management reach and observe every aspect of their business. With the addition of e-commerce to a pre-existing IT accountability system, companies can simplify access to previously collected information for those within the company and for external stakeholders, including partners, customers, and investors. New information could be created and both financial and nonfinancial measures could be integrated into the decision-making process.

The information could also be easily and quickly aggregated and disaggregated to facilitate various decisions. Managers could now measure inputs, processes, outputs, and outcomes in ways never before possible. Cisco's new systems permit outsiders to view on its Web site not only its general business plan but also the company's performance statistics at any given moment.

Seamlessness between internal IT systems and e-commerce gives Cisco the ability to provide such information with relatively little effort. This transparency between internal and external systems also helped Cisco endure many of the pitfalls associated with the technology bust by expanding the role of e-commerce to replace human positions throughout the company.

But e-commerce can be used for more than simply replacing employees. Instead, the information made available through a well-developed e-commerce initiative can empower employees at every level of business. Improved measurement is a key component. Management receives information in a timely manner, which lets it act on up-to-date measures of performance, while lower-level employees can access information at any time and take the initiative based on that information, with or without direct managerial direction. Among the most important aspects of e-commerce as it applies to system management and measurement is maintaining consistency across all company lines. A company implementing a new e-commerce solution should ensure consistency among accounting systems, information technology systems, and e-commerce systems and related measures. However, the implementation of an e-commerce solution also necessitates working to ensure compatibility between the systems of business partners using unified e-commerce solutions.

The uniquely advantageous relationship between Dell and its suppliers would not be possible without seamless internal and external systems that enable a free flow of information and measures between companies. E-commerce can facilitate consistency of information and measurements by cascading information throughout the organization and then externally to other stakeholders.

In addition to measuring the performance of the business, e-commerce brings added importance to measuring the value and functionality of operations. Most e-commerce strategies will have a strong operational component, including cost savings from value chain management and cuts in labour costs for the online channel. Operational measures should be tracked by some dedicated resource and balanced between financial and nonfinancial assessments of operational performance. This analysis can lead to a better understanding of the payoffs of investment in e-commerce initiatives.

CUSTOMER RELATIONSHIPS

Under traditional business models, it may be sufficient to offer customer service during normal business hours, either at physical locations or over the phone. E-commerce dramatically changes those expectations both in terms of company strategy and the customer's perspective.

Near-universal and constant customer service availability is expected for almost any viable e-commerce strategy. Companies must re-examine their customer service practices and make numerous key decisions in moving toward universal availability. Two of the main considerations are the distribution of response tasks between human and automated systems and the operating hours for human responses. Each of these include trade-offs among speed, cost, convenience, and efficiency.

Most e-commerce ventures have developed some FAQ (frequently asked questions) function on their Web sites. This function may consist of rudimentary inquiries only or a highly sophisticated taxonomy of nearly every conceivable question. The nature of the offering and the Web site dictates how sophisticated the FAQs should be, but no company can exhaust the list of possible questions. The challenge then becomes how to provide service to customers who are dissatisfied with the FAQs. A company may choose to provide immediate or delayed email support to customers or may offer a phone line for further inquiries. The company must weigh the value of instant response and satisfaction to the customer against the added costs associated with phone banks or with rapid and 24/7 email response.

Some pure-play companies like Half.com chose to keep the process entirely online and not offer phone service. For traditional companies, however, this strategy is more difficult, as it can inundate the traditional business phone lines with Internet inquiries. Delta Airlines, on the other hand, was able to reduce its phone volume and increase its status among elite customers by moving reservation information online while simultaneously implementing a wireless initiative.

Delta first identified such a programme as "nice to have" but not a necessity, but the company quickly recognized the appeal of wireless capabilities to its elite customers by providing quick access to vast amounts of information. Implementing this programme was not only a cost-saving move, but also a successful effort to appeal to customers who desired this level of functionality.

For companies that do provide phone service in addition to their FAQs and Internet support, a decision must be made on availability. Limiting phone support to normal business hours reduces some of the value added associated with the Web site. On the other hand, labour costs may not justify 24/7 phone service for industries that offer commodity goods. More technical industries, B2B companies, and companies with customized and personalized Internet-related offerings should carefully consider offering a 24/7 service.

Another aspect of customer service practices is the development and implementation of policies on shipping, delivery, and returns. In particular, companies that use physical branches as part of a bricks-and-clicks strategy must not neglect proper training on the traditional commerce side necessary to facilitate e-commerce developments and service. Customer service representatives in physical branches must be thoroughly familiar with the Web site, its function, and its policies.

While e-commerce requires changes and enhancement to customer service policies, it also affords most companies excellent opportunities to refine marketing strategies, selling practices, pricing, and Web site design by observing customer behaviour. Physical branches have more limited opportunities to collect customer data, particularly data from sites where customers can impart complaints or grievances.

When customers shop online, however, their every mouse click is potentially revealing and useful for future improvements in e-commerce service.Although these methods require substantial analysis, companies can draw strong implications and direction about customer behaviour from this data. Unused search results may indicate a problem with the search engine. Aborted purchases may indicate that the checkout procedure is unclear or too time-consuming. Consistent nonpurchase of a product may indicate that more precise information is needed to inspire consumer confidence. Corporations must be willing and able to redesign their Web sites and refine customer processes based on the gathered information as well as direct feedback from the customers. Since convenience is a prime source of competitive advantage, problems with customer service systems must be addressed immediately.

Although shutting down the Web site is undesirable, important changes should be made by closing the site for a few hours in nonpeak time and by warning the customers in advance of this downtime.

Thus, to effectively manage and enhance customer service attributes:

- Companies with an Internet presence should provide any information that a customer might need while online.
- Corporate Web sites should incorporate some form of direct contact mechanism, whether it is as simple as a service phone number or as advanced as online chat capabilities.
- Companies should ensure that the Web site easily connects to any other aspect of the company service that a customer might need information about, ranging from traditional brick-and-mortar locations to shipping policies.

PAYOFFS OF E-COMMERCE

We have examined how various organizational inputs and processes can impact the outputs of e-commerce. We have examined leadership, strategy, structure, and systems both in the corporation generally and related specifically to e-commerce. We have also seen how these key factors of success can be successfully managed in a formal process to improve customer acquisitions, customer loyalty, cost savings, channel optimization, and value creation.

Although these outputs are important, the resource allocation decision should rely on understanding the impact of e-commerce decisions and actions on the outcome of improved corporate profitability.

Many researchers and managers have recognized the need to identify and measure the impacts of corporate actions and to provide a better analysis of the return on investment (ROI) of e-commerce expenditures. However, the appropriate metrics have not been well developed. The framework presented here provides the necessary specificity to identify both the causal relationships that lead to e-commerce success, and related measures. In this way, both general managers and IT and e-commerce professionals can more effectively evaluate the success of e-commerce and the potential and actual payoffs of e-commerce investments.

Managers now can also examine the interrelationships among the characteristics of e-commerce success discussed here. The causal linkage analysis illustrates the importance of leadership, strategy, structure, and systems and highlights the specific managerial actions that lead to success. Some writers have suggested the need for more measurements of the effectiveness of IT. They note that corporations have overlooked economic rationality in justifying IT expenditures and instead have leaned toward a strategy that resembled an arms race, where firms acquire the best and most recent technologies to outpace others, regardless of the results.

To assess the payoffs of e-commerce investments, companies must implement systems that evaluate the impact of e-commerce initiatives on financial performance and the trade-offs that must be made among competing organizational constraints and barriers to implementation. These systems assist senior executives as they develop an e-commerce strategy and allocate corporate resources to support that strategy. The systems also assist e-commerce managers to evaluate the trade-offs and decide which projects provide the largest net benefit to both short-term financial performance and the long-term success of the firm. The careful identification and measurement of the payoffs also permits e-commerce and IT managers to demonstrate the impact on corporate profitability and value creation.

It also provides information for better corporate resource allocation decisions in the CEO's and CFO's offices, based on a better understanding of the ROI—including a fuller understanding of the benefits and costs of e-commerce. Hence, to implement their e-commerce strategy, companies are faced with a significant challenge: to quantify the link between corporate actions in e-commerce and corporate financial performance. Indeed, only by making the "business case" for e-commerce expenditures can managers truly integrate potential e-commerce impacts into their business strategies. Yet, many companies have failed to make a case for e-commerce initiatives. Instead, they have often acted because they had a feeling that it was the right thing to do or because their competitors were making the leap into e-commerce ventures. However, projects put into place for these reasons alone are vulnerable to cost overruns and poor ROI, changes in senior management, or shifting corporate or consumer priorities.

To present a clear business case for e-commerce initiatives, senior managers need to identify the metrics of e-commerce performance and how that performance impacts overall long-term corporate profitability. This increased attention to the thorough identification and measurement of the metrics of e-commerce is echoed in popular measurement frameworks such as the popular strategic management system "balanced scorecard." Frameworks such as balanced scorecard and shareholder value analysis focus on the causal relationships and linkages within organizations and the actions managers can implement to improve both customer and corporate profitability and drive increased value. However, substantial work is required to establish the relationships that relate specifically to e-commerce strategies.

Undeniably, the identification and measurement of the impact of e-commerce strategies is particularly difficult as they are usually linked to long time horizons, a high level of uncertainty, and impacts that are often difficult to quantify. But this analysis is important to improve resource allocation, decision making, and profitability. In recent years, companies have placed increasing importance on the development of performance metrics to better measure and manage e-commerce performance. Software programs and information systems have been developed to provide a broader set of measurement tools to incorporate into new strategic management systems.

Although the need for performance measures for e-commerce has been identified, a large number of specific metrics have not been proposed. E-commerce analysis has typically been operating without measures that permit an effective evaluation of e-commerce benefits, success, or value. This lack of performance metrics has meant a lack of both actual and perceived accountability for firm e-commerce operations to various stakeholders. It also examines how companies can make a compelling business case for e-commerce programs. Senior managers understand how to measure the value of e-commerce and understand the payoffs of e-commerce investments. Its purpose is to answer the question, "Is it worth it?" for companies deciding to start or expand e-commerce projects. This quandary is compounded as senior managers consider the high costs typically associated with e-commerce and the seemingly small percentage of e-commerce or IT projects that succeed. Sometimes the projects are flawed, but often the measures of success are flawed.

Examples abound where companies have attempted e-commerce initiatives and have either failed dramatically or have incurred costs that far outweighed the gains. Though some would suggest that those failures occurred when companies were not so well centered on ensuring that IT-related funds were well spent, companies today face similar questions about the value of their e-commerce initiatives. For most companies, it is not a question of whether or not to invest in e-commerce, but when and how: Should it be a large amount up front, or perhaps a smaller expenditure at a later date? Such decisions are critical and difficult. Key to making these decisions is understanding the causal relationships and identifying and measuring the success of the specific actions that managers can take to drive e-commerce success.

METHODS OF E-COMMERCE STRATEGY

Partial corporate integration takes a slower approach to the implementation of an e-Commerce strategy, while recognizing that full integration between the systems of e-Commerce and the traditional business is ultimately desirable. The decision to integrate slowly and follow market leaders can be due to resource constraints or to a desire to limit the business disruption.

Though the resource constraints can be significant company-wide, often they are imposed on the e-Commerce function because the payoffs of the potential ecommerce investments and the ROI are not effectively calculated. Partial corporate integration, a more cautious strategy, certainly involves all the limitations of follower strategies. Innovation is often limited, as is growth. The

CEO makes these strategic choices, often to avoid diverting employee attention and focus from even more compelling initiatives. Companies adopting this strategy are often encouraged to spend less on IT and to wait for a technology to become mainstream and the trends to become clearer before implementing it.

They also view IT as a commodity available to the entire market, similar to the availability of electricity and other technologies that companies use on a daily basis. While there is some historical merit to this argument, a significant problem is the danger of not doing enough to compete with the IT solutions of other companies. A slower strategy might work for an industry leader, yet enough innovation remains to be accomplished in IT and e-Commerce that the companies able to identify unique opportunities in e-Commerce are going to benefit the most from the nearly ubiquitous presence of the Internet and its related technologies in the marketplace.

	Full Integration	**Partial Corporate Integration**	**Business Unit Integration**
Description	Complete integration of e-commerce throughout all company operations and activities	Promotes the use of e-commerce throughout a company but without full dedication or implementation	Fully implements an e-commerce venture but only for select business units or functions
Benefits	Unified strategy for both e-commerce and traditional business, with e-commerce being given full support	Significant cost savings and reduced risk	Companies are able to modify the characteristics of e-commerce to fit particular business needs
Shortcomings	Does not always adequately consider the potentially broad corporate impacts of cross-channel conflict and cannibalization	Innovation, technological advantages, and potential benefits over competitors are underemphasized	Benefits of integration are not realized throughout company

A partial corporate integration provides support and direction for e-Commerce throughout the organization, monitoring of external customer and competitor e-Commerce activities and needs, without making the major financial or organizational commitment of full integration. Of course, in many cases industry leaders have wasted assets on e-Commerce investments, with no payoff.

Business unit integration uses a building-block approach to determine how e-Commerce can fit within a company's larger business strategy, choosing to fully integrate e-Commerce into one or more business units or functions, rather than throughout the company. e-Commerce may be integrated by business unit, functions, product lines, customers, or suppliers. Essentially, companies look at their business and decide where e-Commerce could fit within different parts of their pre-existing model. An analysis of e-Commerce success stories shows that companies can use a similar model, but often only temporarily, as a way to move toward a fully integrated e-Commerce solution.

Many companies just do not have the resources to fully implement an e-Commerce solution. One challenge for companies adopting this strategy is that some of their competitors may have significant revenue and cost advantages with a more complete e-Commerce integration throughout all of their business units, functions, and operations. Some companies choose to introduce e-Commerce into their strategy slowly, creating stepping-stones that can eventually result in a full implementation of the e-Commerce strategy.

They may include an evaluation of the elements of strategy that can be implemented at any given time. The implementation can be accomplished through a number of different methods, such as the creation of a temporary separate business unit with the sole purpose of developing a company-wide e-Commerce solution as efficiently as possible before being folded back into the larger business structure.

Of course, some companies do not desire, or require, that e-Commerce permeate all aspects of their business structure. Limiting e-Commerce to certain company functions such as HR, payroll, marketing, or customer service may be optimal, but only when these limitations are dictated by the needs of the company rather than by the fears of a company's leadership. In these implementations the process can permit e-Commerce to take hold in particular units or functions that require it while not interfering with others.

Such an approach allows for the creativity of a separate unit model to find the best ways to incorporate e-Commerce in its limited role, while still keeping the project close enough to the core of the company to ensure that the e-Commerce initiative maintains a certain company focus. There are two critical success factors to formulating a coherent e-Commerce strategy: multi-channel coordination and effectiveness.

1. Multi-channel coordination encompasses the wide variety of aspects of traditional business that must be modified to fully utilize the

advantages made available by the opportunities of e-Commerce. This includes a focus on creating value primarily through revenue increases, though cost savings also can be significant.

2. Effectiveness deals not only with the financial characteristics of e-Commerce, but also with the effective use of e-Commerce-related technologies and functions to take advantage of company capabilities. The focus tends to be more on creating value through cost control and operational effectiveness.

THE TECHNICAL ENVIRONMENT FOR E-COMMERCE

Many of the claims for a significant break with the past stem from the more sceptical accounts of post-industrialism and the information-based economy, for example by the sociologist Daniel Bell. Other more enthusiastic and technologically determinist accounts include those of the futurologist Alvin Toffler, who coined the phrase 'Third Wave' to imply an impending information revolution. What they share is the prediction and formulation of the concept of an 'information society'. The problem for commentators like Bell and Toffler (in common with almost everybody else) was an inability to predict the physical agency that would bring the 'information society' to fruition. This agency was the Internet.

The Internet began life in 1969 as a demonstration project linking up four university campuses in the United States. It showed how a primitive file-sharing system worked. Today the Internet boasts in excess of 300 million users, offering the most rapid take-up of any technology in history. For a relatively small outlay on a computer, a suitable telecommunications link (e.g. via a phone line and modem) and an on-line account provided by an internet service provider, individuals located across the globe can access this massive network which has grown at an exponential rate.

The network - the Internet - hooks up the physical infrastructure of computers via cable and wireless links so that users can access rich informational sources (e.g. via the Web) and use interactive forms of communication (e.g. e-mail). However, though the population of Internet users across the globe has grown exponentially, their dispersal is not uniform internationally. The relative density of hosts across the globe is variable. It may be unsurprising to note that the higher concentrations of users are in North America and Europe.

Levels of computers and data services can be shown by measuring Internet access. Network Wizards provide a longitudinal study of the growth of Internet nodes (computers with unique 'Internet Protocol' (IP) addresses) from the network's earliest days. Growth between 1980 and 1987 shows numbers of hosts in the tens of thousands. After 1987, when the US funding body NSF (National Science Foundation) started to work with the Internet, the growth leapt into the hundreds of thousands: many non-US academic sites and scientific and research bodies linked up at this point. The next pulse of acceleration of this growth came when the World Wide Web appeared in 1990. Rapid growth rates ensued, especially after 1993, when the graphical browser called Mosaic appeared, and the scale of change moved into the millions. From an almost unknown medium at the beginning of the 1990s, the Internet by the year 2000 was heading for 100 million *hosts* (i.e. unique computers linked up) across the world. Gartzen (2001) estimates that in broad terms the number of users is due to grow from around 300 million in 2001 to around 1 billion in 2005.

In addition to these *fixed* hosts that link individual desktop computers to the Internet there will be *mobile* hosts linking up mobile phones to it using wireless technology. In predictions offered in May 2001, phones labelled as 'Third Generation' (3G) in Gartzen's 'ball park' are due to amount to 1 billion by 2005.

This potential rapidity of the Internet's growth creates problems for its continued deployment. Notwithstanding the assumptions underlying these forecasts, even the current global downturn does not detract from the problems associated with the growth of Internet usage. This issue will become sharper if the 'digital divide' is not overcome. That is, between countries that are hardly wired, as in the developing world, and those with maturing virtual infrastructure, for example in the advanced economies.

The Internet - an *inter*connected series of *net*works - began life as a project supported by the US Department of Defense's Advanced Research Project Agency (ARPA). Based on an original concept (the use of a multi-nodal network) developed by the Rand Corporation in the early 1960s and added to by bodies such as the UK National Physical Laboratory (which had developed packet switching ideas), the objective of the research was to provide the United States with a communications network that would survive in the event of a nuclear conflagration. This product of the Cold War was a network purposely designed to offer resilience during a hot war of massive destruction such that it would continue to function whilst 'in tatters'.

Up to this time, network paradigms had offered a central node by which messages could be routed (on a circuit-switched basis). A paradigm is defined as a set of theories, concepts, methodologies and practices usually associated with particular forms of knowledge.

For example, the natural sciences and social sciences have complementary but sometimes opposing paradigms. So the implication was that if this one central node were to be destroyed, then communications on a continent-wide US basis would have been impossible. In order to circumvent such an emergency, the need was established for a network whose technical architecture was based on multiple nodes, and whose messages could be distributed as packets of data.

As long as every computer linked to the network could be uniquely identified, then messages broken up into packets (each with a header detailing message destination and source) could be routed across the network via diverse nodes and could be reassembled at the destination computer. In-built system resilience meant that if elements of a message were not present for reassembly (identified through gaps in packet sequences), an automatic request would be generated for retransmission. The events of 11 September demonstrated the robust nature of the Internet: where fixed and mobile telephony failed to function in parts of Manhattan after the deadly attacks on the World Trade Centre, e-mail continued to get through.

One notable feature of the Internet's tremendous growth is based on the fact that core software elements were given away by suppliers for free. Mosaic - the first graphical browser - was distributed via the Internet and magazine CD-ROMs to all who wanted to use it at no charge. Its authors (who worked at a university department in Illinois) received no royalties for this work.

In the same manner, the underlying software operating system of the Internet - TCP/IP - was also available free to anybody who could hook up to the Internet. TCP/IP is a set of protocols or technical definitions, developed by Vinton Cerf, which, when rolled out across a number of networks in 1983, allowed their inter-linkage and the coining of the term 'Internet'. TCP (Transfer Control Protocol) and IP (Internet Protocol) handle packet disassembly/ reassembly and computer addressing respectively.

Central to the development of the Internet is the root democracy. The ARPAnet was developed for operation under cataclysmic conditions. Whatever remnant nodes that existed on a network were required to function. One way of helping to maximize success was to keep any processing tasks as simple as possible. So once the interrogation of a packet's destination is adduced, a routing computer does little more than pass it on. At root, therefore, the Internet evinces 'packet switching democracy': all packets are equal under TCP/IP. In the event of a network disruption, therefore, all packets would be delayed equally.

This inherent lack of packet prioritization has significance for any time-critical or contiguous operations, and thus the efficacy of the Internet can be called into question, not least by commercial interests. This treatment of message packets is defined by the IP protocol in its fourth version (known as IPv4). Though a new version, IPv6, allows packet prioritization, it is not yet pervasive. For some commercial interests, delay in introducing this prioritization will be significant, and ultimately have an impact on the growth of e-Commerce.

While TCP/IP has provided the 'glue'of the Internet, until 1993 it was mainly the preserve of a 'high priesthood' of academics and scientists who used detailed knowledge of protocols to exploit Internet applications. Only with the emergence of the World Wide Web - or 'the Web' - did individuals with little knowledge of such protocols manage to participate in this electronic medium. Initially the Web was text-based only.

The relative simplicity with which new users can hook up to the Internet, given telecoms access, has meant its vast and dispersed take-up, such that demand peaks can lead to network congestion and the so-called 'World Wide Wait'. Innate human perception of delays in response times means that 'waiting' for more than a second can be intolerable for some. Nevertheless, the response of suppliers has not been slow, as the vast investments in Internet connectivity make clear. However, the very success that the Internet enjoyed in its rapid take-up led to so much conceptual and financial hyperbole during the late 1990s that speculative activities intended to reap vast profits from vast investments reaped vast losses instead.

On so much technical configuration does human response lie. If nothing else, the dotcom crash had the effect of sharpening the eye for the detail of the Internet's case. In a fundamental degree that case is shaped by technical protocols. Where once the examination of such arcane documents may have been the preserve of technical departments, now they are examined in boardrooms. Many are aware that technical protocols govern the way they undertake business, and that tiny changes to protocols, for example, can have disproportionate effects on business prospects. The ability to influence the technical standards of Internet technologies is therefore to permit some control over financial destinies.

3

The Law of E-commerce

INTRODUCTION

Of greater significance, and the subject of this Report, are those areas of the law that apply specifically to e-commerce. This may be due to the fact that 'old' law applies in an unusual way to e-commerce due to the unpredictable (at the time that law was made) nature of the transaction.

Or it may be due to the presence of 'new'law, which, though it may not have been formulated to deal with e-commerce exclusively, clearly has it in contemplation as the main target of its intended regulation. The list that appears below contains those areas of law that are of particular (and in some cases exclusive) interest to e-commerce businesses:

FORMATION OF CONTRACT

How does the law of offer and acceptance apply to an online transaction? In other words, how will a contract be formed in the virtual world? Will a web page that displays a product for sale be an offer or an invitation to treat? This issue has yet to be decided by the courts.

INTELLECTUAL PROPERTY RIGHTS

Much of the value in an *idea* for an e-commerce website can be tied up in the Intellectual Property Rights (IPR's).It is essential, particularly when trying to attract seed money from venture capitalists, that these IPR's are delineated and transferred to the trading vehicle. They may be owned by a number of different people and so IPR assignments will need to be executed at an early stage.

In any event the value of IPR's is notoriously underestimated by businessmen. Appropriate steps must be taken to protect this value and to take steps to safeguard any brand name and associated goodwill.

COPYRIGHT

Copyright is of course comprised in IPR's, but there are some specific considerations in relation to copyright that need to be looked at. We know that the law of copyright protects literary and artistic works and that these are the sorts of works that comprise a web page. So far so good. But what about links from one web page to another?

Could they constitute breach of copyright? Of course in most instances, there would be no complaint because a link from one website to another would generate increased traffic and this surely is the objective of websites. But in one case a newspaper's website contained a link to the news section of another newspaper's website. It was held in an interim application to the court that this could constitute copyright infringement. The reason for the case was that the link bypassed the front (or home) page of the other website and so the users did not get to see the advertising messages on that home page — this technique is known as deep-linking. Sites that undertake deep-linking should be aware of the potential legal challenges that could arise.

DOMAIN NAMES AND CYBERSQUATTING

The fact that every website must have a unique Internet address means that many commercial enterprises will be disappointed in their desire for a specific domain name. This is the problem that is inherent in a first-come-first-served system of domain name registrations.

Difficulties can arise when one business feels it should be entitled to use a domain name that has already been registered by someone else. Domain names are considered in detail together with the practice known as 'cybersquatting'and the possible methods for acquiring a domain name that has already been registered by someone else.

DATA PROTECTION

This area of the law governs what may and what may not be done with individuals' personal information. In many cases much of the value in an e-commerce business is in its customer database, which may consist of a variety of information including name, address, e-mail address, date of birth, shopping habits, annual household income, etc.

The law establishes a code of conduct (known as the Eight Data Protection Principles) for the processing of such data as well as a right for every individual to see a copy of such data if they request it.

DISTANCE SELLING REGULATIONS

Towards the end of 2000, and in response to European Union legislation, the UK passed the Consumer Protection (Distance Selling) Regulations. These regulations require all UK businesses that enter contracts with consumers 'at a distance' (clearly this includes, but is not exclusive to, Internet transactions) to do two main things that they were not legally obliged to do before.

The first is to provide certain specific information to the consumer and the second is to allow consumers a 'cooling-off' period of seven working days from receipt of goods to return the goods for a full refund.

IT Requi rements

There will be a number of legal considerations which arise from the infrastructure and services which are required for an e-commerce business. Hence there may be purchase or rental of hardware and software, rental of server space if required and a website hosting and development agreement where the hosting is to be outsourced. These topics are considered where relevant throughout this Report.

Law and Jurisdiction

One of the difficulties with an Internet transaction is that the buyer and seller may be in different parts of the world. The question then arises as to which legal system will govern the contract in the absence of any binding express provision. A related question but one which is more complex and somewhat political is which court system will have jurisdiction to hear any relevant litigation?

LEGAL ISSUES IN E-COMMERCE

A comprehensive international legislation system for global e-Commerce does not exist at present and it is not expected in the foreseeable future. Even within the United States, which is so advanced in its use of the Internet, certain e-Commerce legal issues have caused significant disagreements, such as the validity of digital signatures.

While waiting for federal legislation, many states have set up their own laws, which have been widely different in substance from state to state. Organizations such as the UN conference on international trade law have been actively calling for global co-ordination of appropriate legal structures. The most important issues are copyright protection, contractual agreements and privacy laws.

E-COMMERCE GLOBAL STRATEGIES

The organizations practising in the area of e-Commerce are facing a number of d ecisions regarding their global activities. Having analysed the characteristics of the target foreign market, they now face the next stage of developing an international marketing programme.

This would include defining and selecting target segments, positioning the product or service and making the decision to modify the elements of the marketing mix to suit the conditions of the foreign market. For physical goods, the marketing mix is composed of four elements: product, price, place (distribution) and promotion. For services, the marketing mix extends to seven elements with the addition of people, processes and physical evidence.

Given the diversity of the global environment, with differing cultures, customs and competition, the decision facing the e-Commerce marketer is the degree of change necessary within the elements of the marketing mix.

There are a number of pressures affecting this decision, which can be summarized as (1) staying local versus going global, (2) standardization or adaptation.

Local Versus Global

Ten years ago 'pan-European' advertising was all the rage among direct marketing companies in the United Kingdom. A precursor of global communication, it was based on a simple idea, namely that consumers in various countries fall into the same socio-demographic categories, with similar if not identical buying habits and tastes brought about by low-cost cross-border travel. It uses the same imagery, messages, product and brand positioning across all campaigns and all markets. Economies of scale could be achieved and global brands built up, as campaigns could be extended from one country to another.

More recently, globalization has received a few hard knocks, due to changes in customer tastes and timing. Some products achieved global status because they required very little effort in terms of product development in order to be successful in new markets. Others needed extensive redevelopment in order to localize their marketing mix.

A good example is basic office software such as Microsoft Word, which works equally well in most countries, once it has been localized for language characteristics. Other examples are soft drinks like Coca-Cola or imaging products like Kodak, which need only minimal changes of their global campaigns to adapt to local taste. Alternatively, cars are more of a 'lifestyle' purchase.

Consumer tastes in cars vary more widely between the United States, Germany, Japan, Italy, the United Kingdom and India. Achieving substantial economies of scale either in product development or in advertising is more difficult. Ford has been one of the manufacturers most successful in using a modular approach to car manufacturing and marketing. Recognizing that there are strong differences in consumer preferences, Ford has reduced the number of components - and thereby has achieved economies of scale - without affecting the number of options available to customers in each of the seventy-five different national markets in which Ford sells cars.

Ford manages to use a modular approach also in its advertising messages, emphasizing safety in Scandinavia, performance in Italy, design in France and handling in Germany. The Ford brand may be global, but the product and its supporting marketing effort are very much local.

For e-Commerce marketers with global ambitions, the requirements are to find out if the product or service they represent and the way of doing business can be exported in their 'domestic' forms or they will encounter consumer resistance and will need substantial adaptation to suit consumer tastes.

THE RISKS OF GLOBAL WEB MARKETING

For companies that have an established global distribution system the decision to exploit the Internet as a marketing tool needs to be considered with care. Once a Web site is established which has an online purchase facility, there is the risk that overseas customers will cut out the local distributor, place orders electronically and expect price discounts. This was the case of Millipore Corporation of Bedford, Massachusetts, a company with annual sales of $600 million specializing in filtration products for water purification for laboratories and the detection of contaminants in semiconductor manufacturing. With a 'blue chip' list of customers worldwide the Internet clearly offered an effective medium to both communicate information and provide the customer with a purchasing mechanism. However, Millipore faced a massive complication in that, similar to many other multinationals, it charges higher prices overseas in order to cover the additional cost of support services. Having faced the potential dilemma associated with inter-country pricing differentials, Millipore decided to postpone offering an online ordering facility and instead restrict its Web site to providing information with supporting pre- and post-purchase service activities.

Standardization Versus Adaptation

The decision whether to standardize or adapt the marketing mix elements is a major one for any organization operating outside its home environment. Standardization allows the organization to maintain a consistent image and identity throughout the world. It provides economies of scale and is particularly valuable for maximizing impact with the internationally mobile customer. It works best within an identified international segment and with a product of well defined complexity. Global branding and the transfer of new product ideas across boundaries are both possible with standardization.

Standardization has been used successfully in running global promotional campaigns. Transferring campaigns from one country to another is almost impossible, owing to language and cultural differences. Nevertheless, the clever use of pop music as a universal language has allowed Levi's advertising to be successful where others have failed. Coca-Cola has also succeeded with its 'one sound, one sight, one appeal' philosophy which brings it closer to a full standardization position. Benetton is still running their 'United Colours of Benetton' global campaign based on multi-cultural, universal images that appeal globally. Adaptation is nevertheless necessary if the organization is under pressure to satisfy the multiplicity of needs of the global customer to the extent to which it will have to change the elements of the marketing mix.

CHANGING PATTERNS IN GLOBAL DISTRIBUTION

Distribution is the process by which all consumer and industrial goods are transferred from the producers to the end users. The process includes not only the physical handling and distribution of goods and the transfer of ownership from producer to consumer, but also the whole range of buying and selling negotiations between producers and intermediaries, and between intermediaries and consumers. Distribution channels are the ways and means by which goods are distributed from the producer to the end user. The traditional distribution model has been linear.

The producer is the originator of the products, which it builds or manufactures. Wholesalers and distributors bring together the products from a number of manufacturers, then divide them and transport them in small lots to resellers or retailers who deal directly with the consumers. The value added of the distribution chain has been in the dispatch, warehousing and delivering of products.

Sometimes distributors undertake the repackaging and marketing of the products. The chain of intermediaries, who are the wholesalers, distributors and retailers, adds substantial costs to the value chain, which can make the prices to the end user significantly higher than those of the producers. The Internet has been unique in its potential to revolutionize the value chain, as it enables producers to reach the end users directly.

As e-Commerce firms are developing, they will be choosing their entry and distribution modes on the basis of reducing their transaction costs even to the point of internalizing certain activities which have been traditionally performed by intermediaries. The Internet has raised expectations that, in time, producers will sell directly to end users and, in turn, end users will prefer buying direct from the producers. What is actually happening is that value chains are being deconstructed, reconstructed and transformed into value webs, giving rise to a new class of intermediaries, which are the collecting and distributing of information. For example, companies like Yahoo! or Netscape act as information collectors and disseminators, offering e-Commerce new possibilities of doing business.

e-Commerce Distribution System

For Web-based businesses focused on competing in global markets, there is every indication that representatives in the field are necessary in order to facilitate dispatch, the handling of returns and servicing. Companies that deal with consumer goods and have relatively low international volumes that require little service assistance may be able to dispense with any on-the-spot distribution requirements and rely on a global integrated carrier.

Global Exporting

The European Union in its present form has a larger population than the United States. Nevertheless, most of its producers and consumers live and work in a radius of 800 km, equivalent to 12 per cent of the land area of the United States, and for historical and economic reasons, transport in the European countries has been burdened with rules and regulations. For example, a trucker transporting goods from Glasgow to Athens used to spend 30 per cent of his time at border crossings, waiting and filling in up to 200 forms.

These inefficiencies are mercifully now a thing of the past. In order to move goods between EU member states only one simplified transit document is required and many of the custom formalities have been eliminated. However, consignment to countries outside the European Union is still burdened with an array of obstacles, cultural and linguistic, which lead to many companies failing to exploit the opportunities offered by overseas markets. The SME sector is affected in particular, as such companies do not have the resources to spend on overseas sales teams and trade-related computer systems.

TYPES OF LAWS AND REMEDIES

Which type of law do the following involve and what remedy is the court most likely to grant for them:

- Setting up an e-Business retailing goods whilst having no actual stock or capital with which to obtain stock, and accepting orders and credit card payments online without ever obtaining or supplying goods to meet those orders.
- An e-tailer supplying a pair of trainers which fall apart after one month's normal wear as everyday shoes to university, the shops, the bar, etc.
- Replicating the fundamental design of an existing Web site and inserting one's own details instead.
- 'Hacking' into a computer and 'improving' your examination grades.

Your answers should have included the following:

- Probably a criminal offence under the Theft Act 1968 for which the accused would be prosecuted and, if convicted, fined or sent to prison. It might well not be a crime if the accused could show evidence that, at the time she/he took payment, they intended to fulfil the order (e.g. had suppliers lined up, etc., which perhaps then fell through). Note The purchaser would still be entitled to the return of their payment under breach of contract in the civil law, irrespective of the outcome of the criminal case. A civil case under the Sale of Goods Act 1979 under which the claimant would be entitled to their money back (damages) - or a replacement pair/free repair if they so elected.
- A civil case involving breach of copyright and possibly breach of trade mark. The claimant would be entitled to an injunction ordering the defendant to cease such breaches by removing the Web page and damages to compensate for harm suffered as a result of it having been up.
- A crime under the Computer Misuse Act 1990 for which the accused would be fined or sent to prison if convicted.

GLOBALIZATION, JURISDICTION AND ENFORCEMENT

Traditionally, as a general rule, countries may make laws relating only to activities occurring within their jurisdiction and considerable problems of sovereignty arise in respect of laws involving *extraterritoriality* - having effect within another jurisdiction. District Judge Preska in American Library Assoc.*v.* Pataki [1997] said:

The Internet is wholly insensitive to geographical distinctions. In almost every case users of the Internet neither know nor care abut the physical location of the resources to the access. Internet protocols were designed to ignore rather than document geographical locations; while computers on the network do have 'addresses' they are logical addresses on the network rather than geographical addresses in real space.

As all law is essentially territorial and the Web, by definition, is extraterritorial, in that activities within a variety of jurisdictions are possible in one e-Commerce transaction, legal regulation faces considerable difficulties. For example, a US-registered company via an Internet service provider in France may well display a Web page to a potential customer in the United Kingdom. That customer might order a flight from the United Kingdom to Spain and the provision of hotel services and accommodation in Spain. It is clear that all four jurisdictions could have some involvement if problems arise from the contract.

It is possible for a country to exercise jurisdiction over an individual resident within it or a company with assets within that country, but what if others refuse to appear for trial or, having done so, refuse to pay the fine/ damages or obey the injunction? Problems of extradition and of enforcing judgements against a party outside the jurisdiction are very real. Essentially a borderless global technology such as the World Wide Web needs supranational regulation but what body has the authority to make international laws and how could it enforce them? Even the United Nations can be seen as a voluntary club of member nations with very little in the way of sanctions against its members (especially the big and powerful ones), other than expulsion from the club. Its rights over companies and individuals may be seen as even more limited.

In 1980 a UN conference in Vienna adopted the UN Convention on the International Sale of Goods (CISG), which came into force in 1988. It has been adopted by over fifty-seven nations and covers over half the world's trade. It is linked with the North American Free Trade Association and a substantial part, but not all of the European Union. The United Kingdom has not adopted CISG, which also does not apply to goods bought for personal, family or household reasons.

Within the European Union, the Brussels Convention on Jurisdiction and the Enforcement of Judgements in Civil and Commercial Matters 1968 applies. In the United Kingdom the Civil Jurisdiction and Judgements Act 1968 provides that the Brussels Convention shall have the force of law. In consumer sales the consumer can be sued only in her/his own country of domicile but may elect to sue either there or in the seller's country of domicile. In non-consumer sales, a contracting party can be sued only in her/his country of domicile or the country where the transaction/delivery should have taken place, if that differs. The 1980 Rome Convention covers the subject of applicability of law and is applicable in the United Kingdom under the Contracts (Applicable Law) Act 1990.

Essentially, the convention states that the parties may elect the law by which their contract is governed. If no such election is made, the law of the country where the contract was made applies. Frequently in e-Commerce, parties are required to click on an icon to show that they accept the other party's standard terms and conditions, which might well specify the country's law to be applicable. Software is often shrink-wrapped and the packaging states that end-user licence conditions apply and that by opening the packaging one accepts the terms and conditions of that licence. This is not infrequently backed up by a requirement during installation to click indicating acceptance of the end-user licence terms and conditions.

The EU Distance Selling Directive 97/7, which came into force in English law on 1 November 2000, applies if the negotiations and contract are completed by distance means (e.g. through the Internet) by a purchaser buying as a consumer from a seller supplying in the course of a business. The consumer must, before the contract is concluded, be provided with information on the identity of the supplier, her/his address, the main characteristics of the goods/services, price, delivery costs, arrangements for payment, the period for which the price remains valid and the right of withdrawal.

This must all be provided in a downloadable form. The right of withdrawal is for a minimum of seven working days' cooling-off period without need for reason or financial penalty for having done so, but does not apply in relation to personalized goods, audio/video recordings, software/periodicals/magazines, etc., that have been delivered, or where performance in relation to services has started.

Until relatively recently domain name regulation was governed by US government agencies. This arose because the Web was developed in the United States and many large commercial players internationally are US corporations. In the United Kingdom, Nominet UK took over the domain name registration process in 1996. By 1998 it became clear that the Net was fast expanding into an international medium for commerce, education and communication and that a global system of management was desirable. At the prompting of the US government, the Internet Corporation for Assigned Names and Numbers (ICANN) was established in 1998 as a non-profit-making group of business, academic and technical interests to regulate the allocation of intellectual property address space and to manage the domain name system. It has limited powers and is in effect an attempt at self-regulation by Internet stakeholders. Currently the Web would seem to be governed, if it is *de facto* governed very much at all, by a mixture of individual national laws, co-ordinated national laws or cross-border conventions and self-regulation from the more powerful stakeholders connected with the Internet. No one model can meet all the requirements. The national law model has jurisdictional and enforceability problems, and national laws may easily be outflanked on the Net by consumers/suppliers simply going elsewhere to get or do what they want. The cross-border model has problems of authority and enforcement and would require a large and efficient bureaucracy. It shares with the self-regulation model the fundamental problems of democracy, accountability and the worries of domination by one/a few powerful groups or countries looking to their own interests rather than those of the wider community. It may also be that the interests of the community at large will be difficult to define, as debates on freedom of speech and protection against pornography and corruption illustrate.

The ingenuity of those seeking to avoid regulation will almost certainly equal that of those seeking to regulate, and each door closing may be matched by another one opening. Methods such as encryption may well make it difficult for those seeking to control even to know who those evading their measures are, let alone to impose constraints upon them. Spinello says there is 'a power struggle between a frustrated state and a newly empowered Internet community' with 'cyberspace at the epicentre of that struggle'.

PROBLEMS OF EXTRATERRITORIALITY IN PRACTICE

In Germany in 2000 a Holocaust revisionist, Frederick Toben, was convicted of offences under laws against denying the Holocaust and against spreading Nazi propaganda. Toben had denied that millions of Jews had been killed by the Nazis during the Holocaust. The denials had been made both in pamphlets and on Toben's own Web site. The German Federal Court denied Toben's appeal against his conviction, stating that German national law on this topic applied to the Internet even when the content had originated outside Germany and was put there by a non-German national (an Australian), provided that the site was accessible in Germany. It was not clear to what extent the ruling applied to anyone other than individuals - such as ISPs.

There is clearly a moral/ethical problem here over freedom of speech/ expression and control of dangerous/offensive propaganda. There is also the problem of extraterritoriality. In France in 2000 the International League against Racism and Antisemitism and the Union of French Jewish students applied to the French courts for an order to prevent Yahoo continuing to display on its auction site advertisements for Nazi memorabilia. Despite Yahoo's claim of no jurisdiction because its site is based in the United States, the French court issued an order requiring Yahoo to take all measures to make impossible the sale of Nazi memorabilia through its Web site to French citizens.

Yahoo has announced that it will take such measures but has asked the US courts to rule in principle on the validity of a French court ruling on a US ISP. The French government and courts clearly have a right and the power to regulate the conduct of its nationals in France and to prohibit offensive activities, but to what extent can any country prevent the effects of the Net when it is provided by a foreign national from outside its boundaries?

ENCRYPTION AND PRIVACY RIGHTS

One stumbling block to greater use of e-Commerce in areas such as e-Banking and e-Shopping is public apprehension about security flaws and the safety and privacy of data necessarily disclosed to your trading partners by trading in this way. To what extent is such data secure - either in transmission or when held by the other party - and to what extent can third parties get access to it?

The dangers of a third party getting unauthorized access to your credit card number are obvious, although worries about disclosing such data online are strangely inconsistent with happily giving waiters, shop assistants and those involved in telephone sales the card, or details of it, as many of us do regularly without a second thought. Having said that, a study revealed that 59 per cent of companies with Web sites that were surveyed had experienced one or more security breakdowns in 1997.

Article of the European Convention on Human Rights and Fundamental Freedoms 1953 - now enshrined in UK law by the Human Rights Act 1998 - includes a right 'to respect for ... private and family life ... home and ... correspondence'. This would seem to give a green light to those who argue for freedom of speech and privacy on the Net. Unless protected by encryption, communication on the Internet is akin to communication on a postcard - open to any who choose casually to read it, including administration staff at any of the servers through which it passes and potential hackers. The defensive measures that are put in place to prevent this may reduce the likelihood of unauthorized disclosure, but not all systems are as secure as they should be and probably no system is totally protected against determined and increasingly sophisticated hackers. A totally secure encryption system does, however, raise problems for governments.

CASE STUDY: BREACH OF PRIVACY THROUGH HACKING

Raphael Gray, a teenager in South Wales, claimed in January 2000 that he was on a mission to expose the dangers of shopping on the Internet. Using a well publicized flaw in Microsoft's Internet Information Server (not having detected a new flaw for himself), Gray wrote a programme that flooded the Web site with data, causing a buffer overflow and making the data on the site insecure. This flaw had been publicized in security bulletins on the Internet but many e-Commerce organizations had failed to patch their systems. Gray extracted credit card details from the databases and told Web sites using

Microsoft Internet Information Service that they were vulnerable. Many ignored him, so Gray published the numbers, names and expiry dates of 6,000 credit cards on the Internet.

Gray was caught by means of reading the server logs to discover when and from where the hacks were done and then the logs of the ISP Gray had used to see who was logged on at that time. However, the damage had been done, and it cost Mastercard and Visa £2 million to reassure customers and replace their cards, and those 6,000 were considerably inconvenienced in the interim with no credit card available to them. Gray was apparently of low self-esteem and had a medical condition caused from a blow on the head. The court accordingly sentenced him to a three-year probation order linked with treatment for a mental disorder.

Many of the advocates of a totally free Internet would regard such hackers as playing a game, their only crime being curiosity, or a prank producing a little e-graffiti. A seventeen-year-old from Hereford hacked into a national rail Web site and that of Lloyd's of London and posted messages saying 'No trains will be running over the millennium due to Y2K problems' and 'The UK caught the Net boom but forgot about security' respectively. In December 2000 he was convicted of two breaches of the Computer Misuse Act and conditionally discharged for twelve months.

In June 2001 Owen Goddard was charged with posting bogus information on an Internet site - Interactive Investor International - which said (falsely) that Mercury Asset Management had sold its shares in Minmet - a mining exploration group. This caused Minmet shares to halve in value and wiped £70 million off the company's value.

The FBI in the United States had considerable difficulties in breaking up an international child pornography ring because everything was on encrypted computer files. An uncrackable secret communication system would also seem like heaven for criminals and terrorists and hell for law enforcement agencies and governments.

With the increasing ease of collecting, processing and transferring personal data about anyone comes the fear of invasion of privacy. Developments like these led to laws such as the Data Protection Act 1998, which sets out a framework of law regarding what data may be collected, kept and disclosed or transferred, and gives the data subject rights of viewing and correcting data held on her/him.

Nevertheless, with the use of encryption, an Internet user may well achieve a greater degree of privacy for communications than is available in respect of postal or telephone communication. Barker and Hurst argue that 'cryptography is surely the best of technologies and the worst of technologies. It will stop crimes, and it will create new crimes. It will undermine dictatorships and it will drive them to new excesses. It will make us all anonymous and will track our every transaction'. Encryption is now an everyday facet of e-Commerce and can provide confidentiality and authenticity of information transmitted and can validate that it has not been subject to intrusion during transmission or disclosure to unauthorized parties. Digital signatures can be created by encryption so as to authenticate the sender of the information. Easily used encryption software is available in all computer shops and even, in the case of PGP (Pretty Good Privacy), free over the Internet for personal use.

Many would see legitimate uses of encryption and secrecy as including commercially confidential information, military and governmental secrets, confidential advice and counselling to clients and even reports of human rights violations and war crimes. Different countries have different views about encryption. For some 'the absence of consensus harms not only the growth and development of e-Commerce but also the possibility of providing a stable and trustworthy environment for Netizens'. In a 1997 communication paper, *Towards a European Framework for Digital Signatures and Encryption,* the European Commission thought that there were few criminal cases using professional encryption and that it was unlikely that the use of encryption could be effectively controlled by regulation. In 1999 the EU Directive on a Community Framework for Electronic Signatures sought to legitimize the use of electronic signatures within the European Union, and allowed for voluntary but not compulsory certification schemes. The European Union has not yet managed to reach a common proposal, let alone a policy, on the thorny problem of encryption.

In 1996 the UK government in a discussion paper on *Regulatory Intent Concerning use of Encryption on Public Networks* proposed the introduction of licensed Trusted Third Parties to hold copies of all private encryption keys and thus facilitate key recovery and verification. The Labour government elected in 1997 in its own Secure Electronic Commerce Statement in 1998 followed the same idea on a voluntary but not legally compulsory basis, but those who chose not to use Trusted Service Providers would not have a presumption of authenticity. Quite how voluntary such a system is in such circumstances is, to say the least, debatable. However, a House of Commons select committee report on *Building Confidence in Electronic Commerce* said, 'we can see no benefits arising from the government's promotion of key escrow or key recovery technologies' (HMSO 1999).

Eventually the UK government passed the Electronic Communications Act 2000, which replaced the previous idea of compulsory licences with a voluntary approval regime. The industry adopted self-regulatory kite marking and was threatened with an imposed registration scheme if the voluntary system proved ineffective. An industry-devised scheme, the T scheme, has been drawn up. The Act also gives UK legal approval to all electronic signatures.

The Regulation of Investigatory Powers Act 2000 concerns powers of seizing and disclosing communications data. Decryption powers are granted in Part III, although there must be some power under which the original seizure is authorized.

Purposes for authorizing seizure include preventing any crime or disorder, but also health and taxation, and can be extended by statutory order (i.e. no need for a new Act to extend them).

If the authorities seize encrypted raw material the Act includes powers to require the possessor to hand over the key but such powers need the written permission of an independent judicial officer in most cases, and regard must be had to both necessity and proportionality before notice is granted. The exercise of the power to grant such notices is kept under review by the Covert Investigations Commissioner. The disclosure of text rather than the key will also be an acceptable response in most cases, unless the handing over of the key has specifically been demanded, and is proportionate in the circumstances. There is a defence to the crime of failure to disclose or facilitate access if it is not reasonably practicable (which must be proved by the accused), e.g. that she/he never had the key or no longer had it at the time of the request.

The Secretary of State used his powers under the Regulation of Investigating Powers Act 2000 to make the Telecommunications (Lawful Business Practice) (Interception of Communications) Regulations 2000, which authorize the interception of telecommunications by, or with the consent of, a person carrying on a business (including government departments and public authorities) for purposes relevant to that business and using that business's own telecoms system. The controller of the system must make all reasonable efforts to inform potential users that interceptions may be made, thereby getting their express or implied consent.

One quite often is played a pre-recorded message to the effect that the conversation may be recorded for monitoring for quality assurance purposes. Such interceptions are authorized for establishing the existence of facts; ascertaining compliance with regulatory practices applicable to the system controller in her/his business; to ascertain the standards which are achieved by those using the systems as part of their duties; monitoring to see if the communications are business or personal; to prevent/detect crime or in the interests of national security. This will often be done in the form of monitoring employees' e-mails and telephone calls. Monitoring by concealed CCTV or tape recorders will be justified only in very limited circumstances - such as where a crime is suspected and blanket monitoring cannot be justified - said Elizabeth France, when she was Data Protection Commissioner. Provided the employer makes every reasonable effort to inform staff of any intended monitoring and the interception is proportionate and for legitimate business reasons then it probably will not breach the Data Protection Act or the Human Rights Act.

Data Protection

The position in the United Kingdom is governed by the Data Protection Act 1998, which was the United Kingdom's response to the EU Data Protection

Directive 95/46/EC. The Act is coming in over a period of time until 2007 and replacing the 1984 Act. All EU member states have fundamentally the same laws regarding data protection. There are eight Data Protection Principles under the Act:

- Personal data shall be processed fairly and lawfully. Schedule 2 says processing may be carried out only where the individual has given her/his consent; where it is necessary to perform a contract with the individual; when it is required under a legal obligation; or when it is necessary in the legitimate interests of the business and not prejudicial to the interests of the individual. Sensitive data - defined by Schedule 3 to include matters on racial/ethnic origin, political opinions/religious beliefs, trade union membership, health, sexuality and criminal convictions - can be processed only with explicit consent (i.e. the individual has positively opted in).
- Personal data shall be obtained only for a specified and lawful purpose(s) and should not be processed in a manner incompatible with that. A data processor must notify the Data Protection Commissioner (formerly the Data Protection Registrar) for inclusion on a publicly available database. There will be exemptions from such notification where processing is 'unlikely to prejudice the rights and freedoms of data subjects'.
- Personal data shall be adequate, relevant and not excessive for the purposes for which they are obtained under principle 2.
- Personal data shall be accurate and, where necessary, kept up to date. The data subject may, on payment of one reasonable fee, request to be given details of all of the data on her/him, the purposes for which it is being kept, the source of and any potential recipients of it. This *must* be supplied within forty days of the request. The data subject can ask the processor to correct/erase/destroy any inaccurate data and this can be enforced by a court order.
- Personal data shall not be kept for longer than is necessary for the notified purpose for which it was collected.
- Personal data shall be processed in accordance with the rights of data subjects including the right to have details of it, to have it corrected, to know its source and likely recipients, and to know the logic behind any decision-making process of which the data is likely to be the sole basis which significantly affects her/him - e.g. allowing her/him credit in a proposed hire-purchase/credit sale transaction. The commissioner may issue an information notice where it is suspected that a principle has been breached, or an enforcement notice where there is evidence that a principle has been breached. The data subject may also prevent the processing of data for the purposes of direct marketing or where such processing would cause her/him harm or distress - subject to a public interest defence.

Catherine Zeta Jones and Michael Douglas tried to use this right to prevent illicitly obtained photographs of their wedding being published when they had sold exclusive rights to take and publish photographs to another rival magazine.

- Appropriate technical and organizational measures must be taken to protect against unauthorized/unlawful processing of data and against accidental loss/destruction/damage to personal data. These measures must ensure, in the light of technical developments and the cost of implementation, a level of security appropriate to the extent and nature of the harm that breach of this principle might cause, i.e. the greater the extent or the nature of such harm the greater the expense and precautions that ought to be taken.

This will include matters such as reasonable steps to ensure the reliability of any employees, etc., who might have access to the data. If data is processed by another on the data controller's behalf, the controller must order the processor (with evidence in writing of the order) to take all reasonable steps to check the reliability of the processor and of their systems, as well as issuing the order.

BS 7799 may assist data processors to check the adequacy of their security regimes. This should apply not only to persons with authorized access, but also to others who might gain unauthorized access (e.g. other staff, cleaners and repair persons, where there are insecure passwords or they are left in obvious hiding places).

- Personal data shall not be transferred outside the European Economic Area (essentially the European Union plus Norway, Iceland and Liechtenstein) unless the country ensures an adequate level of protection for the rights and freedoms of data subjects in relation to processing personal data. Many states outside North America and the European Union may not comply with this. Adequacy or otherwise will be judged in the light of the nature of the data, the country of origin and destination, the purposes for which the data is being processed and the levels of protection and international obligations of the destination country.

Section of the Data Protection Act makes it a criminal offence 'knowingly or recklessly without the consent of the data controller to obtain or disclose personal data ... or procure the disclosure to another person'. There are defences in relation to disclosure necessary for the purpose of preventing or detecting crime or where it was required or authorized by law.

4

E-Management and Internet

INTRODUCTION

Before proceeding to look at the law of e-commerce, it is useful to consider some particular aspects of e-business management. There is no doubt that, for the managers of any commercial enterprise, the Internet presents the most significant universal challenge that has yet been presented in the history of commerce.

It is tempting to think of the Internet as merely an electronic expression of what has gone before: e-mails replace typed letters, websites replace glossy brochures and electronic invoices replace their paper equivalents. But the Internet is not merely a more efficient replacement for existing systems. Its significance lies in its ability to be not merely a communications device, but a market, an information system and a manufacturing tool.

It allows managers to do not only what they have done before communicating with suppliers, advertising products and services, collecting customer data and obtaining payment more efficiently, cheaply and comprehensively, but also opens up significant new possibilities for the core operations of every business.

Of course it is the potential to increase productivity and cut costs that is a most attractive feature of the Internet, and this must not be overlooked. Suppose, for example, you are a car manufacturer. Traditionally you have obtained orders for new cars from a network of showrooms that have in turn obtained orders from their customers. Where outsourcing has been required, you have placed orders with your suppliers.

Assembly takes place, the car is customised to the customer's requirements and is shipped to the dealer. With the Internet comes the possibility of the customer placing their order online. They can choose their accessories and colour scheme and create a virtual image of how the car will look on-screen before proceeding with their order. Direct electronic communication of the order eradicates possible mis-communication in, and later arguments over, choice of specification. The delivery date can be electronically calculated and arrangements for payment can be finalised. The manufacturer's automated system will communicate electronically with suppliers so that the alloy wheels, or whatever has been selected, can be delivered precisely when needed for fitting to the vehicle. The finished product can be delivered via an intermediary dealer or direct to the customer.

E-MAIL

The spread of electronic communication brings transparency and openness to the management process. The ease with which an e-mail can be forwarded to hundreds or thousands of people changes the nature of communication — one must now assume that not just the recipient will read an e-mail that is sent to him. It is no longer possible to hide behind mountains of paperwork or to 'lose' a letter to which it is currently not desirable to respond.

It is common knowledge that the ability to send and forward e-mails causes two main concerns for employers. The first is that time will be wasted — some employees spend several hours each week in sending e-mails to friends. The second is that the employer will incur some liability as a result of the content of such e-mails. Both these concerns can be met by an 'e-mail policy', which should be clear and comprehensive.

It should set out the employer's attitude to e-mail and explain that employees'e-mails will be monitored (if this is desired) to ensure quality of service and appropriateness of communication. The presence of such a policy should have the effect of employees exercising some caution when sending and forwarding e-mails.

It should also mean that embarrassing incidents such as the Norton Rose 'blow job' e-mail debacle can be avoided. It should be noted that the monitoring of employee e-mails has data protection and privacy implications that are beyond the scope of this Report.

A related issue is that of pornography. Pornographic images are popular with employees but cause great concern for employers. Not only do they waste employee time, they cause offence and clog vital server space. They could also lead to liability for the employer. To avoid the sort of situation experienced by Orange when it dismissed 30 employees for downloading and distributing pornographic images, a clear statement should be made to employees of the employer's attitude to this activity.

To stem the flow closer to its source, the business should consider installing software capable of screening-out unwanted material.E-businesses should remember that an e-mail is a business document in the same way as is a letter or a fax. E-mails must therefore comply with the requirements of the Companies Act 1985, namely that the following information must appear:

- The full name of the company;
- The registered number of the company;
- The address of the registered office; and
- The country of registration of the company.

Human Resources

Given the current climate of short-term working practices and the need to have efficient and productive staff, e-businesses need to focus on staff attraction and retention. E-businesses, generally speaking, need fewer but better staff. This may require a review of working conditions, working practices, pay structures and benefits. The e-business revolution has, significantly, created new jobs that did not exist in the offline economy — examples include website designers, knowledge management officers and e-business managers. Workers in e-business are increasingly flexible, many working from home or onthe-road. Rather than being feared, such practices should be embraced by businesses.

Not only do they lead to a lowering of overheads (heat, light and a desk in the office are not required for mobile workers) but they can create greater satisfaction and loyalty amongst staff. Appropriate communication infrastructures should be employed so that staff are kept fully informed of events 'back at the office'and are able to communicate with other staff members, as well as customers and suppliers. Where sales teams spend much of their time out of the office, they too should be kept fully informed and accountable.

The lack of office presence of individual employees and the globalisation of businesses mean that the 'drink after work' and the 'training weekend' become increasingly difficult. Many businesses are developing corporate portals for their business to employee (B2E) communications. Such portals can prove invaluable in providing information and training to employees.

Larger companies can additionally use the portals as an online job market and to provide maps of buildings and photographs and locations of staff. Some companies motivate employees to log on to the portal on a daily basis by posting the share prices of the company or by displaying a list of employee birthdays for the relevant week. A section of the portal can be used for selling the company's products to the employees.

The Internet can be used for recruiting staff. Potential job applicants can be given up-to-date information on vacancies, be taken on a virtual tour of the business and be invited to apply online. Communications between the HR department and job applicant can be undertaken by e-mail. The expense of using a recruitment agent can be saved.

CUSTOMERS

The Internet gives rise to the possibility of a wider marketplace. Customers may now be located anywhere on the planet but have equal access to the marketing material of the business. Systems should be set up to deal with this new global presence.

Better information on customers is available from the monitoring of their activities whilst visiting the website. Using cookies it is possible to 'personalise' the content of the site for each particular customer. Knowing that a customer lives in Oxford, for example, it is possible to display a banner advertisement for an Oxford-based pizza restaurant on your homepage.

Were a different customer to visit the homepage, the advertisement would be of a different kind. Location-specific and targeted advertising have data protection implications and detailed proposals should be submitted to a data protection lawyer before procedures are implemented.

As the technology grows, so do customers' expectations. Customers will expect to be kept informed of the process of their order and will want more information than would have previously been available. Electronic order tracking systems should be available to customers online to provide them with this information. DHL, for example, has a system which enables a customer to see the location of their package at each stage of its journey and to know the precise moment that it is 'signed-for' by the recipient.

MANAGEMENT OF DOMAIN NAMES

No serious commercial enterprise is without a domain name. Indeed the number of domain names that have been registered during the past five years could be graphically represented by an exponential curve. By 1995 approximately 100,000 domain names had been registered. At the beginning of 2000 this number had increased to 6 million. At the time of writing the number of domain names registered stood at more than 40 million.

Commonly there are no pre-conditions for registering a domain name and no restriction on the number of domain names that can be registered. In the case of start-ups or new ventures for existing businesses, it is important to register the chosen domain name as soon as possible, and certainly before any publicity about the business is released to the public.

There have been several cases in the past few years where a company has sent out a press release concerning a new business venture, including the proposed business name without having secured the domain name. The same day a member of the public who has seen the publicity surrounding the venture has registered the proposed business name as a domain name. Mediation with Nominet or dispute resolution with ICANN can produce a satisfactory resolution but will inevitably be expensive and time-consuming.

E-commerce businesses are advised to register all ccTLD variations of the domain name that relate to those countries where the client expects to do business as well as all gTLD's that are available. This prevents someone from registering the same SLD as the business, albeit with a different TLD.Businesses should also register all variations of the name, for example using hyphens where the SLD consists of more than one word or even common misspellings.

This prevents anyone from taking unfair advantage of the goodwill in the business by engaging in the activity known as cybersquatting. An appropriate and sensible commercial strategy for domain name registrations, coupled with relevant trade mark registrations, can reduce the risks posed by cybersquatters. It should also be remembered that a domain name is not a property right as such. Rather, a domain name registration allows the registrant the exclusive use of that domain name for the period of registration. Registration periods are commonly either one or two years. It is vital that renewal is made otherwise use of the domain name will be lost.

Trade Marks and Branding

For the protection of a business or its product or service, the registration of a trade mark or service mark should be considered. An infringement action can then be brought against anyone using the same or similar mark in respect of a similar business in the jurisdiction of registration. Where brand protection is not available by use of a registered trade mark (due to, for example, the business being unable to comply with the strict requirements of the registration process) some protection may be available from that branch of the law known as 'passing off'. This section considers the law of trade marks and passing off specifically in the context of protection of domain names.

Trade Marks

The fundamental difference between a trade mark and a domain name is that there can be several identical trade marks registered in different parts of the world, or even in the same jurisdiction, by different people. Each identical trade mark can relate to a different type of goods without any possibility of the trade mark use constituting an infringement. By contrast there can only ever be one of each domain name, as such names are necessarily unique. Whilst use of an identical domain name to one registered by an e-business is therefore impossible, registration and use of a similar domain name by a third party is not unlikely. For example, although we may register the domain name, pwcarey.com, this does not stop someone else registering the domain name p-w-carey.com or pcarey.com.

In other words, the domain name registration system offers no protection against the registration of similar names. An action for trade mark infringement on the other hand can be brought against not only those persons who use an identical mark in relation to similar goods or services, but also against those who use a similar mark in relation to similar goods or services. E-businesses should therefore aim to support the protection of their brands by registering a trade mark for their domain names in each of their principal trading territories. Trade mark registrations can be undertaken by law firms or trade mark agents. It is possible that use of a domain name by one person may constitute the infringement of a registered trade mark of another. The claimant must show, under s10 TMA 1994, that there has been use of an identical mark in relation to identical goods/services or use of a similar mark in relation to identical/similar goods/services where there is likelihood of confusion.

PASSING OFF

Where goodwill in a business is being used by another for their own benefit but that other is not using an identical or similar registered trade mark, the business may be able to bring an action for 'passing-off'. An action by one business against another or against an individual in the tort of passing off usually requires a misrepresentation in the course of trade, which leads to financial loss.

An exception to the rule that to succeed in a passing off action the claimant must show that the defendant was using the same or similar mark in the course of trade was established in the context of domain names in the case of *BT and Others v. One in a Million Ltd* (1999) FSR.

In the case, brought by BT, Virgin, Sainsburys and others, the court held that the 'mere creation of an instrument of fraud' could amount to passing off. One in a Million Ltd was forced to give up its interest in certain domain names that it had registered such as sainsbury.com, virgin.com and bt.org. It had registered these domains in the hope of selling them to the relevant companies for a profit.

Some would argue that the companies should have had the foresight to resister these domain names themselves and should not expect the law to rescue them from their lack of commercial awareness. Nevertheless the court showed a willingness to adapt the common law to the changing commercial environment.

The laws of both trade mark infringement and passing off are difficult to prove and in any event litigation takes a good deal of time and money. For these reasons businesses that have found that others have registered domain names that they feel should in fact belong to themselves have chosen to engage in dispute resolution as an alternative to a court action.

CYBER SQUATTING AND DISPUTE RESOLUTION

Cyber squatting is the activity that involves the bad faith registration of trade marks as domain names. Where an e-business finds itself to be the victim of a cyber squatter there are a number of potential courses of action. In appropriate circumstances the cyber squatter can be sued in a court of law for infringement of a registered trade mark or in the tort of passing off. An alternative, and often cheaper and faster procedure is to enter into domain name dispute resolution.

Dispute resolution is a useful alternative to litigation for those cases where a claimant feels that they should be entitled to use a domain name that has been registered by someone else. Such a situation commonly arises under the existing procedure for domain name registrations, which is essentially a 'first-come-first-served'system. In most cases anyone can purchase the exclusive right to use a domain name, provided that no one has registered it beforehand. The *One in a Million Case* showed that it is possible to obtain a court order for the transfer of a domain name, but litigation is inevitably costly and time consuming. The Internet Corporation for Assigned Names and Numbers (ICANN) set up a dispute resolution system for the top-level generic domain names (.com,.net and.org) in December 1999.That system, known as the Uniform Dispute Resolution Policy (UDRP), has proved very popular and successful.

It is administered by four bodies (the best known of which is the World Intellectual Property Organisation) and frequently results in a domain name being transferred to the claimant. This section considers the dispute resolution procedures of ICANN and Nominet (which administers all.uk domain names).

ICANN DISPUTE RESOLUTION PROCEDURE

The important thing to bear in mind is that domain names are not property as such. The registrant's rights to use a domain name derives from the contract that it enters into with the registration authority. As far as gTLD's are concerned, the registration authority is ICANN (Internet Corporation for Assigned Names and Numbers). ICANN set up a Uniform Dispute Resolution Policy (UDRP), which became operational on 1 December 1999. The UDRP applies only to those domains administered by ICANN i.e. the three gTLD's.com,.net and.org. ICANN has subcontracted out the job of hearing and adjudicating on the disputes to four bodies, the best known of which is the World Intellectual Property Organisation (WIPO). The UDRP relates only to an 'abusive registration'

This means that applicants will only be successful where they are able to show that:

- The disputed domain name is identical or confusingly similar to a trade mark or service mark in which the applicant has rights
- The registrant has no rights or legitimate interests in the domain name
- The domain name has been registered and is being used in bad faith.

Unfortunately the UDRP does not provide any guidance on how 'confusing similarity' is to be assessed. A 'legitimate interest' can be demonstrated by the registrant by showing some use or preparatory steps to use the domain name dating from prior to any notice by the applicant; evidence that the registrant is commonly known by the domain name or evidence that the registrant has engaged in a legitimate non-commercial use of the domain name.

'Bad faith', the most important element of the UDRP, can be shown where the registrant's main purpose in registering the domain name was to sell it to the applicant; where it was designed to prevent the applicant using its trade mark as a domain name or where there was an intention to attract users to the registrant's website by creating a likelihood of confusion with the applicant's mark.

It should be noted that bad faith can be shown not only by a demand for money, but also by a request for services. In a case involving the domain name uwyoming.com the respondent wanted free tuition for his daughter at the University of Wyoming, and in the gearmagazine.com case the respondent demanded the contract to build the complainant's website. In both cases the complainants were successful in getting the domain names transferred to themselves.

If the applicant is successful at the arbitration hearing (which is by written submission, no live witnesses) then ICANN will immediately transfer the domain name to the applicant. By way of example, Julia Roberts was able to obtain reregistration of the domain name juliaroberts.com in her own name by using the UDRP.

By contrast Bruce Springsteen failed in a similar application for brucespringsteen.com, largely because the registrant was able to show legitimate use (for a Bruce Springsteen fan club website).

DISPUTE RESOLUTION FOR.UK DOMAIN NAMES

Nominet, the UK domain name registry, has announced its intention to radically update its dispute resolution procedure for applications by claimants against cybersquatters.

The principal criticism of the Nominet system to date has been that it does not allow transfers of the disputed domain name into the name of the claimant. Under the new system, to operate from Autumn 2001, Nominet will be able to remove the existing name from the register and replace it with that of the claimant.

The new system proposed by Nominet for all.uk domains is modelled on the UDRP but has some interesting differences.

At present the dispute resolution system available from Nominet, the second largest of the country code specific domain name registries, is a mediation service. It is free of charge and is undertaken by written submissions by the parties. Of the 1,200 mediations dealt with by Nominet since it began the service in 1997, approximately one third have been successfully resolved. Of the two thirds of claims that are not amicably resolved by the parties, the remaining alternative is litigation. Nominet will currently withdraw or suspend a domain name (but not transfer it) in the following circumstances:

- If the name is administered in a way that is likely to endanger the operation of the domain name system.
- If the basis on which the domain name was registered has changed.
- If Nominet finds that the name is being used in a manner likely to cause confusion to Internet users.
- Where Nominet UK has been informed that legal action has been commenced regarding use of the name.
- Where Nominet UK is of the opinion that one of the above is likely to occur.

The need for a new dispute resolution system arises out of increased public awareness in the activity known as 'cybersquatting' and the desire for a quick and effective procedure for the transfer of a.uk domain name which has been registered by a third party. There is also, according to Nominet, a perception that cybersquatting threatens the principles of a first-come-first-served registration system, and that self-regulation is preferable to an enforced solution.Under the proposals Nominet will continue to offer a mediation service for disputed domain names but the mediation will 'time-out' if it has been unsuccessful after ten working days.

The application will then be automatically referred to an independent expert who will be appointed in a 'cab-rank' fashion from a list held by Nominet (under the UDRP applicants can choose particular experts — there may be up to three experts deciding each case).

A fee — likely to be in the region of £500 to £1,000 — will be payable to Nominet for use of the service and all decisions of the experts will be published.In order to succeed in its application for domain name transfer, a claimant will be expected to show that the registration is 'abusive'.There is to be a two-stage test for abusive registrations. The claimant must show that:

- They have rights in respect of a name or mark which is identical or similar to a domain name.
- The registrant has and/or is using the domain name in bad faith.

This test is similar to that under the UDRP, except under the latter, the claimant must additionally show that the registrant has no rights or legitimate interest in the domain name. Under the UDRP where the mark of the claimant is not identical to the domain name, the claimant must show that it is 'confusingly similar', as opposed to merely 'similar', to the domain name.

The central requirement for both the UDRP and the Nominet proposal is that the domain name be registered (or used) in bad faith. However, although the burden of proof under both schemes is on the claimant, the standard of proof is different. Under the Nominet proposal, the claimant will be expected to prove, *beyond a reasonable doubt*, the bad faith of the registrant.

Bad faith is commonly shown by a clear motive to siphon business goodwill away from the claimant or an attempt by the registrant to sell the domain name to the claimant at a grossly inflated price. It is unclear how the higher standard of proof will affect claims for the transfer of.uk domains.

THE MOBILE INTERNET

The growth of the mobile Internet now exceeds that of the PC version. Mobile communications offer considerable potential to marketers because of their unrivalled combination of:

- Instant response;
- Personalized content (as each customer has a unique telephone number);
- Scope for geographical location tracking.

The potential for mobile networks is particularly high in developing countries that do not have an established wired telephone network and hence no established PC-based Internet services. In the Philippines, for example, SMS messaging has recently taken off rapidly, and mobile Internet services therefore offer huge marketing opportunities in these emerging markets.There has been a lot of hype recently about the potential of location-based technology in particular. However, current services are very basic, and it is important to remember that there is some way to go before they become sufficiently reliable and useful to have a broad appeal.

For example, variations on the scenario whereby a customer is called on their phone and advised of a special breakfast offer just as they walk to work past a Starbucks outlet, have been heralded as the ultimate in personalized promotional campaigns. There are a number of practical difficulties, though, such as customers' reluctance to be bombarded with intrusive advertising messages and the challenge of communicating effectively with the wide range of mobile devices and standards currently in use.The usefulness of wireless devices has recently been improved by new standards such as Jini and Bluetooth that connect wireless devices to other electronic products:

- Jini (www.jini.com) allows mobile phones, PCs and personal digital assistants (PDAs) to collaborate as part of an intelligent network, without the need for the correct device driver to be added to the operating system before a new device can be used.
- Bluetooth (www.bluetooth.com) is particularly useful for linking mobile devices because it does not require any wire connections. For example, it could allow a user on a mobile in a car to transfer data from an office PC directly to a home printer.

Keynote systems (www.keynote.com) recently launched a mobile performance measurement service to compare the services offered by all the major UK networks. It can measure delivery times, network comparisons, handset performance and geographic availability, thereby allowing content providers, networks or manufacturers to judge how successful their services have been. It also allows consumers to benchmark performance and make informed purchase decisions. In addition, for a detailed comparison of the characteristics of different mobile technologies, see Smith and Chaffey.

Mobile phones are now rapidly evolving and becoming 'pocket portals' that provide a range of personalized services including email and text messaging with just one monthly bill. Before discussing some of the recent and pending innovations in this area, we shall review developments over the past two or three years.The first mobiles to offer Internet access, using Wireless Application Protocol (WAP), were introduced in 1999. The information displayed had to be especially formatted for a small screen area, and the limited functionality fell well short of the often extreme levels of industry hype.

The telecommunications industry broke one of the central rules of marketing, which states that promotional campaigns should 'under-promise' and 'over-deliver' rather than the other way round. Users found that navigating between pages on a mobile phone could be an extremely laborious process, for which they were paying by the minute for connection charges. During 2000, many early users abandoned mobile commerce after disappointing experiences.

While mobile commerce is useful for 'distress' purchases such as parking, actually browsing the Web on a mobile phone is hardly a straightforward and stress-free experience. However, there have been successes to date, notably with mobile banking and gambling services.'Second-generation' mobile phones introduced early in 2001 offer faster connection speeds and are starting to carry advertising.

High response rates are currently enjoyed by advertisers, and the most successful campaigns have been run by companies such as the *Sun* newspaper, which has used the mobile channel to advertise competitions being run in the paper itself.

In other words, the *Sun* is using online advertising to drive its traditional core business - which is offline newspaper sales. Mobile advertising still represents a very small percentage of company promotional spend in comparison with more traditional media such as radio and television, but the figure is increasing. Business services via mobile channels are currently few and far between, but early experiments are under way with order placing, stock-checking availability and order tracking to facilitate supply chain integration.

The much-hyped but still awaited third generation of mobile communications (3G) is expected to deliver sound and images and be 'always on'. Auctions held in 2000 for the licences to operate 3G services netted the UK government over £20 billion, but since then the share prices of the 'successful' telecommunication firms that purchased them have been severely dented.

The technology competing with WAP is called Short Message Systems (SMS), and it is currently by far the more successful in terms of user numbers. SMS is a derivative of numeric paging technology, which has been in existence for many years, updated for two-way communication:

- In 1998, mobile phones had a 20 per cent market penetration in the UK and some *1 million* text messages were sent.

As with the growth of the PC-based Internet, it seems that communications with staff and customers are currently adding most value at this early stage, while the widespread acceptance of mobile transactions is still some way away. One must also bear in mind that not all these applications will be relevant to all companies all the time, and in most cases they will complement rather than replace existing channels.

The key skill for marketers is to focus on the particular aspects of mobile marketing that will add value to customers in their specific industry contexts. We will now examine each of these areas in turn, drawing upon a number of examples to illustrate this important point.

CONTENT PROVISION AND ADVERTISING

Mobile advertising is expected to grow exponentially following a slow start in the difficult economic conditions of 2000-1. The long-anticipated 3G technology will offer far more scope for creative advertising than the small black and white text-only screens that have dominated the market until recently. It seems to be commonly accepted that busy professional people do not want their important business interrupted by marketing messages on their mobile phones.

However, we all at least tolerate advertisements while watching movies ... so firms that specialize in placing advertisements on mobile firms are at the moment focusing their advertisement placement on mobile entertainment services rather than on business ones. Placing adverts in mobile games that users are playing when they have time to spare is likely to be more acceptable than if a user is interrupted while trying to link up remotely to a company for business purposes.

In exchange for the entertainment value in the game, it is reasonable to expect that the customer will tolerate (and, companies of course will hope, respond to) the advertising message. For example, Stone reports that Mobliss, a US-based wireless marketing agency, worked with Tribune Media in turning its 'Jumble' brand (a scrambled-word game) into a multi-player wireless game.

It was also an effective advertising tool because the words used in the puzzles could be directly related to the advertiser's company or product. The advertisements can be displayed as either graphical images or text and themed to correlate with the creative campaign that the advertiser is running offline. In either case, with mobile Internet access, customers also have the ability to click a button and be connected directly to the advertiser's call centre.

Mobliss has also launched a snow report system at www.mysnowreport.com where customers can go online and build in their preferences for particular resorts. Then a text message detailing snow conditions can be sent to the customer's phone. By forming partnerships with companies like the travel agency Moguls that are trying to reach the skier demographic (high income, high expenditure), a customer is able to check out the snow conditions at a resort, and then follow an advertiser's link that is offering a discounted package trip to that resort.

Then another link will connect the customer to the call centre to speak to a ski-travel agent. In these circumstances, the customer is more likely to perceive the advertisement as a benefit rather than as just a nuisance.

Targeting is very effective because if a user is enquiring about snow conditions, then almost by definition they are themselves a skier. In addition, the fact that the overwhelming majority of people currently using mobile Web services are males aged 20-39 with incomes over £30,000 is of course very appealing to advertisers.

Traditional magazines have been experiencing a fall in advertising revenues over the past couple of years due to the global economic slowdown.

The ability to offer interactivity through SMS can make a publication more appealing to companies seeking to place advertisements, while at the same time winning new readers for the magazine itself.

So, for example, a company seeking to run a mobile advertising campaign to promote its brand could:

- First, rent a database of readers of a particular magazine that fit the demographic profile of their target group;
- Second, send text messages promoting a competition linked to the brand that is set out in the paper-based magazine.

Stone (2002) reports that a few companies have begun sending coupons as messages to wireless devices in order to unload 'perishable' services such concert seats or restaurant tables. He describes the example of PlanetHopper, a small company based in New York, which is focusing upon the entertainment industry.

It has partnered General Cinemas, theatres and Shecky's guide to bars and clubs to provide the wireless coupons. By advertising in cinemas and in some 200 New York bars and restaurants, it drew some 20,000 users who opted in to get the promotional messages. The key to success is 'opt in' messaging, as people's tolerance of spam messages falls. *The Economist* (2001) recommends that to avoid giving offence, mobile advertisements must:

- Be optional (meaning actively requested by users);
- Be personalized;
- Be moderate in volume;
- Be free to the recipient;
- Offer a means to unsubscribe.

The article goes on to report on a recent initiative by a mobile advertising company called the Mobile Trial, in which advertisements as text messages had an average response rate of 10-20 per cent. This is much higher than usual rates for direct mail (3 per cent) and Internet banner advertisements (less than 1 per cent).

MOBILE COMMERCE

Mobile commerce - meaning the actual purchase of items from the mobile Internet - is expected to grow rapidly over the next few years. (www.forrrester.com) suggests that worldwide revenues could reach $200 billion by 2005. Be warned that we have heard wild projections before - in connection with the potential revenues likely to be generated by dotcoms, for example - so do not read too much into these figures. Before getting carried away in another round of Internet euphoria, think about the recent high level of negative publicity about mobile theft, which highlights the problem of security. Steps have recently been taken by the major market players to address this issue. In early 2002, a common database of stolen phone numbers was established so that the handsets could be disabled to prevent unauthorized purchases being made. Remember also that many people are still reluctant to undertake PC-based commerce, let alone transact through a mobile phone. Growth in mobile commerce is likely to be driven by alliances between banks and telecommunications companies. Both parties have particular strengths which if brought together can add considerable value. Banks have a banking licence, credit verification skills and an established retail network. Mobile operators provide a modern brand image and the infrastructure of a mobile network.

Both have a large customer base upon which to draw. While some companies (notably Vodafone) have made public their objective to provide financial services when restrictions on the allocation of banking licences are lifted (in 2002), others believe that the partnership route is the way forward. So far, banks have taken a cautious approach and built their mobile capabilities for small numbers of customers on a trial basis.

They now face the challenge of scaling up the infrastructure to cope with larger volumes of users. Abbey National, for example, offers e-Banking via the Genie mobile portal, which can be accessed by WAP phones over any service network. According to Bansal (2001), the bank's strategy is to develop partnerships that enable it to offer electronic banking across all technology platforms. These alliances offer customers the security of dealing with an established brand, which can be significant in building the necessary trust for mobile banking to really take off.

INTERNAL COMMUNICATIONS

Remote workers can use wireless devices to access office systems and marketing information held on the corporate intranet. Such services are useful for logistics companies needing to keep track of their drivers' location and also to send SMS messages with reminders and alerts, for example of schedule changes or traffic problems. Salespeople operating in the field can update customer records or request specific information automatically. Although the potential for the mobile Internet to enhance communications between staff or between staff and customers is considerable, adapting the corporate security systems to allow access through the mobile environment can be a significant headache, as can the practicalities of integrating mobile channels with existing IT systems more generally.

MOBILE CHALLENGES

Leung and Antypas (2001) note how the current mobile landscape resembles the first-generation Internet in the mid-1990s in terms of the key business challenges:

- *Bandwidth*. Many innovative services such as real-time video streaming will not be feasible, given the limited bandwidth currently available, and will remain what the authors refer to as 'pipe dreams' for the foreseeable future. The problem may be eased somewhat - although by no means fully addressed - by the arrival of 2.5G and 3G handsets promised for 2002.

- *Interperability*. Cellular carriers currently have different systems and standards that are not compatible with each other. GSM (Global Service for Mobile), TDMA (Time Division Multiple Access) and CDMA (Code Division Multiple Access) are available on different carriers in different areas, meaning that communications with customers may need to be channelled through each carrier for its specific area.
- *Equipment*. The mobile cannot compete with the desktop in terms of display, computing power and keyboard facilities. The displays are currently available only in black and white, and support very limited animation. There are no cookies to recognize passwords and personalize greetings, and if the Internet connection is broken, then access cannot be resumed from where it was last used because the application will restart.

Case Study: The Mobey Forum

The Mobey Forum, (www.mobeyforum.org) was established in May 2000 to develop and promote mobile technology in financial services, in search of a secure and customer-friendly solution to the issue of mobile payments. The Forum aims to ensure that users will be able to pay for goods and services as easily with their phones as they can with credit or debit cards today. Its mission is to encourage the use of mobile technology for services such as remote banking and share-dealing. The Forum advocates a 'dual chip' phone, one for the mobile service and one for banking transactions. This means that the financial services provided will be independent of the telecom provider.

Users are expected to treat the phone as they would a wallet, as it will encompass facilities for:

- Receipt storage;
- Electronic ticketing;
- Promotional coupons;
- Making payments.

A series of trials are currently under way. By working closely with European standardization bodies, the Mobey Forum aims to avoid fragmentation of the mobile commerce market by a multitude of competing standards. It is also putting across the message that if mobile payment services are to thrive, the key customer needs of security, convenience and usability must be central to developers' agendas.

Case Study: Is the Future of E-commerce Mobile?

In Japan, most business people have to commute every day and will spend a good part of their working days in densha or chikatetsu, the Japanese public transport system. As a result, mobile communication devices such as PHSs (Personal Handyphone System), mobile phones and pagers have become very popular and are being supplied in a wide variety of models. The PHS, developed by Japan's NTT, is a lightweight portable wireless phone that can function as a cordless phone at the user's home and as a mobile phone elsewhere. It can handle voice, fax and video signals. Users can send and receive email and even develop their own Web pages on tiny mobile handsets.

At the Information Technology Conference in Taiwan held in June 2000, Tadashi Sekizawa, the CEO of Fujitsu, claimed that the mobile Internet - defined as an intelligent transmitting system that can link with any Internet-accessible hardware or satellite system - will gradually replace personal computers as the most important application in the electronic commerce era. Japan is an exceptional player in the mobile field, having developed its own unique hardware system. The service is not delivered via desktop personal computers, laptop computers or digital televisions, but by using mobile phones and PDAs.

NTT Mobile Communication network, Japan's leading mobile phone operator, and its competitors Nippon IDO Tsushin and DDI Cellular Group, are already providing mobile data services such as home banking, news headlines, restaurant guides, weather reports, cinema schedules and fortune-telling to the Japanese market.

NTT DoCoMo, one of the most advanced companies in the telecommunication's industry today, is currently introducing the first 3G mobile phone service. The 3G mobile phone service will be the first step for Japan into the 'Evernet' (a Japanese term for universal access to the Internet, irrespective of place, time and equipment). NTT DoCoMo is using a technology called FOMA (Freedom of Mobile Multimedia Access) which will provide more freedom in terms of speed and quality than the WAP technology developed in the West. The company has already begun offering its hit 'i-mode' wireless Internet service to the US market through its partner AT&T Wireless. The service will be tested first in the Seattle area before being expanded nationwide early in 2002. It will allow US users to exchange email, check stock prices and find restaurants, movies and other information from their cell phones.

NTT DoCoMo is set to expand rapidly, having bought a 16 per cent stake in AT&T Wireless in 2000, as well as minority stakes in KPN Mobile NV of Netherlands, Hutchinson 3G UK Holdings, Taiwan's KG Telecom and Hutchinson Telecom of Hong Kong. Kiyoyuki Tsujimuru, Managing Director in charge of global strategy, was confident the i-mode would be a hit overseas: 'Cell phones in the United States and Europe are still like 13-inch black and white TV sets. There is a huge gap in technology. People see colour displays and are stunned.' US users will be able to access a wide variety of i-mode sites such as CNN for news or Disney for their characters. There are already 40,000 i-mode sites operational in Japan. The variety and the quality of the information displayed makes NTT DoCoMo one of the first in the world able to offer advanced forms of wireless technology allowing for video, audio and other data-rich transmissions.

DIGITAL TELEVISION

Interactive Digital Television (iDTV) looks similar to PC-based Internet but is delivered through a television set and can be operated using a remote control. From a standing start in 1999, market penetration by 2002 is currently around 40 per cent of UK households and is projected to rise to 95 per cent by 2010, according to a Netpoll survey. Leading providers include Sky Digital, ON Digital, Telewest and NTL. One of the key drivers for this surprisingly rapid growth has been the provision of free set-top boxes by these platform providers. Services currently provided include home shopping, email, video, banking and travel. Forrester Research (2001) predicts that more people will access the Internet through a television than through a PC by the end of 2004.

Advertising through this mechanism can be interactive, as viewers can respond immediately to request further information or to sign up for a promotion. Digital television has helped increase the fragmentation of viewers, as there are over 200 channels now available in the UK. This means that advertising can be easily targeted to tighter niche audiences, for example through exposure on sports, cooking or health channels.

Advertisers can develop their own television channels in order to incorporate content provision and communicate with their customers less intrusively. For example, the PC version of Boots' digital health channel, Wellbeing, is also automatically accessed if you type in 'www.boots.co.uk'. Specialist digital television channels also provide more focus for sponsorship deals.

Domino's Pizza, which is represented on satellite, cable and the Web, is one of the early success stories of iDTV. e-Commerce transactions represent 4 per cent of its total business. Management credit the firm's sponsorship of *The Simpsons* as pivotal in building Domino's iDTV business. This activity has given Domino's a brand recognition figure of 98 per cent in multi-channel homes.

The UK government is currently pushing for total digital television penetration, and there has been talk of switching off the analogue signal by as soon as 2010. By the end of 2001, the number of digital television owners in the UK reached the same level (36 per cent) as the number of Internet users in the country for the first time, according to e-MORI's Technology Tracker (www.e-mori.co.uk).

While the number of new users seeking Internet access is levelling off, digital TV ownership more than doubled in 2001. In social groups AB and C1, PC-based Internet access far outweighs digital television ownership, but the ratio shifts in social groups C2 and DE, in which twice as many households have digital television as have Internet access via PC. The relationship between social class and choice of Internet access mechanism.

Fewer than half of digital television owners have so far used interactive services such as shopping, banking, gaming or email. This is because PCs have been traditionally viewed as information tools and are a logical choice for accessing the Internet and using online consumer services. The television, however, is viewed as an entertainment tool, and the biggest driver for digital adoption so far has been improved picture quality and a greater choice of channels, with little attention being paid by consumers to the advantages of interactive services.Smith and Chaffey (2002) note the following advantages of iDTV to marketers:

- Direct-response mass-market advertising;
- Highly targetable;
- Moving buyers through the complete buying process;
- Audience engagement through interaction;
- Brand-building and positioning reinforcement;
- Brand-building through community-building;
- Customer service - reduction of bottlenecks;
- Security – less risk associated with TV than Web sites;
- Controllable - highly measurable;
- Cost savings.

These authors go on to recommend five key steps to making iDTV work in practice:

- Start small; test out advertisements first on a small scale and see what reaction is gained.
- Develop your own content area or micro Web site linked to iDTV.
- Design for the lowest common denominator to maximize the number of people who can make use of your service.
- Grow your offer over time to include purchasing or personalization.
- Form partnerships or build a team for the future to ensure that the necessary skills are available.

However, despite the rapidly increasing volume of viewers, actual purchase transactions have been slow to take off. Forrester Research notes that many retailers currently using iDTV as a channel to market are planning to pull out when their contracts come up for renewal. The main reason for their dissatisfaction is weak sales. The Forrester Research report points to a poor visitor-to-purchase ratio of only 2 per cent. Also problematic is the location of transactional sites within 'walled gardens', which are dedicated interactive channels that are separate from programme content. The challenge is to find ways and means of driving consumers to these interactive channels and encouraging them to carry out transactions. Although a shake-out of unprofitable business is probably inevitable, the iDTV medium is slowly evolving, costs are falling and interactivity becoming less 'clunky', suggesting that opportunities will present themselves to companies prepared to take the longer view.

'Push' technology is the name given to a broad spectrum of products that automate the delivery of information to the user. Many Web sites are currently based upon 'pull' models, whereby users seek out the information in which they are interested. In contrast, push technologies create automated communications relationships whereby products can be aimed at users who have expressed an interest and given permission to be sent targeted material.

V-Commerce (short for 'voice') allows users to conduct self-service transactions alternately using the web and the telephone. This initiative is being led by the V-Commerce Alliance, which consists of a number of Internet and telecom companies. For example, a consumer would be able to make an airline reservation over the Web, and then later call a specific number to obtain departure gate or frequent-flyer information - or, before ordering a new computer online, speak to a customer service representative to check which model would be most suitable for their requirements.

Speech recognition is becoming increasingly common in US call centres, particularly in the banking and airline industries. It is also being adapted as a 'hands-free' input device for cars in Europe and Japan, as the motor industry recognizes that voice is the safest way for drivers to interact with in-car technologies (The Economist, 2001b). Nissan already sells a premium model that uses voice instruction to control audio, temperature, navigation and lighting. The new technologies promise to deliver access to information and services on a permanent basis anywhere that there is a telephone connection.

It is only in the past year or so that the necessary computing power has become small and cheap enough to fit into mobile devices in a cost-effective way. In addition, the (admittedly slow) spread of broadband access to the Internet in public places is fuelling the demand for instant information. What is also generating interest is the way in which speech recognition is improving the quality of information services by eliminating the need for telephone queuing and badly designed menu-driven voicemail systems.

Apart from call centres, other opportunities for telephone-based services using speech recognition include:

- Self-service banking;
- Catalogue ordering;
- Weather and stock market reports;
- Email collection;
- Virtual personal assistants (VPAs).

In order for the telephone and the Internet to be merged effectively, common industry standards need to be achieved so that Web pages can handle voice. In October 2001 the World Wide Web Consortium (www.w3.org) - a voluntary organization that sets international standards - released a draft version of VoiceXML for this purpose. At the same time, however, a new platform was created by such key players as Microsoft, Intel and Philips to develop a rival standard called SALT (Speech Application Language Tags). It remains to be seen which of these will prevail.

Virgin plans a new service (www.virginunlimited.com) that aims to sell everything from cars and toasters to holidays at big discounts. It will offer postcode-specific advice on financial services and household utilities at the lowest prices. In order to provide this service, the company has established partnerships with a number of consumer durable wholesalers and also providers of specialist niche products. Consumers will be able to ask product providers to compete for business by stating their requirements. The company that offers the best price and terms will win the order.

Consumers are often frustrated at having to deal with different service providers for each channel, which necessitates separate billing arrangements, passwords and email addresses. Consequently, they will migrate to services that allow them to personalize a single service for use on multiple devices. Looking ahead, Java TV (still at a very early stage of development) will bring together television and computing technologies to enable broadcasters to deliver value-added services to a range of Java-enabled devices.

This means that the Internet will be rendered 'device independent' and customers will be able to switch their viewing from television to PC or mobile - anywhere and at any time - as their circumstances dictate. The organizational challenges associated with developing and integrating effective multiple channel operations should not be underestimated.

CHALLENGES OF MULTI-CHANNEL MARKETING

The usage of various Internet access mechanisms has developed over the past few years. At this early stage, companies need to address a number of challenges when considering the development of multi-channel strategies that allow customers to access online content from a range of devices:

- The extent to which they should invest in these relatively untried technologies, with little indication of likely customer demand or long-term prospects for making money.
- The need to 'repurpose' content for each tool. For example, trying to display a Web site on a WAP screen means that graphics and pictures are lost, and different coding is required. Smith and Chaffey also note that switching between PC and iDTV is problematic because Web sites are designed to be viewed in 'lean-forward mode' from two feet away, but iDTV in 'laid-back mode' from more like eight feet away. Navigating with a mouse is also very different from navigating with a remote control device.
- The unique properties of each medium in terms of the user experience delivered. For example, mobile transactions are likely to be for low-value or distress purchases, because the amount and quality of information that can be displayed to the customer on screen is limited. In contrast, the PC allows huge volumes of data to searched and displayed, and so is best suited to situations where the customer wants to carry out extensive research before making a purchase. Digital television offers yet another dynamic; although it

is still in its infancy, early usage suggests that purchases may take place in a more collaborative, impulsive and social context than through the other channels.

- Whether they should offer all their products or services across each medium (and if so, the extent to which customization is necessary and/or appropriate) or 'mix and match' according to the characteristics of each channel and the specific message to be delivered.
- The need for *integrated* online and offline marketing campaigns. Smith and Chaffey (2002) describe how MTV asked viewers to send in SMS text messages to provide comments and vote for their favourite video. MTV then played the winning video together with the comments live. The event was promoted through offline magazines read by the target audience, and the paper-based advertisement demonstrated a text message on a phone explaining how to take part.
- How to manage the necessary internal information processing that will allow the company to achieve a unified view of customer activity across all channels. For this to work, a central database is necessary to provide up-to-date customer details to all channel operators. Remember that customers' expectations are continually rising and they may expect to use a combination of channels to effect just one single purchase ...

It should be clear from this brief discussion that the technical ability to offer multi-channel access is just the starting point. Considerable investment needs to be made in the back-office computer systems and business process integration necessary to actually make it work in practice.

The difficulties are even greater for small firms with limited financial resources, or those with legacy computer systems that cannot be easily integrated. However, for those that succeed, the potential for combine multi-channel offerings with *personalized* content provides an enormous marketing opportunity.

THE GENIE MOBILE INTERNET PORTAL

Genie was launched in 2001 as the world's first exclusively online mobile service. Genie's UK mobile service operates on the BT Cellnet network and is therefore now part of O2. BT Cellnet is one of the largest UK mobile networks, with over 8 million customers, and offers 99 per cent coverage of the UK population.

Genie is the UK's leading mobile Internet company, with over 3 million registered users of the Genie Internet portal. It provides free text messaging and free access to WAP. The mobile Internet is the technology that allows users to view information, play games and manage personal email via a WAP phone. WAP stands for Wireless Application Protocol and is the worldwide standard enabling WAP mobile phones to access the Mobile Internet. Genie Mobile Internet provides a number of services available on WAP phones:

- Email - the ability to read, reply and forward emails;
- M-Commerce - you can now buy books and CDs;
- Information - the latest sports scores, current news and gossip;
- Enquiries - flight times, cinema times;
- Entertainment - games, competitions and reviews.

Mobile phone and Internet services are integrated so that customers can access information on a PC or via mobile phone.

The Genie portal itself runs at significant loss, but its services appeal to the key market segment of early-adopter mobile phone users. Members of this group are predisposed to purchasing new gadgets, understand the rapidly developing terminology and issues surrounding mobile developments, and also happen to spend the most money on mobiles.

Any mobile user can register on the site - they do not necessarily have to be using O2 networks. By permission-based marketing to these registered Genie visitors, special deals can be offered to get them to switch to the O2 network.

At this stage of market development, the key selling points as far as users are concerned relate to content (in the form of information and alerts about share prices, skiing conditions, sports results, etc.) rather than transactional commerce.

The Genie brand has high awareness ratings despite low advertising spend. According to *Campaign's* dotcom weekly awareness survey, Genie is ranked tenth in the UK, with an awareness rating of 27 per cent, just behind the Easy Group on 32 per cent and ahead of Wellbeing on 20 per cent. Genie is promoted on the major portals such as Google, MSN and Yahoo!, and pays for prominent placements on search engines so that a banner is invoked should a surfer conduct a search for 'mobile phone', for example.

Genie aims to leverage value from its mobile services by offering customers special deals through partnerships with banks and ISPs as part of a 'closed' network. This business model is superior to many 'open' network portals because partner firms will either pay for preferential access to Genie customers or at least provide content for free. Genie customers who want to access services from companies outside the partner network have to pay extra for the privilege. To illustrate how this works, consider the example of mobile banking.

Genie provides secure links to eight leading banks to enable customers to access their bank accounts via their mobile phones on the O2 network. Within the next twelve months, customers will also be able to trade stocks in this way. Hence there is scope for the major stockbrokers to be 'plumbed in' to the partnership to make the entire contact, share purchase and payment transaction from the bank account a seamless and immediate process for the customer. If such a service is available, why would a customer want to look elsewhere for a stockbroker? Stockbrokers, therefore, will pay for a preferential placing in the Genie portfolio, and indeed several may compete with each other - with the best positions on the listing commanding the highest fees.From the partner firms' perspective, there are three key drivers for associating with Genie:

- To obtain additional revenue from existing customers by offering an alternative channel to access the company;
- To expand the customer base by appealing to new market segments (for example people who use their mobile phone to bet with Ladbrokes through the Genie gateway have a very different demographic profile from that of Ladbroke's traditional customer base relying upon the firm's network of betting shops);
- To reduce the costs of servicing their customer base. This is the key driver for banking partners, for example.

To illustrate the potential of mobile services to reduce costs (and in some cases change the partner firm's entire business model), consider the example of a recruitment agency for temporary staff. In the past, such a firm would rely upon a team of office-based employees to make telephone calls to perhaps hundreds of registered individuals to advise them of newly received employment opportunities and sign people up as required. This could be an expensive and time-consuming exercise if large numbers of staff were required.

By sending a text message simultaneously to the entire labour pool database requesting those interested to call in and sign up for the job, the entire cost structure of the business is altered. The staff employed to recruit would only have to answer calls from people accepting the work, rather than make a large number of outgoing calls touting for business. In the near future, the acceptance procedure will also become Web based, thereby reducing the need for human intervention still further.

THE INTERNET AND THE WORLD WIDE WEB

Prior to the Internet, World Wide Web and its associated technologies, the impact of technology for the purposes of business transactions had been peripheral. The Internet and the World Wide Web have fundamentally changed commerce. Commerce's basic mode of communication, written and verbal communication between a business and its customer or business and its suppliers or partners, remained unchanged since Adam Smith's first observations on economic markets.

Electronic communication, in the form of digital mainframe computers and microcomputers (personal computers) connected to the Internet, has radically transformed commercial activity for customers and businesses alike. The transformation has been so fundamental that new terms such as 'e-Commerce', 'e-Business', 'e-Markets' and the 'new e-Economy' are freely used to describe the modern phenomenon of Internet-based commercial activity.

e-Commerce may be described as the sharing of product and service information, developing and maintaining human commercial relationships, and transacting business over the Internet and the World Wide Web.

Technologies such as telephony have influenced business activity in the past, but their influence has not been revolutionary. Such technologies have not fundamentally changed how businesses organize themselves and how they interact with their customers, suppliers or partners. In contrast, the Internet and the World Wide Web have revolutionized business activity.

- Provides an introductory description of the current IT, Internet and World Wide Web technology underpinning e-Commerce;
- Comments on its implications for business and e-Commerce;
- Explores potential future developments in Internet and World Wide Web technology that will affect e-Commerce.

This introductory reading on e-Commerce technology should enable you to describe Internet and World Wide Web technology to enable e-Commerce. Critically, the reading should enable you to state and understand the main elements of an e-Commerce system architecture and assess e-Commerce security technology for confidentiality and payments.

Memex

The Internet's evolution has encompassed over fifty years of technological and conceptual development. The original concept of the Internet is attributed to Vannevar Bush. He worked in a team of engineers during World War II in the United States. His experience of working in an expert team of scientists led him to think about the problem of processing and sharing information among the team. His solution was the invention of a machine called Memex (MEMory EXtension). He envisaged that Memex would work like the human brain, which finds information by association. His ideas provided the conceptual framework for subsequent work on developing the technology of the Internet and World Wide Web.

ARPAnet

The Internet began in 1969 as a communications medium project of the US Department of Defence, and its associated academic and research agencies. It needed a network of computers to enable collaborative work among the different agencies. In its original form, the Internet consisted of a decentralized digital network that connected defence, research and academic mainframe computers.

This network was called the ARPAnet after the agency that led the project, the department's Advanced Research Projects Agency (ARPA). The purpose of the ARPAnet was to connect various government and related computers, and in the event of disaster or war to preserve the integrity of information passing between these important government agencies. ARPAnet was privatized in 1990, and as it was gradually released to the public domain it began to be transformed into the Internet that we know today.

The World Wide Web

Around the same time, Tim Berners-Lee, a research scientist working at the European CERN physics lab in Switzerland, conceived the World Wide Web and released it to the public domain in 1991. The problem that Tim Berners-Lee faced was how to share research knowledge among scientists who used different brands of computers and associated software at CERN. He developed the method of hypertext link for connecting information stored on different computers. In his words, his motive for inventing the Web was: 'If everyone had the same information as me, my life would be easier.

The original idea for linking electronic documents was Ted Nelson's. He coined the term 'hypertext' in the early 1960s. Marc Andreessen developed the first graphical browser for the Internet. It enabled people seeking information on the Internet to find it quickly and efficiently.

A major effect of the Internet and the Web over the 1990s was to enable executives and business strategists to develop new ways of doing business electronically. These new electronic approaches are termed e-Commerce 'business models'. Business models that combine the use of the Internet and Web technologies with fundamental business transformation are referred to as 'e-Business'.

The term e-Business is used to describe a business that shares its production or service information with customers and business suppliers or partners, fosters the development of customer relationships electronically, and enables business to be transacted from personal computers or other electronic devices, such as mobile phones or personal digital assistants (PDAs). One of the most successful e-Commerce business models is the US company Dell Computers.

It has a $14 million per day Internet-based revenue stream, or a quarter of its total revenue. Though a survey by NOP in 1999 revealed that only 15 per cent of the companies surveyed used the Internet for making online sales, Gartner Research predict that 97.5 million US users will adopt e-billing and online account management by 2005.

INTERNET AND WORLD WIDE WEB TECHNOLOGIES

The microcomputer or Personal Computer (PC) forms the basis of e-Commerce. The Internet would not have the wide reach that it has into peoples' homes in the absence of the PC. Most office PCs are linked to a computer network and PCs at home are connected to the Internet via modems or dedicated data transfer cables.

Local area Networks and Wide area Networks

PCs on local area networks (LANs) and wide area networks (WANs) are connected to the Internet. LANs and WANs are digital computer networks that connect PCs to enable sharing of information between separate computers.

LANs are limited to a geographical area such as an office, whereas WANs connect computers over a wider geographical area. The computers on a LAN or WAN share information in the form of addressed packets of data.

The capacity of a single computer is increased by connecting it to a LAN or WAN, as it can share computer programs and information. A computer that is linked to a network can download and use computer programs and share storage and printing facilities, and take advantage of network capabilities for sending and receiving data and information.

Client-server Architecture

A computer on a LAN or WAN that provides resources like application programs or printer connections is known as a 'server'. A server provides other computers known as 'clients' on the LAN or WAN with software and other resources. This set-up is called client-server computing architecture. A server that is linked to the Internet is called a 'host computer'.

A server computer is capable of running server software, which needs to be compatible with the network operating system. The client and server are independent and perform specialized tasks to process information and run computer applications.

If you use Microsoft Word on your computer, the client, it is probable that a server will have provided the Microsoft Word software for you to use. The client-server architecture is the basis of the Internet too.

The Internet and Protocols

The Internet is the sum total connection of LANs, WANs and stand-alone computers around the world. The term 'Internet' is short for 'inter-networking' or an interconnected set of networks. It is the global network of computers, whether the computer is on a LAN in an office, or a WAN in an industry extranet, or an independent computer in a private home. An Internet-connected computer is known as an Internet host computer. The Internet is also known as the 'Net', the 'Information superhighway' or 'Cyberspace'.

The set of rules for moving information over the Internet is called a 'protocol'. The transmission control protocol (TCP) is used for sending large amounts of information between host computers on the Internet. Vinton Cerf wrote the basic ideas for TCP on the back of an envelope over lunch, and in 1983 the core protocols of the Internet transmission control protocol/Internet protocol (TCP/IP) became the standard protocol for transmitting information over the Internet.

Intranet

An intranet consists of networked internal connection of computers owned by an organization and makes use of Web technology. An intranet may be mounted on a LAN or a WAN. An intranet makes use of Internet technology such as TCP/IP, HTML, Java and HTTP to make it interoperable and to provide it with Web capability. The basic elements of an intranet are a computer network, a computer designated as a server containing server software and the Internet protocols TCP/IP.

An intranet offers several benefits to an organization: improved sharing and communication of information, open standards and cross-platform collaboration. For example, a car manufacturing company may connect its information systems on purchasing with its accounting information systems to form an intranet for sharing and processing information between two departments in the company.

An intranet is a company's own internal information transfer system that offers: e-mail, communication among different computers, connection to remote offices, a Web browser interface and special-interest news groups. For e-Commerce, an intranet is used to provide a corporate image and unified 'experience' for a customer that combines product information, ordering and customer care.

Extranet

An extranet is used for business-to-business (B2B) e-Commerce. It is the networked connection of computers of two or more companies. It is a private communication system to support trade and is used for communication and transactions between business partners, suppliers or special customers. For example, a car manufacturing company may connect its computers with its various suppliers of components for the cars it makes. Another example is the airline industry's OneWorld network, which enables customers to transfer seamlessly between airlines to reach their destinations.

Design principles

Intranets and extranets share the same design principles formulated for the Internet. The Internet design principles are:

Interoperability. There are varying operating systems that control computer functions on the many different computers on the Internet. Normally a given operating system cannot communicate with a different one. A standard to enable varying operating systems to communicate with each other was introduced by the US Department of Defence, which originally financed the Internet. Interoperability means that independent implementations of Internet protocols can work seamlessly.

Consequently, operating system developers such as Microsoft or Apple incorporate software into their operating systems that enables them to operate with other computers over the Internet. Internet-compatible systems use the TCP/IP common protocol for communication. Interoperability for e-Commerce means that companies and customers do not have to purchase and upgrade software from the same vendors. Their computers will be able to communicate over the Internet because of the standard protocols.

Layering. The Internet can be regarded as a series of layers of software. The structure of the Internet is layered. It is a five-layer system consisting of: interconnect level (National Access Points, NAPs), national backbone providers, regional Internet providers, local Internet service providers, and the business and consumer market.

The bottom layers of software, interconnect and network, are concerned with operating the computer hardware. The higher layers, business and consumer market, come closer to the needs of the person using the Internet.

The most relevant layer is the layer that processes the information required by the Internet user; this is called the 'application' layer. These different hardware and application layers need to communicate with each other and they do so by using well defined interfaces. The Internet layering standard has resulted in increased reliability of Internet software and it is invisible to the Internet user.

Simplicity.The layering has resulted in simplicity of software design. Each layer is concerned only with its own functionality, making its design simpler. For example, the layer concerned with physical devices like mouse operations are hidden from the higher layers that process information. This kind of simplicity has contributed to increased software reliability too.

Uniform naming and addressing. Each Internet host computer has an Internet Protocol (IP) address that uniquely identifies it on the Internet from the millions of other computers also on the Internet. The IP address is expressed in a uniform format or 'dotted quad'. An example is: '17.10.2.3'. As the dotted quad is not meaningful to humans the domain name system (DNS) is used to provide a symbolic name for the dotted quad. An example is: 'sol.brunel.ac.uk'. The DNS is capable of translating the symbolic name into the required IP address to enable Internet operations.

End-to-end protocols. The Internet does not process information. It enables the transfer of 'packets' of information between computers. This is called end-to-end protocol. The Internet enables the transfer of information or 'content' of the packet. The transmitting or receiving computers, known as the 'end' system, do the actual processing of information.

The combined use of the Internet, intranets and extranets by companies has resulted in the term 'virtual organization' or 'networked organization'. The virtual organization is to be contrasted with the physical organization; the latter is restricted by geographical, physical space. Companies can combine computer-networking technology with information technology (IT) and information systems (IS) to develop a network of computers that can capture, process and share information and knowledge in virtual or cyberspace, where time and space are defined differently from physical time and space.

Amazon.com may be classed as a virtual organization. Virtual organizations tend to be flatter because access to information and knowledge is potentially open to all employees who have access to a PC.

THE WORLD WIDE WEB

The World Wide Web, also known as the 'Web' or 'WWW', consists of pages of information depicted as text, graphics, sound, or video clips. A Web page may contain Java applets - Java programs that are downloaded from the server and run on the local computer. The Web consists of over a million Web servers, and an untold number of Web browsers. What distinguishes the Web from other computer media is its ability to link Web pages dynamically; this is known as hypertext links or simply links. The Web combines computer network technology with hypertext to provide a 'global information system'. One Web page can be linked to another by a hypertext link and the user merely has to click on the link to display related information. A link appears as highlighted on the Web page. It is this hypertext linking capability of the Web that makes it a powerful source of information. The Web is a client-server architecture system, and a Web user can access the Web servers with a Web browser such as Netscape or Microsoft Explorer.

Hypertext

A document on the Web is composed using hypertext technology. Hypertext is an electronic document system that can be read non-sequentially and interactively. The reader does not have to read it like a book, she/he can click on hyperlinks of related information. The Apollo space programme to record its documentation used a hypertext system. e-Commerce Web sites are built using hypertext documents, and other hypermedia.

Hypertext Transfer Protocol

The Web differs from the Internet by the protocol it uses to transfer information between computers. The Web uses the hypertext transfer protocol (HTTP) to connect and transfer hypertext documents stored on Web servers, also known as Web sites. All the computers on the Internet that use the HTTP protocol compose the Web.

The Web browser

A Web browser is a graphical interface for searching, accessing and viewing hypertext and multimedia files on the Web. The first browser, called Mosaic, was invented by the US company Netscape Communications, founded in 1994 by Marc Andreessen. He set himself the problem of transferring sound and pictures over the Web. His solution was the first graphical Web browser.

It allowed basic functions such as retrieving and displaying hypertext files. The growth of the Internet and the Web is largely because of the invention of the graphical browser which makes it easier for people to search and view information. Two popular browsers are Netscape Communicator and Internet Explorer. They are more sophisticated than the original Mosaic browser and enable e-mail messaging, HTML authoring, and extensions such as scripting, plug-in and multimedia.

INTERNET SEARCH ENGINES

The Internet is unarguably the most voluminous information store in the world. Finding information on the Internet requires complex computer algorithms. These algorithms form the backbone of Internet search engines designed to help people find the information they want. Organizations need search engines to find information about customers or business competitors or partners. Search engines are computer programs that locate specific Web pages, files or multimedia items stored on the Internet. Search engines such as Google or Autonomy use different algorithms or techniques to search for Web pages.

UNIFORM RESOURCE LOCATOR

The uniform resource locator (URL) is the address of a particular Web site on the Internet. It consists of domain names and a pathway that locates a particular host computer that is connected to the Internet. An example URL is www.yahoo.com or www.dell.com. A URL consists of the protocol that is to be used to make the Internet connection (the WWW in the examples), the name of the host computer ('Yahoo' or 'Dell') and the domain (.com). In the case of commercial companies, the name of the host computer connected to the Internet is usually the registered name of the company.

HYPERTEXT MARK-UP LANGUAGE

Hypertext mark-up language (HTML) is used to author information on a Web page. HTML documents are text files that are interpreted by a Web browser. The browser reads the HTML file and interprets the HTML instructions. The browser has to do this interpretation each time a hypertext file is loaded. A Web page can be divided into 'frames' or sub-pages.

Each frame is used to display separate but relevant information designed by the Web author. Multimedia can be facilitated by extensions to HTML or by 'plug-ins' or add-on programs that make the Web client more versatile to deal with additional media types. An example of extension is Secure HTTP that enables sophisticated encryption and decryption algorithms for sensitive e-Commerce data like payments for transactions.

It takes time to learn to write HTML code. Authoring tools are available for automatically converting documents in Microsoft Word to HTML files, ready to load on to a Web server. Hot Dog Pro, Adobe PageMill and Microsoft FrontPage are examples. A Web site consists of one or more Web pages linked together by hyperlinks. The contents of a Web site are known as 'content'. HTML is not capable of processing or interacting with Internet users. To process data captured through a Web form JavaScript is required.

MULTIMEDIA

Multimedia is a tool capable of providing the transfer of sound and images like pictures over the Internet. Multimedia applications require lots of memory and bandwidth - the physical capacity of data cables to carry and transfer data. For example, one minute of music requires 5 MB of data. The transfer of sound and images in real time requires special software which is added to TCP/IP and HTTP protocols. On the client end, a player is required to interpret the data and render it into sound or images. Multimedia Internet Mail Extensions or MIME is an Internet standard for multimedia Internet e-mail. MIME enables e-mail to be cast as types consisting of HTML, text, images or video. Example MIME types are: image/jpeg, video/ mpeg or application/pdf.

JAVA, APPLETS, JAVASCRIPT AND INTERACTIVITY

The Internet is popular because it is interactive. Interactivity means that the Internet user (or client) can actively request information from and provide information to the server. Such interactivity is important for e-Commerce applications. CGI script and JavaScript provide interactivity on the Internet. Java is a programming language originally intended for programming consumer electronic devices like microwave ovens, dishwashers or electronic clocks. As there are many manufacturers of these products, Java's developer, Sun Microsystems, designed Java to be ubiquitous, meaning that it should be operable on any manufacturer's device.

Virtual Java machines that are independent of PC operating systems interpret Java, a feature that makes it ideal for Internet programming. Java programs created for the Internet are called applets. Java applets are embedded in HTML documents. An applet is a Java programme that is executed on the client machine. It is loaded by the Web browser and restricted to prevent security breaches. The applet is executed on a Java virtual machine in the browser.

JavaScript, originally called LiveScript, was developed independently of Java by Netscape to provide interactivity. It is used to process data captured via forms on the Internet and to create interactive Web sites, and both the server and the client side use it. JavaScript is embedded in HTML and is interpreted by a browser. Web pages that contain JavaScript can be transferred around the Internet, because JavaScript is platform-independent or interpreted. ActiveX is a competitor of JavaScript. Scripts can be used in e-Commerce to validate service or product order form entries.

Common Gateway Interface

CGI programs are text files that consist of line or programming code similar to JavaScript; such programs are called CGI script. Pear is an example of CGI programming. CGI is used to create interactive Web sites that pass information from a Web browser to a server using a form, very useful for organizational needs. A form is a document that is created to interact with a user, take data from the user and send it to the server for processing, usually via a database.

INFORMATION SEARCH ON THE WEB

In the e-retail literature, much is made of the *similarities* between the new electronic ways to sell goods to consumers and the traditional ways (bricks). One can talk about e-stores, e-shop fronts, e-shoppers, e-malls and so on. We highlight some of the *differences* between clicks and bricks.

These differences arise from the totally different technologies which are used in a clicks store compared with a bricks store, and the totally different approach used by e-shoppers to find goods and services, to compare prices and to generally browse around. The essential concept is *search* - the process by which e-shoppers find information about products and services.

BACKGROUND TO SEARCHING THE INTERNET AND THE WEB

The Internet is a worldwide network of servers and machines, originally set up (as the ARPAnet) to facilitate information exchange between US government contractors and university researchers . From the earliest days of the Internet, a major activity has been *searching* for information. As the Internet grew, a variety of tools were set up to help users perform searching to find the required information. Nowadays, the focus of activity is the World Wide Web, which uses Internet technology with an improved user interface, making huge amounts of information available to the end-user, often a home computer user. Much of this information is about products and services for mass distribution provided by e-retailers. The interface employed by most users is a graphical Web browser, typically Microsoft Internet Explorer or Netscape Navigator.

In practice much of the information is textual in nature, with graphical layout (such as the use of lists) to provide structure and additional graphics to provide other information and 'decoration'. Although much has been made of the idea of e-malls, where a group of e-shops congregate together like a conventional shopping mall, the typical user experience involves focusing on a specific website often linked to one company's offerings.

SURVEYS ON WHAT PEOPLE DO AND WHERE PEOPLE 'GO' ON THE WEB

A computer scientist would say that what e-shoppers actually do is to use a Web browser to examine data from the Web rendered into graphical images. A typical user would say something rather different - the experience is that you explore a virtual world and that at any moment you are at one 'place' in that world.

From then you might explore the place more deeply or move on to other places which are linked. Many surveys have been done to help us understand why people use the Web. There are four primary motives for Internet use: researching (in the most general sense), shopping, socializing and generalized surfing (for enjoyment). Shehan (2002) carried out a cluster analysis of types of Internet sessions, finding that 'I need to find some information' was a significantly stronger motivation than all others. Visiting news sites, using search engines, searching for product information and using online databases together accounted for 34 per cent of users' online time.

Searching for product information alone accounted for 7 per cent of online time, compared with only 1.7 per cent spent e-shopping. Eighty-five per cent of all Internet traffic comes from 13 major search engines. Information search is important for consumers and it is important for e-retailers too: in a US study, the use of the Internet to search for information was the strongest predictor of e-shopping intention. In addition, information search improved shoppers' attitudes towards e-retailing a nd helped overcome the perceived barriers to e-shopping. Similarly, Fink and Laupase (2000) carried out an experiment with 30 Australian and 30 Malaysian participants who evaluated selected websites. They found evidence of a relationship between products and services and news stories. The authors argued that the impact of products and services displayed could be maximized through the presence of news stories providing information about recent developments.

We referred briefly to our study investigating shoppers' motivations in e-shopping. The respondents were a sample of 150 undergraduatestudents. Enjoyment was one of the main motivations and 'involvement' was one of the most important enjoyment dimensions. In line with previous work drawing attention to 'variety seeking', the most popular sites were Amazon (www.amazon.co.uk), CD WOW (www.cd-wow.co.uk) and eBay (www.ebay.co.uk), i.e. 'hedonic' e-retailers .Amazon and eBay are the UK's top two sites in terms of audience numbers.

It is particularly strong on involvement, with visitors spending on average 1 hour and 11 minutes on the site, one of the longest of UK e-retailers. Visitors return to the site frequently to check on items they are buying or selling. There is also a feedback feature on sellers that helps to build trust, and eBay is one of few UK e-retailers to achieve over one billion page views per month.

Such sites enthusiastically embrace the 'involvement' aspect of enjoyment with features such as chat rooms, bulletin boards, customer written stories and product reviews, suggestion boxes and personalization of the website offers. In short, many of the features that make these sites involving, enjoyable and successful are based on satisfying shoppers' needs for information in one form or another. Some e-retailers use surfers' needs for information as a successful method of directing traffic to their sites. For example, outdoor equipment supplier L L Bean (www.llbean.com) provides information on national parks, and chemist/ drugstore Boots specializes in nutrition and health information.

SEARCHING AND FINDING ON THE WEB

Shoppers, then, spend a lot of time *searching*, and e-retailers are, of course, most interested in what they *find* ('Seek, and ye shall find!'). They would like shoppers to find information on their products and services at their virtual store, and to find (and execute) ordering and payment processes. They thus need to understand what technologies the shoppers use, and how they use these technologies, in order to improve the chances of sales and services on the Web. Thus, e-retailers who can help satisfy surfers' wants for information have a head start in selling to those customers.

THE AVERAGE WEB SESSION

Let us consider what average users do in an average Web session:

- The users sit down and start their Web browser, often set up so that the initial screen (the home page) points to some major website, and it displays a list of links to other sites and services. For example, the home page might be set to the Yahoo! main page (www.yahoo.com). Possibly they might decide to *focus* immediately on some site they know about and type in the Web address (URL) or use 'favourites' or 'bookmarks' to access that site.
- Otherwise, they look through the home page visually and *evaluate* the list, and make some decision based on what they are interested in.
- They might then decide to access a *search engine*, for example Google, (www.google.com) and, by entering suitable search phrases and hitting the Search button, instruct the engine to produce a list of relevant web pages with a brief summary of their contents. Having got that list, it is then scanned and evaluated.
- They might decide to examine a *directory system* related to their search goals, and scan through that and evaluate items.
- The process of scanning through lists for relevant items and/or using search engines is repeated until the relevant items are found. If nothing suitable is found, the search is refocused or *abandoned* at any point, or the search goals may be refocused from information retrieved, deliberately or not (some advertisement might pop up). The users might even go directly to some site, even if it does not come up on a directory or search-engine list, if they know the Web address (URL).

Let us now examine these in more detail.

They are:

- Focus
- Directories
- Search engines.

FOCUS

Suppose you want to purchase some hair conditioner. If you go down to the local town centre and locate a major shopping mall or high street area, you have expectations as to what you might find there and the ways you can quickly locate items of interest. For example, you would expect to be able to find a chain pharmacy store in a few minutes - in the United Kingdom, a branch of Boots or Superdrug. Having found such a store, you would expect to locate quickly a section with hair products and, equally quickly, a range of shampoos and conditioners. What you might also do is use some sort of directory (possibly the Yellow Pages) to locate stores of interest.

Compared with the bricks experience, an e-shopper on the Web operates in a rather different way. On the Web, a user starts up a Web browser with some initial page, perhaps that of their Internet service provider. They then start searching for the item required, following appropriate links. Almost certainly they will use some sort of Web search engine. Obviously, we need to design web pages so that they are usable and attractive to the user. Nielsen (2000) has written extensively on website usability, and has pointed out a number of important considerations.

A prime component of making sites usable is clarity and focus. If the user finds the site difficult to use, and the design messy and unfocused, they will abandon the site and turn to searching elsewhere. Neilsen suggests some standards to create user consistency, good design and relevance, leading to a unified user experience across the site.

DIRECTORIES

People like lists, from the Seven Wonders of the Ancient World to the Top 20 pop songs. Directories are lists compiled around some specific topic, such as the telephone directory and trade directories. In the early days of the Web, people (editors) compiled lists of the most popular sites. As the number of sites grew, the lists became rather long. To improve accessibility, they were split into categories and sub-categories. Well known Web directories include Yahoo! (www.yahoo.com) and MSN (www.msn.com).

Let us consider Yahoo! in a little detail. Yahoo! is compiled by human editors who also create a short description that is shown alongside the link to the Web address. The editors categorize the topics logically, in a way a search engine does not. For example, a category listed on the Yahoo! main page might be *Shopping*. This might lead to *Electronics*, which might lead to *Cell Phones*. This might point to a list of cell phone items e-shoppers might be interested in. This hierarchical arrangement ensures that shoppers can fairly quickly get to items in which they are interested.

Improvements in search engines mean that directories are losing some value, but they are still useful for locating groups of relevant websites on a similar topic. It should be noted that directories of this nature can be very wide in scope, or they could be more focused, in the nature of a trade directory. To ensure contact with potential customers, e-retailers might consider something much more focused. One point: note that Yahoo!, for example, is rather more than just a directory. It includes a search engine (formerly, the

Google engine), and a range of services such as mail and instant messaging. Such a service, which acts as a 'port' to many other Web and Internet services, is known as a *portal*. Portal owners hope that users will use their portal as their home page and point of departure, hence making them targets for selective advertising and other delights. This does make portal sites attractive (if expensive) places to place web banners and other advertising material. The big portals are hard at work implementing a 'Search, Find and Obtain' model across information, shopping and entertainment channels. The effectiveness can be demonstrated by usage figures: MSN and Yahoo! are the most popular websites worldwide, each with 83 million users .

SEARCH ENGINES

Search engines on the Internet have been around some time. The first ones actually did a 'live' search of remote file systems holding documents (FTP servers), looking for filenames which matched search terms. When the Web became popular, researchers built Web search engines to try out new software and hardware on the huge amounts of data that became available. Later on, these experimental systems were commercialized. Well-known commercial search engine systems are Google (www.google.com) and AltaVista (www.altavista.com.).

There are actually *two* sorts of search engine involved.First, programs called 'crawlers' gather information about websites. This is done by starting with a list of 'well-known sites' and from there searching the sites they reference. This is an automatic process. The HTML (HyperText Markup Language) code corresponding to each web page is scanned for links to other sites. In the HTML, such a link will appear like this: If this link is followed, the corresponding web page will also have links, and these too are followed. This process is continued, until millions of web pages are accessed. Each page is analysed for content. What this means is all the information in the page HTML - the title, the text of the body of the page and any additional information tagged on to the page (metainformation) - is extracted and examined for relevance. All this information is then put into a database (also called a catalogue or index).

This process is repeated at regular intervals, possibly every two weeks.The database is indexed on content, and is made available to the e-shopper via a Web interface. Given some *search term*, such as 'shampoo', the database is searched for matching terms and the corresponding page URLs are retrieved, together with the page titles and summaries of the page contents. This information is then formatted into a web page which is returned to the e-shopper. So the user inputs the word 'shampoo' and obtains a page of references to websites involving that term.

A few technical points:

- Following of links from any one page is only done to a certain 'depth', which means that it is important to put significant information on the Home Page or just a little 'below'.

- *Web crawlers* see a web page split into 'frames' as a number of pages, and therefore explore these less deeply than pages without frames. Frames are best avoided if you want Web crawlers to extract as much information as possible from your pages.
- Web crawlers are not clever enough to deal with databases (for example, catalogues) which might be accessed from your pages. Really significant information should be able to be accessed as plain HTML pages, rather than by using some catalogue systems. Catalogues are really meant for human users.

Note that the process of database construction is automatic, but guided by concepts such as *well-known sites* and *relevance*. It is also possible to notify a search-engine system of a site for inclusion, which again guides the crawler. Websites that meet the criteria are added to the index whether they have been submitted for inclusion or not.

Popular Search Engines

Google (www.google.com) is the world's most popular search site, accounting for 60 per cent of all searches . Google compiles its catalogue of over four billion web pages very week or so. Despite being faster, larger and more efficient than competitors, even Google indexes only a fraction of the total web pages available.

However, the coverage is very wide. Although most e-shoppers use search engines, the typical user is usually not willing to spend much time formulating search terms, and often gets rather frustrated if the information they require is not returned. They might abandon the search, or perhaps try another search engine. Many systems offer Boolean searching, which means that search terms and phrases can be linked, for example. Digital camera AND Canon AND inexpensive. Some systems also offer the option of fine-tuning the results by allowing the user to input terms used to rank (put in some order of precedence) the returned results.

The average e-shopper is not usually willing to learn how to set up these more sophisticated queries. They want a reasonable set of results with as little work formulating the query as possible. Otherwise, they tend to give up and try some other method. They might use *metacrawlers*, which bring together results from various search engines and directories. Coverage is wide but operation can be cumbersome, with little fine-tuning possible, so these are not that popular.

The most useful systems as far as many e-shoppers are concerned are systems that allow natural language, for example a query such as: Where I can buy inexpensive Canon digital cameras? Systems such as

AskJeeeves (www.ask.com) specialize in such natural language queries. Observation by the authors shows that users often pose their questions in natural language whatever the system! They do this because no one has ever told them that they cannot, and because reasonable results are often returned, since many search engine systems filter *noise words* (such as 'the', 'and' and 'but') and use the remaining words as search terms and for ranking the results. Systems such as Google also make suggestions in an attempt to correct spelling results.

Growth in Search Engine Activity

Most of the growth in e-shopping is being driven by search engines like Google and other sites like the online marketplace eBay. Improved search quality, pioneered by Google, has made search engines an easy and efficient way for people to find things online - and for advertisers to find customers. At the same time, eBay, a haven for small businesses, has become the fastest-growing major shopping site, and much of Amazon's growth has come from serving as an intermediary for independent retailers.

Another example is that of Visa, which noted that online sales, including travel, have increased considerably, much more than sales using Visa cards with traditional retailers. A firm that compiles Internet research, online sales are rising by nearly 30 per cent per year, and soon 100 million people a year are expected to make online purchases.

A Price water house coopers survey indicates that not only are search capabilities and product information important to online shoppers when selecting an online shopping site, but they can help e-retailers turn shoppers into buyers and make the online shopping experience more like the on-land one. Search functions are the most popular online shopping feature. The majority of online shoppers - 77 per cent - have used a search function while shopping online and most of these users are satisfied enough with search functions to use them on a regular basis.

In addition to being the most popular features, survey results indicate that search capabilities and product information are most important to online shoppers when selecting an online shopping site. Search functionality and product information are ranked as the most important online shopping features by 43 per cent and 40 per cent of online shoppers, respectively.

TRUST AND GOVERNANCE: WHO GOVERNS THE INTERNET?

Trust and governance are seen as key concepts in the contemporary business environment. Trust is crucial in businesses that act as intermediaries. For example, when we write or receive a cheque, we take it on trust that the intermediary between the issuer and the recipient of the cheque will honour the payment. In this case, the intermediary is a commercial bank. Similarly, when we buy goods or a service via the Internet, we take it on trust that the goods or service will be delivered at the price quoted.

Governance is a slippery concept that has become current in a number of fields. Essentially, governance refers to the manner in which activities are governed through a set of institutions, practices and procedures. For example, corporate governance refers to the way in which companies are governed in respect of fulfilling obligations to the various stakeholders. Governance will often include legal obligations, but can be distinguished from *government*, which is the formal organization of legally binding functions operated on the behalf of a population, be it local, regional or national. Government includes legally imposed regulations, practices and procedures.

The governance of the Web and the Internet started from the view that it should be a universally available and free resource. However, as the Internet has developed, there is an implication that its governance will shift towards more formal regulation as large corporations come to dominate its activities. No single entity owns the Internet or is wholly responsible for its functioning. It is a decentralized network, whose operation is influenced by a number of bodies and forces, not least large commercial interests such as Cisco and Microsoft which help drive ICT standards and innovation in the market place itself, and as members or otherwise of the various bodies.

Between 1987 and 1995, however, one of the most dominant influences on the Internet and Web was the US National Science Foundation (NSF), which subsidized its use, along with scientific and academic institutions that paid for servers and created Web content. The ethos underpinning the Internet at this point was one of not-for-profit, and the lack of packet prioritization underpinned an essentially democratic spirit amongst its user communities.

However, with the 'Boucher amendment' of 1992 the US Congress permitted this not-for-profit medium to extend its remit to include for-profit activity. This had an impact in 1995 when the publicly funded NSFNET (whose 'charter' precluded direct commercial activity) withdrew from network backbone responsibilities in the United States to be replaced by private and commercial funding.

In the same year Netscape, which had launched its Navigator browser the previous year, sought share capital through an Initial Public Offering (IPO) and staggered the markets with a 'Day 1' capitalization in excess of $2 billion. It is the year 1995 therefore that can claim to be the birth date of e-Commerce - at least in popular imagination - and from this point the rapid colonization of the network by commercial interests began.

The operation of the Internet in hardware and software terms is based on technical standards produced by a plethora of bodies. Telecommunication standards and other technical specifications have been set by the International Telegraphic Union (ITU) and OSI (representing the French for 'International Standards Organization') for a number of decades. Principal among the bodies that have a prescribed influence on the development of the Internet and the Web are IETF, W3C and ICANN.

The IETF (Internet Engineering Task Force) was created in 1986 to be responsible for drawing up the technical standards for the Internet and comes under the aegis of the Internet Society (ISOC) - created in 1992 - which assumes overall responsibility for the organization of its development. The World Wide Web Consortium (W3C) focuses on the development of the Web (a subset of the Internet) and was created in 1994. It is chaired by the Web's original creator, Tim Berners-Lee. The Internet Corporation for Assigned Names and Numbers (ICANN), created in 1998, controls the accreditation of domain name registrars that undertake the business of registering Web sites. Decisions made by these bodies determine how Internet and WWW operations take place, and by definition what products and/or services are to be successful in the market.

Indicative of the self-view of these organizations is a statement from ICANN:

ICANN has no statutory or other governmental power: its authority is entirely a consequence of voluntary contracts and compliance with its consensus policies by the global Internet community. It has no power to force any individual or entity to do anything; its 'authority' is nothing more than the reflection of the willingness of the members of the Internet community to use ICANN as a consensus development vehicle. Other than in their own terms, no major legal statutes charter these bodies or determine their membership or procedures.

ISOC, IETF, ICANN and W3C are bodies that determine their own existence, their own charters and their own procedures, and tend to have memberships composed of established figures in the Internet world, whether from academia or from industry. The claimed ethos of these groups is to further the development of the Internet on the basis of consensus.

ICANN, however, has attracted conflicting views since its incorporation in 1998, when it took responsibility for the Domain Name System (DNS), IP address space allocation and the Internet root server. The significance of this is high-lighted by David Post, who observes:

Any entity responsible for, and exercising control over, the root server data-bases possesses immense power over the future development of the Internet itself, and will, accordingly, be subject to immense pressure to act in ways that may be contrary to the best interests of the Internet community as a whole. Devising ways to prevent arbitrary, oppressive, or self-interested actions by this entity is a task of deep, of truly constitutional importance to that community.

Whilst the technology creates the physical mechanism by which the Internet functions, the determining of domain names (e.g. www.abc.com) along with their unique numerical identities (e.g. 234.5678.901.234) gives ICANN the power to create definitive and addressable electronic spaces, central to the establishment of Internet and Web entities. Without them commercial enterprises would be unable to establish any Web presence.

The issue of trust and governance is central to the business environment for e-Commerce. From a system of governance that was essentially self-regulating we are moving towards a market structure in which a few large firms are starting to dominate. From economic theory, this is akin to market structures that are oligopolistic - markets dominated by a few large firms that formally or informally collude - and monopolistic - markets dominated by one large firm. Despite the low cost of entering Internet-based markets, the resources and infrastructure needed to sustain larger volumes of business suggest that firm size and market consolidation in the form of mergers and take-overs will become characteristic features. In this scenario, some form of government regulatory intervention is inevitable - the admirable roots of the Web as a free resource then being under-mined by the imperative of avoiding monopolistic dominance of the Web and the Internet by large corporations.

The other side of the regulatory governance coin is trust. Given that the Internet establishes a new set of intermediaries between consumers and producers, producers and producers, trust is essential for sustaining the basis of e-Commerce and e-Business.

Consumers can inspect, check and then buy goods at their local mall at a given price instantaneously, whereas there is the virtual intermediary of purchasing on the Internet and the physical intermediary of getting goods delivered. There is also the issue of credit and payment card security, which at present is higher in conventional shopping outlets. The beauty of the Internet for the consumer is that it reduces search costs. One can search various outlets to compare the availability and prices of goods and then visit one local mall to purchase them.

Similarly, for producers, transaction costs are transferred to the consumer as the latter provides details of preferences, tastes and prices he or she is willing to pay, thereby allowing producers to identify their markets more clearly. The issue of trust and governance is thus central to developments in the business environment for e-Commerce as the Internet and other media, particularly television, are increasingly adapted for B2B and B2C transactions.

MEASURING E-COMMERCE

Measuring the value of electronically mediated business has become an important activity in its own right. Fraught with difficulty, it is one which has to date produced wide divergences in terms of predictions, many of them prepared by those with a material interest in promoting e-Commerce and e-Business. It is also one where the danger of double counting is most frequently encountered. One source of data is the University of Texas at Austin, where Barua *et al.* identify four levels of the 'Internet economy'.

- *Layer 1: The Internet infrastructure layer.* This includes trade in products and services that provide for the electronic infrastructure. It encompasses Internet backbone providers (e.g. Nortel Networks), Internet service providers (e.g. AOL), networking hardware and software (e.g. Cisco), PC and server manufacturers (e.g. Dell), security vendors (e.g. Norton) and fibre optic manufacturers (e.g. Corning).
- *Layer 2: The Internet applications layer.* This includes products and services that build upon the infrastructure layer and make it technologically feasible to undertake business activities online.

Categories include all software applications such as browser and server software (e.g. Netscape, Microsoft), multimedia (e.g. Macromedia), Web building (e.g. Adobe), search engines (e.g. Google), databases (e.g. Oracle), on-line training (e.g. Assymetrix, ilearn.to) and consultancy (e.g. Scient).

- *Layer 3: The Internet intermediary layer.* Internet intermediaries seek to increase the efficiency of electronic markets by facilitating the meeting of buyers and sellers and their interaction. Categories include Web portals (e.g. Yahoo), brokerages (e.g. Schwab), content aggregators (e.g. ZDNet), market makers (e.g. IFX) and online advertising brokers (e.g. Doubleclick).
- *Layer 4: The Internet commerce layer.* This layer concentrates on Web-based commerce transactions. It includes the new 'e-tailers' (e.g. Amazon.com), manufacturers (e.g. Dell), fee/subscription-based providers (e.g. Forrester) and online entertainment (e.g. AOL Time Warner) and professional services (e.g. KPMG).

This is a useful approach to measuring the Internet economy. The difficulty is untangling what is attributable to the 'new economy' and what is attributable to the 'old economy'. In fact, this example is as problematic as trying to separate out manufacturing from services: a common mistake among politicians and journalists.

There is also the problem of double counting. In national income accounting, each successive stage of production adds value to the previous stage. For example, coal is mined and then sold to make steel. Steel is made from the combination of coal, iron ore and lime. Steel is used in the production of, say, beams for buildings, which are manufactured and then sold to construction companies to be used in buildings which are then sold or leased to clients. At each stage in the production value is added.

The value of the coal, iron ore and lime is added to the net increase in value of the steel, what it is sold at less the cost of the material inputs. The value of the steel beams less the cost of the steel inputs is then added and finally the value of the buildings less the cost of the steel beams is added to produce final national income made up of the value added at each production stage.

This method avoids double counting and it is this kind of approach that should be used in measuring the value of the Internet economy, notwithstanding the general problem of disentangling conventional economic transactions from those associated with the Internet. Although the taxonomy is a useful way to think about measuring the 'Internet economy', the necessary corrective. It shows that the contribution of B2B and B2C to national income was very small in 1999, just before the peak of the so-called productivity miracle in the United States.

The significant slowdown from the end of 2000 and subsequent recession in the United States, the fall-out from dot-bomb phenomena and events after

11 September 2001 show that the brave new world of the virtual economy was as susceptible to the business cycle and political shocks as the so-called old economy. In the words of Public Enemy, the US rap band, 'Don't believe the hype. '

DRIVERS AND BARRIERS FOR E-COMMERCE TAKE-UP

The principal driver for the take up of e-Commerce is economic. If we accept what corporate forecasters such as Forrester and IDC predict, then more than 80 per cent of the growth of electronically mediated trade in the period 1999-2004 will be via B2B e-Commerce. At root, this take-up is driven by transaction costs.

As an example, banks feel that the cost of processing a financial transaction via the Web can be as little as 1 per cent of that performed at a branch using traditional paper methods. So once fixed costs such as equipment and telecommunication lines are found, the marginal cost of servicing transactions on the Web can be very low.

For a relatively small outlay, companies and individuals can hook up to the Web and access sites that are dispersed across the globe. This fact has contributed to an explosion of infrastructural and service provision on the Internet and prompted many commentators to enthuse about the potential it holds for the traditional economics of location. Frances Cairncross (1998), for example, asserts that the communications revolution removes geographical boundaries to trade. 'No longer will location be key to most business decisions. Companies will locate any screen-based activity anywhere on the Earth, wherever they can find the best bargain of skills and productivity. '

However, though the Internet can facilitate market growth for individual companies, commentators point to more complex factors at work in terms of location. Pratt cites New York's 'Silicon Alley' as a cluster of software developers that could locate in a disaggregated manner if they wished but choose to retain close physical proximity.

Whatever the reasons for this and the nature of the particular business function, it suggests that commentators such as Cairncross are ignoring the potential value of social interaction and informal face-to-face networks that clustering might imply. In the case of the City of London, Europe's largest financial centre, large international financial institutions, law and accounting firms and business services providers seek to locate in close proximity.

The underlying logic is associated with external versions of economies of scale and scope. That is, the ability to explore large and different transactions in the same place. Other key factors are the ability to easily recruit specialist labour, access to informational and transport infrastructure and, perhaps more important, the development and sustaining of a powerful innovation environment in which new financial products are developed. Richard Sennett, the American sociologist, has pointed out that in an apparently global era, the leading international economic and business activities are still crowding into the world's major cities. Whatever the claims made for an imagined virtual future, place still matters to business and society. The cost of computing power has declined over the past thirty years to such an extent that claims are made that the power of the multi-million-dollar mainframes supporting the Apollo mission to the moon at the end of the 1960s can now be contained within a desktop computer costing less than $1,000.

The precipitous increase in the power of 'microchips' has followed a pattern first predicted by Gordon Moore, a co-founder of Intel, in 1965. 'Moore's law' reckoned that the power of chips would double at intervals of every eighteen months to two years. The effect has been that, in relative terms, the cost of ICT is now so low and its power so great that companies have little financial reason to avoid taking up Web-mediated business if they so wish. Once installed, all that a user needs is an account with an Internet service provider (ISP). At the height of the dotcom boom, there were hundreds of ISPs on the UK market offering access to the Internet, and pricing reflected their relative quality of service.

Globalization and Competition

Globalization has engendered as much debate about the new economy. For some, it represents a cleavage with the past. For others, the hype does not measure up to the reality and is merely a different version of the past, this difference being due almost entirely to the evolution of information and communications technology (ICT) and the subsequent speeding up of economic transactions.

Leaving aside the influences that pervade under the notion of 'global culture', economic globalization can be defined in the following way:

- The development of and access to markets, the organization of production, corporate decision making and consumer strategies on a global scale.
- Capital markets operating through electronic media twenty-four hours a day.
- The development of transnational corporations (TNCs) in which there is significant foreign ownership and whose board of directors has a large proportion of foreign members.

The reality is a little more mundane. The world appears to be made up of three large economic blocs, the Americas, Europe and East Asia, each accounting for around a third of the world's income, and the United States, Germany and Japan being the largest constituent national economies. If one looks at a mapping of Internet traffic, its volume and frequency tend to mirror telephone and airline traffic, the largest amounts being between the three largest economic blocs. Large parts of Asia, Africa, Latin America and Eastern Europe are bypassed. For these regions of the world, the 'digital divide' is more appropriate than the 'digital revolution'. It also suggests that the world's economy is characterized more by regionalism than by globalization.

What has afforded a more global perspective is the manner in which ICT developments, deregulation and liberalization have opened new markets and productions sites around the world. The general level of production costs has been lowered, and increased international take-overs and mergers by large corporations have generated large economies of scale and scope.

As a result, there has been a tendency towards the over-supply of goods, partly rendering a low inflationary environment and a much more intensively competitive environment. In such an environment, new modes of market access with the possibility of lower transaction costs, such as the Internet, have been beneficial to firms' international strategic position, at least in the short term.

The key issue for international firms' strategies is still the development of new business models arising from the development of technology rather than market change being driven by the technology itself. Like the proclamations of the new economy, globalization is long on promise and short on delivery.

Political Imperatives

The political imperatives that both drive and arise from the prospect of the Internet economy are relatively easy to understand. Political cycles and the longevity of politicians' careers tend to rest on achieving economic growth and full employment.

Any prospect of short-cutting the achievement of these twin goals, for example by the evolution of the new or Internet economy, is often greeted with quasi-religious fervour. By also embracing the ideology of globalization the political elites can escape blame for any of the local social costs, whilst taking credit for the creation of local benefits in the form of inward investment, employment creation, innovation generation and so on.

Added to these aspects is the development of e-Government in which many of the public administration's operations could be transferred to online media. In the United Kingdom, the government has set up the Office of the e-Envoy to encourage and develop e-Government activities. In the United States, the federal government's Office of Commerce has undertaken similar activities.

In the European Union, politicians and business proponents have been arguing for the speeding up of further telecoms liberalization so that high-speed Internet access is provided directly to small and medium-size enterprises (SMEs) and individual subscribers. An EU summit held at Lisbon in March 2000 created an over-ambitious timetable when Member States demanded that incumbent telcos should allow access to rival service providers from 1January 2001. Incumbent telcos have been laggard in this. At the same summit, the UK Prime Minister, Tony Blair, boasted of the United Kingdom becoming the leading knowledge economy in the European Union by the end of the decade.

Apart from these examples, governments in general in the advanced economies account for about 40 per cent of national income. They are large purchasers of private goods and services, invest heavily in infrastructure and information systems and employ large numbers of people. They also initiate and underwrite big technology research and innovation programmes and projects under the rubric of building and sustaining the knowledge economy. Therefore, the political imperative driving the Internet economy is both concrete and abstract.

Barriers

Physically, before users can begin to address linking up to access the Internet via an internet service provider they must have a telephone line (or some other kind of communications link). In many economies, telecoms provision has increased significantly as the result of deregulatory policies that have seen competition introduced into telecom markets.

Once physical connectivity is possible, you can begin to exchange electronic communications across a global network by virtue of an account with an ISP. Initial ISP hook-ups provided speeds of data transfer of nine kilobits per second (kbps) - or 9k - but successive jumps via 14k and 28k generations have seen the establishment of a 56k standard.

Computers work at a digital granularity with all messages and their modes of communication (text, audio, still and moving images) being decomposed into streams of noughts and ones. The telephone system though was originally designed for voice. So, for data transfer to take place, computers were obliged to communicate via the network using sound. Thus the 56k modem converts a digital signal from the computer (composed of noughts and ones) into an analogue signal - sound - for delivery along the telephone system as a stream of sounds of two discrete pitches. The fact that further modem standards have not been developed is indicative of the apparent physical limit of 'acoustic coupling'.

While the demands of asynchronous communications such as e-mail, on-line chat and simple Web pages can be accommodated satisfactorily within 56k, such data transfer rates are not sufficient for synchronous communications such as video-conferencing or 'video on demand'. Thus wholly digital transfer technologies such as ISDN (128k) and ADSL (from 500k) have come into focus and are seen as the means of opening up multimedia - and hence e-Commerce - delivery to domestic premises and small firms. Such bandwidth had only been available to large companies using leased lines before this.

Though deregulation of telecoms markets had seen the development of digital communications in trunk networks, their extension to the 'last mile' of telecom networks (i.e. from local exchange to domestic or small firm premises) occurred only in the late 1990s. For competition to prevail, two physical developments must occur. At the exchange the physical unbundling of copper wires is required. This 'unbundling the local loop' allows digital equipment to be hooked up to individual lines by alternative telecom providers. At the domestic or small firm premises, the installation of a digital adaptor is required. However, political imperative has not led to the desired opening up of the local loop market, with ex-monopolist telcos such as BT and France Télécom failing to act with the speed the regulators envisaged. As a result, high-speed services are not as prevalent as proponents of e-Commerce desired.

With 20:20 hindsight, it seems clear that incumbent telcos would not vote for reductions in their revenue streams with gusto. In the United States, however, where unbundling began in the mid-1990s, the liberalized telephony and data services regime was to allow regional telcos to enter long-distance markets and permit long-distance telcos to enter the local loop market, so long as access could be gained to individual subscribers by any service provider. Purton (2001) observes that while US service providers were allowed to enter each other's markets in exchange for giving up exclusive service provision in their own markets, in the European market there had been no such *quid quo pro*.

Further comparison of US *v.* European markets shows that in the United States, subscribers pay a flat fee to their telecoms provider for line rental. After paying this fixed cost, there are no further charges for calls using local exchanges. In Europe, on the other hand, local market practice saw the establishment of per-minute charging on local networks from the 1960s onwards.

There is an impact on Internet use of 'unmetering' and 'metering'. Metering inhibits Internet use owing to the ongoing financial penalty of maintaining a presence on a line. An unmetered approach promotes potential Internet use owing to a user's indifference to the quantity of time spent maintaining a presence on a line - at least in financial terms.

Technical Problems

The Internet protocol IPv4 was not designed either to handle very large numbers of unique addresses or the different levels of 'Quality of Service' (QoS) that different forms of media and hence e-Commerce require. The Internet has become a victim of its own success, and it is assumed that all IPv4 addresses will be exhausted by the 2005-11 period (Pouffary 2001) if predictions about the total number of devices that will be attached become true.

This includes extra fixed links such as printers, cookers and fridges and mobile links including 3G phones, vehicles, ships and planes. Whereas businesses with the necessary resources can avoid traffic problems on the public switched telephone network by leasing telecom lines to guarantee QoS levels, the Internet works on a 'one size fits all' approach. Mathy *et al.* (2000) note that it was originally designed primarily to move files between computers. For this there were no strict time requirements - termed *elastic* - and a 'best effort service' was adequate for the task of delivering e-mail and Web pages. However, applications such as video-conferencing are much more demanding and require on-demand, guaranteed and immediate delivery of data packets.

These have *inelastic* service requirements, and imply a more complex set of service quality attributes than IPv4 can offer. IPv6 has been designed, however, to allow service discrimination, and data packets are forwarded depending on their prioritization.

E-COMMERCE POLICY

There are bodies at international, regional and national levels that seek to promote the take-up of e-Commerce. The principal international bodies come under the auspices of the United Nations and include the World Trade Organization (WTO), the World Intellectual Property Organization (WIPO) and the United Nations Committee for International Trade and Law (UNCITRAL).

This latter body has drawn up the UNCITRAL Model Law for Electronic Commerce that supports the commercial use of international contracts in e-Commerce, and offers technical advice to governments on this. The Model Law creates rules and norms validating the practice of electronic commerce, seeks to make electronic documents and signatures legal and supports the admission of electronic evidence into court proceedings and arbitration.At a European level, the European Union has drawn up a number of directives that aim to provide a legal framework for e-Commerce within the European Union. The member countries are obliged to follow these directives by creating new legislation in order to harmonize the legislative framework across the single market.

These directives include:

- *The Electronic Signatures Directive.* This defines the requirements for electronic signatures and their certification in order to ensure a minimum level of security in e-Commerce dealings. The United Kingdom passed the Electronic Communications Act in 2000 that amended in the region of 300 laws so that any reference to documents, writing and signatures would now include their electronic equivalents. However, to get this Act through Parliament, the UK government was obliged to remove controversial provisions on encryption keys. Public Key Cryptography has both public and private keys that allow the encryption and decryption of data and is seen as critical in the provision of secure e-Commerce transactions.
- *The Conditional Access Services Directive.* This aims to safeguard against the unauthorized use of conditional access services, and to make illegal, for example, technology that allows decryption of satellite television services when no contract exists with a service provider.

- *The Data Protection Directive.* This seeks to harmonize the rights of individuals and the obligations placed on organizations with regard to the use of 'personal data' gathered in e-Commerce activities. Additionally a prohibition was created on the export of such data to organizations in countries without similar provision. A potential problem that would have seen much of the trade between the European Union and the United States being deemed illegal was averted by use of a 'Safe Harbor Agreement' which sought to bring some level of accommodation in data protection terms between the two bodies. The United States places greater emphasis on the 'freedom of information' in its legislative framework and this comes into conflict with a European focus on the right of an individual to relative privacy. The United Kingdom's 1998 Data Protection Act updated the 1984 Act of the same name in line with this.
- *The Misleading Advertising Directive.* This seeks to prohibit the use of advertising on EU Web sites that is either misleading orlikely to mislead consumers.

• *The Distance Selling Directive.* This seeks to protect those buying products or services on the Internet within the European Union, and to provide seven day 'cooling off periods' during which consumers may choose to withdraw from agreed transactions. The directive does not apply to financial services or a number of product types and services such as auctions or short-life products. In October 2000 this directive was mirrored in the United Kingdom when the Consumer Protection (Distance Selling) Regulations Act was brought into force.

5

E-Commerce and Leadership

INTRODUCTION

Success in e-commerce has become almost synonymous with the names of a few CEOs and leaders of successful companies, such as Michael Dell, Jack Welch, and Jeff Bezos. In the absence of clear guidance on e-commerce strategy and implementation, a cult of personality has developed in popular press discussions of e-commerce.

Without a clearly defined approach and methodology for the formulation and implementation of an e-commerce strategy, this kind of leadership-worship was the closest anyone could come to defining what actually led to e-commerce success for these companies.

Now, we have the opportunity to step back and appreciate the full range of critical factors that contributed to early cases of e-commerce success. Leadership is one factor, but leadership shouldn't be any more or less important in e-commerce than in any other aspect of business strategy.

Still, it makes sense to discuss leadership as a precursor to formulating strategy and designing structure and systems.

The special conditions associated with e-commerce make the discussion of leadership excellence especially critical. The individual roles of the CEO, CIO, and CFO concern more than an organization chart or delegation of responsibilities. In e-commerce, the coordination between these leaders becomes as important as their actions. Failure to achieve this coordination will undermine any hope for corporate e-commerce integration.

We can identify the aspects of leadership that are applicable to all businesses wishing to implement an e-commerce strategy. Leadership occupies the first link between the inputs of the traditional business and the subsequent process elements of e-commerce strategy, structure, and systems. Placing it here emphasizes the role that leadership plays in moving from traditional strategy, structure, and systems to those in e-commerce.

Leadership is about both people and actions. Each of the major leadership roles in a company—including the CEO, the CIO, and the CFO—requires a person with a positive, reasoned approach toward e-commerce.

Just as the CFO should not trivialize the importance of IT, neither should the CIO exaggerate the role of technology over strategy. These leadership roles require technical competence related to the business operations, IT, and e-commerce, as well as a positive attitude. Knowledge and experience in the uses of technologies and an understanding of the implications of the use of technology in specific business operations are necessary for e-commerce leadership positions. Some major assessments must be made by the company's leaders before they can consider the formulation and implementation of an e-commerce strategy. An assessment of competitive position is often particularly challenging in a dynamic e-commerce environment.

Strong traditional competitors may be currently irrelevant if their e-commerce strategy is undeveloped, but that can change quickly. Weaker traditional competitors may be able to use e-commerce as a catalyst to make the gains they couldn't make in traditional brick-and-mortar business. Pure-play Internet companies may already have established themselves in the industry or may be in the process of moving into the industry. Disruptions in the marketplace can cause additional challenges.

Thus, to assess the proper role for e-commerce, leaders must evaluate the nature of the company's offerings, traditional strategy and business models, and the geographic scope of the company. Though current capabilities may be limited, opportunities for growth in revenue and reductions in cost must be assessed.

With the data, leaders can then properly evaluate the appropriate levels of investment and potential returns. Leadership requires some initial steps to prepare the organization for a transition to e-commerce. Some changes are of such importance that they must be addressed early in the evaluation of e-commerce strategy formulation and execution, especially discussing basic e-commerce functionality and communicating the potential impact of e-commerce on company operations.

First Stage E-commerce Leadership Requirements

Senior corporate leaders must complete the following first stage e-commerce leadership requirements:

- Assessment of the company's e-commerce competitive position
- Assessment and communication of the value of e-commerce to corporate, business unit, and functional operations and necessary technical and integration issues
- Creation of a company culture conducive to the introduction of e-commerce

The following sections highlight each of these aspects of e-commerce leadership with stories of companies that took the first step toward success or failure before the first strategy was ever formulated.

Other discussions and company cases illustrate how leadership impacted the e-commerce successes and features.

LEADERSHIP ROLES

The CEO

In the late 1990s, spin-offs were a popular strategy for e-commerce ventures. Leadership consisted of finding someone, often from outside the company, who would lead the e-commerce venture. Leaders for these ventures were frequently selected because their resumes included technology experience, often without considering their understanding of the business or its environment. The CEO of the brick-and-mortar company, on the other hand, was regarded only as a sponsor, with little involvement expected.

We now know that the appropriate role for the CEO undertaking an e-commerce venture is a highly proactive one with a strong level of commitment and a vision of e-commerce within the company. Instead of delegating the responsibilities of e-commerce to an outside "expert, " leaders must take the steps to transform the company into one that can utilize and profit from e-commerce. These e-commerce transformations are part of an ongoing process that is certainly not complete when a company successfully establishes an e-commerce foothold.

Cisco CEO John Chambers has kept Cisco at or near the top of the market through considerable market fluctuations and changes in the nature of e-commerce, through his willingness to change Cisco according to the demands of the market. Similarly, Amazon CEO Jeff Bezos has consistently altered prices on books and other products to meet competitive challenges. He also began strategic alliances with other merchants such as Target and Toys 'R' Us to better serve Amazon customers and improve profitability. This flexibility is one important key to success in the ever-changing world of e-commerce. Monitoring company and industry changes, along with the constant technological improvements in e-commerce, are critical leadership issues.

CEOs do not need to become technology experts. Instead, CEOs need a basic understanding of how e-commerce works and, more important, how it affects current and potential business models and processes. This knowledge can be easily obtained through interaction with the CIO and senior IT personnel or by interaction with e-commerce savvy leaders at other companies. At Merrill Lynch, the impetus for e-commerce came from the CIO, who convinced a skeptical CEO of the merits of an e-commerce venture through persistent discussions of technology and strategy.

The CEO must also be convinced of the specific potential benefits of e-commerce to the company and begin to take action for the implementation, demonstrating commitment in both communications and actions. For a successful transformation, the CEO must express the appropriate attitude, personal commitment to e-commerce, and understanding of the technical issues to make it clear that the CEO is not ceding leadership to the IT specialists. E-Bay CEO Meg Whitman is credited with transforming e-Bay from an "online flea market" to a "virtual, self-regulating global economy." Leadership is also demonstrated through the commitment of financial resources, including adequate funding for the IT department and the modernization of the company's information systems. E-commerce and IT should be seen as value creators rather than cost centers. The CEO must be also committed to a leadership role in IT planning, facilitating communication between IT and business units and challenging the IT department to maximize business functionality.

The CEO must also emphasize a long-term commitment and ensure that the other senior corporate and business unit leaders are also fully committed to e-commerce. The role requires collaboration of the CIO, CFO, and business unit leaders and a vision for the entire organization. The role of coordination, communication, and motivation with business unit leaders is critical. The business units ultimately have the major responsibility for execution, as it is the business unit leaders who find opportunities for e-commerce value creation. The CEO must take the lead in driving the integration process.

The CIO

The rise of e-commerce has brought far more attention to the role of the CIO as an integral part of the senior management team. Companies that have previously treated their CIO as a technologist face the largest changes as they prepare for e-commerce. For e-commerce to be fully integrated, the CIO's place in the organizational structure must report directly to the CEO or COO. Without direct access to the CEO, the CIO plays a lesser role in influencing strategy, which may push IT and e-commerce into the position of a cost centre. Such factors contribute to the finding that CIO tenure is quite short, compared to that of CFOs.

Even in companies whose CIOs already play an important role in senior management, CEOs should continuously work to increase coordination and interaction between the CIO and other key members of senior management, to increase the visibility of e-commerce initiatives. The CIO should provide both information and analysis and should have a relationship with the CEO that empowers the CIO to challenge both strategic direction and technology usage. Merrill Lynch faced a severe loss in margins as Schwab began to pass Merrill in market value in late 1998 and 1999. It wasn't until then-CIO John

McKinley convinced his CEO to fully embrace online trading while using the company's IT budget to develop its Web site that the company was able to reestablish itself after being a late mover in e-commerce. When Mattel Inc.'s Joe Eckroth took over as CIO, he immediately transferred toy design online to allow virtual models to be zipped electronically to all of the company's factories, cutting development time by 20 percent. In addition, Eckroth installed Mattel's $2 billion licensing programme online to automate and expedite the licensing approval process and significantly increase profitability. To improve the decision-making process in organizations as well as to obtain increased resources for e-commerce, the CIO needs to provide more complete measurements and analysis of the benefits and costs of the business impacts of IT and e-commerce investments. It is important that potential projects are analyzed in a strategic context, and the financial payoffs are clear. More generally, the CIO has a large stake not only in directing business change but also in taking on the role of educator for the CEO and CFO.

While senior business leadership should still undergo specialized training to gain a basic understanding of the technologies associated with e-commerce and IT, the CIO should be capable of explaining the business implications of technology to internal and external partners so that the company makes sound business decisions based upon adequate knowledge. As with the CEO, it is not necessary that the CIO have a specific resume or previous experience in e-commerce. Certainly an understanding of the technology side of e-commerce is necessary. The most important skills for a CIO include the ability to complete an accurate technology risk assessment, to objectively gauge strategic benefits of technology, and to manage the complications of both the technical and the human sides of an e-commerce implementation.

The nontechnical components of an e-commerce implementation are far more challenging than the technical ones. The CIO must have an integrated view of the business and be able to communicate that view to the senior corporate managers, the business unit leaders, functional staff, and many others both inside and outside the company.

The CFO

Many studies have shown high levels of conflict between CFOs and CIOs, and e-commerce is purported only to increase that conflict. The long-term and nonspecific benefits of IT projects, especially those relating to e-commerce, are often seen as anathema to the strict measurement standards of the archetypal CFO. That conflict, however, arises from a misunderstanding of the proper roles of each position and often from a lack of rigorous analysis. For e-commerce to be successful, the CFO must be more sensitive to the challenges of IT and e-commerce, and the CIO must complete more comprehensive financial analysis of e-commerce projects to better articulate the likely costs and benefits.

A formalized approach to understanding and measuring the payoffs of e-commerce activities. The analysis of the causal relationships between e-commerce investments and financial payoffs provides a new basis for discussion between CIOs, CFOs, and CEOs. It also permits e-commerce to fit more effectively into the traditional resource allocation decisions made in the CFO's office. When the CIO's reporting responsibility is to the CFO, the wrong message is communicated to every aspect of the business, from investors, to employees, to customers, especially in an e-commerce context. The CFO must recognize IT's strategic role and its vital role in bringing about business process changes. The CFO must also take the lead in helping the CIO with the methodology, of measuring the payoffs of e-commerce investments. It is only in this way that IT and e-commerce are seen as value creators and can compete effectively for resources within the company.

The CFO need not have the same content knowledge of IT as the CIO, or even the CEO. A modicum of technology understanding, however, is likely to strengthen the CFO's relationship with the CIO and can lead to better-coordinated analysis of project benefits. Alignment is likely to be strongest when the two leaders can move beyond their specific domains and focus on the strategic context. This united front usually also improves the coordination with business unit leaders and improves decision making. For e-commerce to be successful, business leadership must be able and willing to expand their essential functions within the company. While old responsibilities are not to be neglected because of the addition of e-commerce, the new demands of e-commerce are of such importance that senior leaders must assume additional expertise and responsibilities.

DEVELOPMENT OF E-COMMERCE

The literature onf *e-service* has by and large followed the commercial thrust of Internet marketing development. Initially, the most common application by firms and use by users was through the website itself, often a basic overview of the company and more in keeping with having a public relations 'presence' in the e-commerce world. The next most common application was to post more detailed information about products, and conversely this was the second most common use by users. The third wave of application is the now dominant interest in e-selling, that is, the use of the Web to sell or buy goods. This takes us to the fourth and emerging wave, one that is still greatly underutilized, namely e-service.

Essentially, e-service offers the potential for some of the more advanced applications of Internet technology. For example, firms could use intelligent agents to provide extraordinary service, by tracking and datamining previous histories through Internet sites and developing known patterns of users' requirements. Customer relationships can be developed, based on prior 'modelled' understanding of which offers a consumer is likely to respond to. This is a special case of market segmentation to a market of one. As another application of work by Brookes *et al.* referred to in Cravens *et al.* (2000, p. 4), a manufacturer of washing machines could include in its warranty agreement the electronic capability of monitoring the ongoing usage of the machine.

Suppose that, after the machine has been bought, the household has a new baby. If detergent dosage or load patterns place strain on the motor, the machine could have the built-in communication capability to automatically page the manufacturer's service depot. The depot receives a message for a service representative to visit the household and adjust the washing machine before it becomes a problem. In this way, while both the information technologies and the servicing component are largely unobtrusive to the household, they are nonetheless essential to maintaining customer satisfaction and potential loyalty.

The literature has started to discuss e-service, but it is somewhat unstructured. For this reason, a review of the literature plays a particularly important front-end role and we provide a simple classification of the literature to assist. We have included a separate section debating whether self-service is a myth for e-service. Our own position on this matter is made clear. We follow the literature review with a proposed, more systematic, typology of e-service, which could be useful to readers.

THREE APPROACHES TO E-SERVICE

We have identified three types of e-service literature. The first is what we call the *macro* or *very broad view* of e-service, namely that e-service is effectively synonymous with e-commerce. An *intermediate view* of e-service is that we can study the provision of *specialist services* made available by *specialist service providers* that help service Internet users (both individuals and companies). The third perspective on e-service is what we term a *micro perspective,* namely the provision of particular and varied detailed customer services within a site as *part* of the website - user interface.

At the broadest level is the view that e-commerce per se is an electronic service to customers - one that provides greater convenience. This view places e-commerce as an option available to customers, providing another channel of distribution or information. For example, instead of spending, say, an hour to physically access and purchase from a bookstore, the customer has the option to purchase the same electronically. As a further example, a company may use the Web to provide information about the company's offering to assist consumers in their product search, without necessarily enabling the consumer to purchase through the Web.

A related macro view of e-service is the *services marketing* perspective on e-retailing. They argue that e-retail offerings are service offerings and exhibit many of the same characteristics as other non-Internet-based services. They further argue that Internet services can be evaluated by similar criteria, such as responsiveness, empathy and the establishment of trust through courtesy and competency. The principal service provided by e-retailers is a search and evaluation facility that potentially saves time and effort for the consumer. The task of the e-retailer is to provide a website design that caters to different shopping styles, provides evidence to reduce risk and also educates the user in a shopping mode that may differ to what they are used to in conventional retail shopping.

There is now a considerable number of papers that have applied the macro perspective of e-service to a specific industry. For example, Muir and Douglas (2001) have studied how service delivery has changed in legal services with the rise of e-commerce. They argue that the quality of service is potentially improved with the Web. A Web presence allows legal practices to be more transparent and to offer greater access to information for customers by way of improving their services.

It is suggested that this improved communication may lead to a reduction in complaints against solicitors.An *intermediate perspective* of e-service is the provision of *electronic services* from *specialist providers* to users of the Internet and intranets. Thus we have a market (external or internal) in which key electronic services are similar to products and sold or exchanged in a market to general users of the Web. here is a huge variety of specialist firms that offer their services (products) to Web users.

Web designers form a stereotypical group in this category, but also included are all types of suppliers of a wide range of Internet services, such as portal providers or providers of any specific link in the Internet network. For example, consider the commercial services offered by Compuserve, Prodigy, America Online and e-world. The pages of the national financial newspapers are filled with the advertisements of companies offering such Web-enabling services, some claiming to offer an integrated service.Electronic trust services are specialist e-services that provide reassurance and trust to the financial and privacy security of Internet information flow. There is a number of third-party commercial service providers who guarantee protection of either the financial security or the personal confidentiality of information flows.

A special case of this situation is the role of the electronic signature, an issue discussed by Travers (2001), who is particularly concerned with the status, planning and implementation of electronic signatures, in the context of the UK Electronic Communications Act 2000. He argues that electronic signatures can be considered within a knowledge management framework and proposes a six-part system that incorporates people, clients, knowledge matters, business development and training.

Travers notes that the Electronic Communications Act provides:

- An approvals scheme for businesses providing cryptography services such as electronic signature services and confidentiality services;
- For the legal recognition of electronic signatures and the process under which they are verified; and
- For the removal of obstacles in other legislation to the use of electronic communications and storage in place of paper.

A somewhat unusual example of a specialist e-service is the provision of electronic money (Buck, 1997), which could be redefined as a trust-service, but Buck did not do so in his paper. He notes that there is a range of online payment systems, including credit systems (e.g. Payflow Pro), debit systems (e.g. BankNet), token-based mechanisms (e.g. Digicash) and electronic cash schemes (e.g. Mondex). Such mechanisms vary considerably in terms of safety, privacy protection and trustworthiness.

An example of a specialist e-service within an internal market is that of an e-mail-mediated help service (Hahn 1998). Hahn analysed 265 help-service responses from service logs and found, among other things, that users and help-service staff held different internal models for ideal e-mail communication. Users desired a fairly simple exchange of communication, that is, a clear question followed by a quick, simple response. Staff, on the other hand, envisaged the need for a more complex interrelationship, over several messages.

This takes us to the third perspective of e-service, namely the *micro* approach. Perhaps the dominant element in this field is the role of information. Some authors see information-based marketing as a potential competitive advantage. Other scholars see the Web as important for tracking and gathering customer feedback (Sampson, 1998; Sen *et al.*, 1998). Still other writers focus on the role of e-information as an aid to facilitating consumer search.

It is particularly in Merrilees (2002) that a broader perspective is given to interactivity. He embraces a more multi-dimensional approach to the concept of interactivity. Included factors are two-way communication between the e-retailer and the user; the ability of each party to communicate with the other including through e-mail; the ability to personalize the situation for the individual user; and the ability of the individual to control the communication and learn from it.

Finally, there are numerous other Internet studies that emphasize particular aspects of e-service besides information or interactivity. For example Mols (2000), in his study of Danish retail banking, examined the role of more individualized services for consumers and their need for a close relationship with the bank. As a final example of a difficult-to-classify study of providing services on the Internet see Mathur (1998) who takes a financial accounting approach to the topic.

In summary, we have used our three-part classification of macro, intermediate and micro as an initial way of structuring the literature, as it exists. This is not to say that we endorse all perspectives of the literature. In particular we have reservations about the macro perspective. In a sense, the use of the World Wide Web by a retailer to market its organization as an online e-retailer is no more a services marketing exercise than the use of catalogues makes Lands End a services marketer. The *service component for an e-retailer* is the sum total of the ancillary support mechanisms provided by the retailer and the channel intermediaries to aid the Web prospective buyer to select, pay for and receive the merchandise.

The e-retailer may provide services for the consumption of the prospective buyer through the Web channel, but this still does not make the channel a service unto itself. Thus we prefer the intermediate and micro perspectives of initial classification and our empirical research design is more in keeping with the micro perspective. A more refined taxonomy of e-services is developed below.

BRITISH LIBRARY (WWW.BL.UK)

This is a free service provided by the British Library in London that includes a 'turn the page' function. This technology is new to websites and is only available for three articles at the time of going to press. The home page offers a range of services provided by the library and is easy to use with simple menu selection and navigation.

Of interest is the 'turn the pages' of Leonardo da Vinci's notebook. This technology displays a scanned image of the original notebook and allows the user to turn pages using the cursor in a way similar to a real book. To enter this site, select 'turn the pages' on the home page and follow the instruction. To use this facility a Shockwave driver is required and can be downloaded free in two minutes from the same site. This is an interesting site for those who are interested in history.

A SECOND TAXONOMY OF E-SERVICE

We initially used a three-way classification of the e-service literature, namely macro, intermediate and micro, as a way of sorting the literature in this fragmented domain.

Our thinking on this topic has progressed to another proposed taxonomy of e-service. Not all of the aspects covered in this taxonomy are addressed in the empirical part. Taxonomy is put forward as an initial framework that can be debated by interested academics or practitioners.

THE SELF-SERVICE MYTH

Before leaving the literature, it is useful to discuss a crucial issue in the e-service area referred to by Moon and Frei (2000). They give the example of customers visiting a typical airline website and being confronted by a self-service search engine. If they know exactly when and where they want to travel, the website will generate a list of feasible flights.

However, the search process becomes complex if they wish to find the cheapest airfare and are flexible on the dates and destinations. Moon and Frei are sceptical of the usefulness of the self-service approach to e-service and suggest that the customer is likely to have a much more satisfying experience if they call the airline's call centre for handling more complex situations.

Co-production is proposed by Moon and Frei (2000:26) as a better model than self-service for e-commerce. In the co-production model the company undertakes many of the tasks in shopping and buying, relieving the burden on the customer. The new model recognizes that, although customers like having choices, they do not want too many and appreciate pre-screened alternatives geared to their needs.

Co-production also understands that customers want to state their preferences only once. Moon and Frei conclude that e-commerce firms should focus on customer service *not* self-service, and give illustrative examples of companies like Dell Computer Corporation. Dell performs a host of back-end transactions that are invisible to customers, such as grouping products by customer segments and displaying only in-stock items.

The current authors tend to endorse the sentiment of Moon and Frei in that we agree that it would be foolish for owners of e-sites to provide a minimalist infrastructure and simply to let users do their own thing. Our only objection is what to call the 'co-production model'. We are content to keep calling it a *self-service model,* but one that is designed appropriately and optimally.

Indeed, we believe that the challenge is for e-commerce firms to strive for an optimal self-service design capability. For a very interesting and relevant study, see Dabholkar (2000). His review of research into what consumers want from technologically-based self-service options suggests that speed, control and privacy are generally required. However, two additional attributes that positively influence the attitude of consumers towards computer technology are ease of use and fun or enjoyment. Web designers searching for the most effective design are advised to consult Dabholkar (2000).

We should point out that the same issue has been debated with conventional retailing. Some *weak* retailers have taken the view that *self-service* equals *no service* and have provided very little help to consumers, using the opportunity to reduce their costs (in particular fewer sales staff). This approach will only leave consumers frustrated and unable to find what they want and so they are likely to leave the store very unhappy.

In contrast, as Merrilees and Miller (1996) note, for better-performing stores 'self-service' does not mean 'no service'. The best self-service stores, like IKEA, Wal-Mart and many superstores, appreciate that self-service needs to be designed in such a way that it delivers good service, albeit of a kind other than personalized service.

Thus *good self-service design* in *conventional retailing* includes a well-organized store, with good layout, good signage, helpful visual displays and ready access to product information. Merrilees and Miller (2001) have argued that the approach taken by superstores represents a new self-service paradigm of retail service. Broadly speaking, the same good self-service design principles readily transfer from conventional retailing to e-retailing.

E-SERVICE PERFORMANCE

Knowing what is meant by e-service is an important first step in managing an e-retail business. However, it is necessary to take another step, namely the measurement of how well an organization is performing in each e-service activity. At this point it is clear that we only have a limited understanding of which e-service functions are important to consumers and how well e-retailers deliver these services. Some much-needed new research, namely a study of critical incidents in e-service delivery. Our critical incident analysis is followed by an examination of the role of e-service metrics as a management tool. In turn we discuss an alternative measure of e-service performance, namely e-retail service quality.

A CRITICAL INCIDENT APPROACH TO E-SERVICE PERFORMANCE

This section outlines the results of new research initiated especially for this book. A content analysis of 138 e-retail sites was undertaken by four judges in order to assess the nature and effectiveness of e-service across those sites. It was suggested that a good way of getting started might be with book, music, gift and department store sites, because these represent a high share of the e-selling transaction activity. The final discretion as to sites chosen was left to the individual judges. The main criterion for selection as a judge was expertise in analysing e-retailer websites.

Notwithstanding each judge's expertise, further controls were built into the evaluation process through careful briefing and training of the judges. This briefing included careful instruction to make sure that all items were fully understood by each judge and that all judges had the same meaning for each. Another instruction was that each judge was to spend about 10 to 15 minutes moving through the site to understand its features and its content before answering the various set questions. Each site was analysed in the same way.

A survey instrument (protocol) was designed for each judge to use with each site. A wide number of site attributes were assessed on a Likert scale of 1 to 7, depending on whether the judge agreed or not that the site performed well on a particular attribute. There was also an open-ended section of the survey instrument where the focus was on the overall level of e-service for the site, based on a 1 to 7 Likert scale.

On the same page the judge was asked to describe up to three important critical incidents/areas that positively contributed to their assessment of the overall level of e-service. Additionally, up to three important critical incidents could be listed that detracted from the level of e-service.

POSITIVE CRITICAL INCIDENTS

Initially we present the incidents that positively contributed to e-service. We do this in two ways. First we can note those positive facilitators to e-service across the *total* sample of 138 sites. We also break the results into *high-service sites* and *low-service sites*. High-service sites are those sites that were rated highly on the basis of the perceived overall level of e-service, that is, those sites that scored a 5, 6 or 7 out of 7. Those sites that scored 1 to 4 were called low-service sites.

Across the total 138 sites, the three most positive incidents that contributed to e-service were:

- Interactivity and communication (56 per cent of all sites);
- Special offers (33 per cent);

- information (20 per cent).
- The next most important batch included:
- Variety of items for sale (14 per cent);
- Frequently asked questions (FAQs) (a separate type of interactivity) (12 per cent);
- Ease of use (12 per cent).

Other less important facilitators of e-service included security/privacy references (8 per cent), goods delivery (7 per cent) and returns policy (4 per cent). If we compare high-service and low-service sites, we more or less get a similar picture of what is important. One key difference is that the number of positive incidents of good e-service is a lot lower in low-service sites. Thus interactivity and special offers remain the highest two facilitators of good e-service, but the rate of incidence is about twice as much in high-service sites.

For example, in low-service sites there is a 27 per cent incidence of interactivity (compared to 72 per cent in high-service sites) and a 20 per cent incidence of special offers (compared to 39 per cent in high-service sites). A number of key determinants of e-service in high-service sites are downgraded in low-service sites. These include information, FAQ, security/privacy and returns.

NEGATIVE CRITICAL INCIDENTS

Apart from coding those elements of e-service that contribute to the overall level of e-service of a site, we have also analysed those elements that have reduced the overall level of e-service. We have retained the same classification of elements, but now we refer to negative critical incidents. That is, interactivity now refers to a lack of interactivity or a low level of service from this element. The same applies to the other eight elements of e-service.

The pecking order of negative critical incidents that affect overall e-service. The two most important negative incidents are a narrow variety of goods for sale (15 per cent of sites had this problem) and poor delivery service (14 per cent of sites).

Other problem areas of e-service included interactivity (11 per cent), information (10 per cent), ease of use (8 per cent) and returns policy (8 per cent). The other three elements, FAQ, security/privacy and special offers, were rarely mentioned as a negative incident.

We have extended this analysis to a comparison of high-service and low-service sites. As we would expect, the number of negative incidents is almost thrice as great in the low-service sites. Variety and delivery were the top biggest problem areas for both types of sites, but had an incidence rate of less than 10 per cent in the high-service sites (compared to more than a quarter of the low-service sites). For the rest of the e-service elements, the most notable difference in the rankings is that of ease of use. It was the equal third highest problem area among low-service sites, but the lowest (and almost non-existent with a 1 per cent incidence) among the high-service sites.

LOGISTIC REGRESSION OF HIGH-LOW SERVICE SITES

We can extend our analysis from an enumeration of the critical incident elements (as a form of Pareto analysis), to a binary logistic regression analysis in which we can predict which sites fall into the high-service or low-service categories. The dependent variable is binary (either one type of site or the other). The independent variables are the nine dummy variables denoting positive critical incidents and the nine dummy variables denoting negative critical incidents.

Overall the degree of explanation is high, with an adjusted coefficient of determination of 0.53. Nine of the dummy variables were significant at the 5 per cent level. The model predicts very well, with an 88 per cent hit rate.

The six major e-service elements that shunt a firm into either a high-service or low-service category were:

- Positive interactivity incidents
- Negative information incidents
- Negative delivery incidents
- Negative interactivity incidents
- Negative ease of use incidents
- Positive FAQ incidents.

In addition, less important influences were positive information incidents, positive special deals and negative variety of items for sale incidents.

Multiple Regression Analysis of Overall Service Rating

Given that we have recorded the actual overall service rating of the site, on a 1 to 7 scale, we can also analyse the data with conventional multiple regression analysis, with the overall service rating as the dependent variable and the same independent variables as before. This is another way of testing the robustness of our results, although the logistic regression and the multiple Ordinary Least Squares (OLS) are testing slightly different models and therefore we would not expect exactly the same results to be produced. the results. The adjusted coefficient of determination is good, at 0.56. Eight variables were significant. The six most important e-service elements explaining the overall service rating were:

- Positive interactivity incidents
- Negative delivery incidents
- Negative ease of use incidents
- Negative information incidents
- Positive information incidents
- Negative interactivity incidents.

Additionally, positive variety of the offerings had a marginal influence on overall service rating, while positive deals and negative variety of items were not quite significant.

If we compare we see that essentially the same elements are at work. However there are slight differences, with some elements appearing in one table only, and the pecking order changing marginally. For example, a positive FAQ service might elevate an e-retailer into the high-service category, but did not have any discernible influence on the overall rating regression.

E-SERVICE METRICS: A MANAGEMENT TOOL

Our research in the previous section revealed that interactivity was overwhelmingly important for achieving a perception of high e-service. This finding is even stronger when we add frequently asked questions (FAQs) to its role because this is a form of interactivity. In a sense the emphasis on interactivity is akin to the importance of personal service in the conventional literature.

Interestingly, personal service was found to be the most important type of customer service in conventional retailing. Interactivity in the e-context includes two-way communication, the ability of the e-retailer to communicate to the user and the ability of the user to communicate with the e-retailer, responsiveness in answering questions (including the special case of FAQ) and personalization of the process.

Even without measurement, interactivity is clearly a good candidate as a capstone element in a powerful e-service programme. Similarly, we recommend that an e-retailer should audit its interactivity every year or so, along the lines suggested in the previous section (using, say, a critical incident analysis). If interactivity is found to be too low or not as high as desired, then steps can be undertaken to increase it, through, for example, increased customization or other means.

A second key finding of our research study is that interactivity needs to be supported by special offers, information, variety of items for sale and ease of use, as part of an integrated approach to e-service. An e-service audit of an e-retail site should incorporate all components of e-service.

A third key finding of our research is also very important for the practice of good e-service. We have shown that it is not sufficient to create and manage *positive e-service experiences*. Equally, the firm's e-commerce strategy needs to be able to handle *negative critical incidents*. The first point is that *even high-service sites* experience periodic problems in e-service. Show that high-service sites, while generally having a very high (72 per cent) positive incidence of interactivity, nonetheless had a 6 per cent (that is, non-zero) incidence of negative interactivity. The same pattern occurs in the areas of product variety and delivery. Firms need to take steps to continuously improve (that is, lower) the rate of negative incidents. Ideally, more interactivity may need to be built in if all other aspects of interactivity fail - this is the ultimate approach to service-failure recovery. Perhaps it is a toll-free phone service that is needed as a service in the last resort?

A fourth key finding of our research that needs to be carefully considered by websites is that the solution for sites attempting to increase their e-service capability is not simply to *add* more information, an FAQ service or similar facility. Such actions are a necessary, though insufficient condition to becoming a high-service site.

Take information, for example. Information incidents, both positive and negative, were important in determining membership of the e-retailer in a high-service or low-service category and the overall level of e-service of the site. Yet there was only a slight difference (and one that was *not* statistically significant) in the quantity of information across high-service and low-service sites.

This suggests that the problem for some sites is not the *quantity* of information, but rather the *quality* and *relevance* of information. Thus the high rate (20 per cent) of negative incidents about information on the low-service sites may be due to overemphasis on the wrong information, that is, the wrong details, rather than the lack of information in general.

In summary, we suggest that e-retailers should regularly monitor or audit all of their e-service, at least as frequently as annually. The critical incident approach is a simple way of doing this and the method is robust because it captures both positive and negative incidents in e-service. Notwithstanding the merit of this approach, there are alternative ways of evaluating e-service and we turn to one of those in the next section.

E-RETAIL SERVICE QUALITY: AN ALTERNATIVE PERFORMANCE METRIC

Retail service quality entails the application of service quality as both a concept and measure to retailing. The landmark study in this respect is Dabholkar *et al.* (1996). One advantage of using a measure of (retail) service quality is that it represents a composite measure, pulling together a number of components of service, such as personal service, store design and problem-solving.

So, instead of having to say that six or seven or whatever components of service are performing at the individual service level, we can combine our assessment into a composite service quality measure.More recently, researchers have extended their scope of retail service quality from conventional retailing to also include Internet or e-retailing. These studies include Zeithaml *et al.* (2000), Francis and White (2002a; 2002b), Janda *et al.* (2002) and Wolfinbarger and Gilly (2002).

Each study uses slightly different dimensions (or items under each heading) of e-retail service quality, but generally the dimensions include:

- Website design
- Security
- Ordering system
- Delivery system
- Communication.

The five dimensions of e-retail service quality provide an umbrella approach for e-retailers wishing to use an alternative measure of e-service performance. We offer no view as to whether this approach or the critical incident approach is better.

Indeed, e-retailers could quite easily use both sets of metrics to evaluate their e-service, as they complement each other.At the time of going to press a major new article on e-retail quality has appeared, namely Wolfinbarger and Gilly (2003). This article seems to be the most comprehensive and methodical of all of the articles in this field and so we should highlight its findings.

Four components of e-retail quality were identified, namely:

- Website design (navigation, order processing, personalization);
- Fulfilment/reliability (receipt of correct goods, delivery on time);
- Privacy/security (security of credit card payments and privacy of shared information);
- Customer service (responsive to customer inquiries).

In terms of the predictive power of these four components, two of them (website design and fulfilment) were found to be the most important in contributing to overall quality, satisfaction and return purchases.

ADDITIONAL GUIDANCE ON PRACTICAL E-SERVICE PROVISION

A number of practical tools that could help the improved delivery of e-service for e-retailers. First, key concepts, such as interactivity and delivery, have been highlighted as having special importance. Second, the idea of e-service metrics is another practical tool ready for actual use by e-retailers. In addition to these ideas and tools, the reader might wish to consult a number of 'how to' books, including Sterne (1996), Cusack (1998) and Zemke and Connellan (2001).

We have analysed the total number of websites in the sample as well as sub-samples of *high-service* and *low-service* websites. We have also contrasted *positive* critical incidents from *negative* critical incidents. Perhaps an unexpected result, we found that the main e-service elements that drive positive e-service are *not* the same as the elements that cause negative critical incidents in e-service. Interactivity in particular, strongly supported by special offers and information about the product and firm, was the key component of positive e-service. In contrast, negative e-service experiences were most often associated with a lack of variety of items for sale and poor delivery arrangements.

We have suggested that interactivity could be the key capstone element for e-retailers trying to build a powerful e-service programme, with support from information, ease of use, variety and special offers. There is also a need to manage *service-failure recovery*, that is, the myriad of negative critical incidents. This may lead to the ultimate form of interactivity - namely an interactive service that handles the collective failure in all the other interactive mechanisms.

Two different taxonomies or classifications were used to explore the nature of e-services. We also argued that self-service is not a myth for e-services and should not be taken for granted. It needs to be properly designed to genuinely help the e-customer. Further, evaluating e-service performance is important for e-retailers, if they are to fully understand what attributes are needed by customers. Two different ways of measuring e-service performance were given, namely a critical incident approach and an e-retail service quality approach.

LEADERSHIP AND E-COMMERCE

To move forward with e-commerce, the CEO and other senior managers must pursue several initial activities. Leadership comprises words and deeds, explicit and implicit behaviour, control of purse-strings, and leadership by example. Successful e-commerce leadership has four main characteristics, which can be implemented as follows.

- *Commitment at the Top: The CEO and Other Senior Managers Must Embrace E-Commerce.* Implementing an e-commerce plan requires strong leadership at the top of the organization. The CEO and other senior managers must understand the issues surrounding e-commerce well enough to evaluate the organization's strengths and weaknesses and make appropriate decisions on strategy, structure, and systems. The CEO must view IT and its applications as a vital component of the company's strategy and publicly demonstrate this belief through words and actions. The CEO must also adopt the attitude that e-commerce is not optional. The company may decide to have a larger or smaller role for e-commerce and may develop that role quickly or slowly, and it may sell directly to customers or limit its major initiative to the back-end systems, but it cannot ignore e-commerce entirely.
  - Commitment at the top
  - Thorough competitive analysis
  - Significant financial investment
  - Cultural transformation

Many CEOs have become e-commerce believers by discussing the topic with more experienced executives at other companies. For example, a conversation with Michael Dell of Dell Computer led Jack Welch at GE to hasten his company's movement into large scale e-commerce activities. Others, such as Howard Lester at Williams-Sonoma, have been convinced by believers within their own firm through some positive pilot e-commerce projects. In any case, the CEO should begin an earnest dialogue with people who understand e-commerce to learn about its successes and failures in relevant industries.

Other leadership roles are also important. The CIO must be a proactive member of the senior management team who communicates well with the

CEO about the usefulness of IT applications. Rather than serving strictly as a technologist, the CIO must also be a strategist. The CIO should serve in a leadership role in cross-functional teams that combine business units, IT, and e-commerce.

The CFO needs to understand the strategic role of IT in the business and consider its ramifications in funding decisions. Other members of the senior management team should have an active role in e-commerce, in a direct advisory role when it relates to specific relevant areas of responsibility and in a support role for other areas of the company. If possible, senior management should include persons who have prior e-commerce experience.

- *Thorough Competitive Analysis: Determine Company's E-Commerce Position.* In crafting an appropriate e-commerce strategy, it is vital for the company first to understand its e-commerce position relative to competitors. At this point, there are few industries where there has not been a first mover in the use of e-commerce.

  Even in industries where traditional companies have been laggards, pure-play companies have stepped into the void with varying levels of success. In fact, in most industries, a pure-play of some type was the first mover.

This existence of a first-mover competitor does not mean that other companies in an industry cannot gain competitive advantage over their traditional competitors by making significant e-commerce investments and efforts. CEOs who find themselves in an early-mover position should continue to invest and innovate to maintain their advantage. Charles Schwab built a significant advantage over competitor Merrill Lynch, despite having been preceded online by pure-play competitors such as E*Trade.

If a company is a late mover into e-commerce, it can still desire to be the first to provide a particular service, combination of services, or other unique value proposition. Catching up, however, often requires a very high level of investment and a willingness to explore new business models and processes. Regardless of position, a CEO must adopt a broader mode of thinking about competitors because in e-commerce, industry boundaries are more blurred and competition can come from unlikely sources.

- *Significant Financial Investment: Determine Appropriate Role of E-Commerce.* Once the CEO has evaluated the company's e-commerce position relative to other industry members and specific competitors, a decision must be made as to the appropriate role of e-commerce within the company.

  Given the increased usage of the Internet by leading companies in most industries, the senior managers will typically need to move forward with expanding or at least maintaining the company's current e-commerce position relative to its competitors.

The relevant decisions include whether the company is going to sell online and, if so, how its offerings will compare with its traditional offerings. It should also consider the geographic scope of its e-commerce sales, since the Internet permits unlimited worldwide access, which can introduce a myriad of complications and challenges. The extent to which e-commerce will be utilized in procurement and distribution must also be considered, as well as internal functions such as human resources, accounting, and marketing.

Of primary importance is that the company determine appropriate levels of IT activities and provide for appropriate levels of IT funding. This approach requires taking all necessary steps, including acquisitions or strategic alliances, to ensure that the company's IT capabilities are sufficient for a successful e-commerce venture.

The CEO must then work with other executives to ascertain the amount of investment necessary to fully implement the chosen e-commerce strategy. Investment decisions should be primarily strategic, and returns should be viewed, including the measurement of both short-term and long-term value creation, with a broad view of potential impacts.

- *Cultural Transformation: Determine Implementation Needs.* Since structure and systems can be used to implement strategy, most systems decisions are made after an e-commerce strategy has been formulated. But at an attitudinal level, cultural transformation will usually begin even earlier.

  Senior managers have a responsibility to establish a minimum level of IT acceptance and competence throughout the company by demonstrating and communicating commitment and creating appropriate training programs. Some companies will be better prepared for this transition than others; senior managers must carefully consider the required preparation and the implications for implementation speed.

To rapidly implement an e-commerce strategy, IT and e-commerce basics and the purpose of e-commerce must be understood. Communicating purpose is one of the most important actions of a CEO. Employees must realize that e-commerce represents an important challenge and opportunity rather than a threat.

Whether the e-commerce strategy is to be implemented within a month or a year, a sense of urgency is required. The CEO must present e-commerce as having the power to transform the organization in a positive way. Equivocation at every level, from the CFO's hesitation to fund technology to the salesperson's fear that e-commerce will decrease personal commissions, must be avoided. That does not mean reckless risk-taking to move forward, but it does mean a committed acceptance of e-commerce throughout the organization.

STRUCTURE OF E-COMMERCE

After formulating an e-commerce strategy, senior managers must develop a plan for implementation. The company's organizational structure may at times conflict with the goals of e-commerce, and senior managers must anticipate these conflicts and act accordingly, whether by changing the structure of the traditional organization or by creating new structures specific to e-commerce. These considerations span the areas of financing, management teams, and operations. A final consideration is the use of strategic alliances .

- *Internal Investment: Maintain Full-Equity Interest in E-Commerce.* The company faces a decision about equity for the e-commerce venture, whether to retain complete ownership in the e-commerce venture or to spin it off as an independent company.

  The lessons are clear. Many high-profile failures occurred in traditional companies that tried to imitate the pure-play model by spinning off. Investment in the venture should be made from within the firm, and reliance on outside capital typically seems like an indicator of trepidation about e-commerce on the part of senior management.

Spinning off e-commerce was popular in the early period of e-commerce, and the results have generally been disastrous. Building up large market capitalizations through IPOs was a popular trend, but it has become less desirable in a weaker and more skeptical stock market. The vast majority of these companies, including Wal-Mart, Kmart, Barnes and Noble, and Staples, have bought back the stock from equity partners and folded the e-commerce spin-offs back into the company.

- Internal investment
- Integrated management teams
- IT know-how from within
- Strategic partnerships

The other main justification for spinning off was that the company lacked the experience needed to pursue e-commerce or that additional investment capital was necessary. While it may be true that stand-alone firms sometimes find it easier to quickly develop e-commerce expertise, integrated e-commerce ventures in large organizations can also do this. Since e-commerce capabilities are becoming an increasingly important core competency, companies should develop the expertise and control the e-commerce operation inside the company through a full integration into business units and functions.

- *Integrated Management Teams: Innovate without Spinning Off.* From the distribution side, e-commerce should often be seen as simply another sales channel and thus changes in the management structure are kept to a minimum.

  In industries that already have multiple channels such as banks (i.e., physical branches, ATM) and catalog businesses (e.g., Nordstrom), an integrated structure is particularly relevant. With full integration, business functions such as marketing are easy to coordinate and organizational territorial conflicts are reduced. A less ideal but still viable alternative is to create a separate business unit for e-commerce. Many companies that began with spin-offs and then brought e-commerce back within the company chose to adopt separate strategic business units (SBUs).

Many companies have started their e-commerce operations with entirely separate management teams, often proposed to increase the focus on innovation and e-commerce, under the premise that e-commerce will not be given enough attention or independence by senior management at the parent organization. These management teams have often been established far from company headquarters, have had loose organizational cultures, and have been led by independent leadership often drawn from pure-play or other entrepreneurial companies.

Certainly innovation, flexibility, and creativity are needed to drive a successful e-commerce operation. But we have seen that this can occur successfully within traditional organizational boundaries. A formal set of management control structures and systems is necessary to balance the desired empowerment. When separate business units are established, they should function primarily to coordinate the full integration of e-commerce throughout the business units.

As with other organizational functions, it is sometimes desirable initially to establish a central organization both to drive and to coordinate these new activities. But, as the function matures, it should generally be more fully integrated into the business units. The separate functional units and the integrated functions within the business units may need unique structures and systems including unique performance measures and compensation and reward systems, but this customization of the organizational structure can be accomplished within existing organizational boundaries. There is no need to spin off core capabilities and detach valuable corporate assets.

- *IT Know-How from Within: Building Future Capabilities.* Not every company, especially those late to e-commerce, will have invested well enough in IT to develop e-commerce independently. Many e-commerce companies, even those with strong IT departments, have chosen to outsource e-commerce because of the necessity of speed. Speed is indeed a powerful motivation for outsourcing, but outsourcing should be used to catch up, not to give up. Although outsourcing may be used initially to create e-commerce solutions, the company can reassume control over e-commerce and IT and eventually can use the e-commerce systems for traditional commerce as well. Staples followed this approach in attempting to catch its IT-leader rival, Office Depot. Staples invested heavily in IT to build technology close to its core capabilities, but also created a sole-sourcing partnership to avoid delays in more peripheral areas of the business.

Another alternative is to acquire IT capabilities by purchasing a small IT firm and integrating the firm while the e-commerce solution is being implemented. UPS has followed this approach several times in its attempt to hold its IT leadership position over rival Federal Express, and UPS has been able to continually roll out new services while integrating its acquisitions.

Other companies, however, have made the mistake of selling equity to venture capitalists and then relied on these partners for all of their IT needs. Barnes and Noble made this mistake and then was hamstrung further when Amazon sued them for a patent violation related to their Web platform. Borders and Toys 'R' Us have taken the dramatic approach of having a competitor, Amazon, run their Web site for them. Companies must learn from these mistakes and not place themselves in such a precarious position with respect to IT.

- *Strategic Alliances: Moving beyond Core Competencies.* Although companies are advised to maintain equity interest, management control, and IT integration, traditional businesses can benefit from alliances with online companies in other ways. These relationships are most beneficial when the arrangement gives the traditional company access to supply-chain management, peripheral offerings, and customer bases.

Supply-chain management is a particularly useful area for partnership when the company cannot simply supply online customers from the same distribution channels as physical stores. Wal-Mart, Kmart, and Target have all made such arrangements to deal with their general merchandising businesses. CVS also simplified its procurement process for its Web site by entering into a partnership with Merck.com.

To provide peripheral offerings that will be available only online, alliances have also proven to be a successful approach. Neiman Marcus partnered with several luxury retailers to create a limited-scope "luxury portal" of high-end goods within its Web site. CVS partnered with WebMD to provide medical advice to complement pharmacy services.

Finally, traditional companies can gain access to large online customer bases by making strategic alliances with portal and ISP companies. Wal-Mart and Kmart entered agreements with AOL and Yahoo respectively to co-brand Internet service packages that would bring their customers online and to their site in particular.

Traditional companies may also profit from providing a physical presence to online companies that are realizing the inevitable trend toward integrated channels. Target has agreed to house E*Trade kiosks and customer representatives in its stores, in what has been a beneficial relationship for both parties. For E*Trade, the Target deal was just one aspect of a bricks-and-clicks strategy that culminated with the building of a New York super-centre.

STRATEGY OF E-COMMERCE

In designing an e-commerce strategy, it is critical to recognize what the

Internet changes. Not every value proposition in traditional commerce can attract customers in e-commerce, and not every traditional strategy is a viable source of increased profitability. The best strategies do not ignore the fundamental properties of the Internet and the behaviour of its users.

The organization must develop strategies for e-commerce operations that are consistent with overall corporate strategy. (Since this is a dynamic model, the order of appearance of these elements may be different. Strategy may precede leadership and resource commitments and structure and systems already in place may constrain the strategy decision.) The goals should include an increase in customer acquisition, enhanced channel optimization, improved customer loyalty and retention, and capturing value for the organization.

- Well-positioned online brand
- Online-friendly offerings
- Reliable customer service
- Cross-channel coordination

Four strategic moves areOp2:

- *Well-Positioned Online Brand: Acquiring Customers and Building Trust.* The simplest way for companies to initiate e-commerce operations is to transfer the brand name to the Internet, using the company's name as the domain name so that existing customers and potential new customers can easily find the company's Web site.

  The company can then advertise the Web site in various physical locations and in all print publicity materials. All letterheads, business cards, other types of business publications, and traditional advertising media should include the Web site address.

  In-store signage, kiosks, advertising on bags, and other materials have also been successful in drawing customers to the online channel. Large online marketing campaigns are likely to produce click-throughs and hits, but not customers, and have typically proved to have poor payoffs.

A brand name will draw customers to the company's site and can help assure customers about the quality of the offerings, the accuracy of the information, and the security of the Web transactions on that site. The brand name can also promote customer loyalty. The company must continue to provide the level of service and security that the brand name implies, or it will fail to attract repeat online customers and may even damage the traditional brand.

If the company's traditional brand is centered on price competition, it must reevaluate this strategy for e-commerce. Price competition is rarely a viable source of profitability in e-commerce. Search costs for comparing prices are negligible online, and price wars have typically led to prices decreasing to just at or above cost.

The Internet also offers easy access to stores that offer price differentials, because customers do not need to travel any physical distance to get to any given store. Only in limited contexts should companies expect to achieve long-term competitive advantage based on price.

- *Online-Friendly Offerings: Product Selection and Differentiation.* The company must decide what products to offer on the Web site. Companies such as Office Depot have found that they are able to provide more total products to customers through Web sites. Physical store space limits the number of inventory items available in stores, while the Web enables the company to provide a larger product offering. Even when integrating their offline and online brand management, a company should not feel compelled to offer precisely the same products online as in its physical stores. The ability to offer a large quantity of products, especially in retail industries, is a major inducement to acquiring an online channel.

Further, it is fully appropriate for a company to eliminate online offerings that are simply unprofitable or otherwise inappropriate. General retailers such as Wal-Mart and grocers have used price minimums, margin requirements, and category restrictions to limit their online offerings. Some companies also require a minimum total purchase on their Web site.

Companies should also consider peripheral offerings in addition to those provided by the company's physical facilities. Such additions are especially appropriate for companies in service industries and companies with large business-to-business (B2B) components. For example, Office Depot's business services offerings are a strong complement to its office supplies business.

Another differentiator is offering customers the ability to obtain unique or uniquely tailored products or information. Customization can be a powerful differentiator because it allows customers to control the product or service choices, and loyalty can be built partly due to high switching costs. Personalization gives customers their very own version of the site that can include information and recommendations based on the customers' prior purchases and demographics.

- *Reliable Customer Service: Inspiring Loyalty among Customers.* Building trust online requires more than a strong brand; it requires strong customer service practices that emphasize the convenience of the online channel. The customer must trust the company and its Web site. Trust can be built through assurances of privacy and transaction security and by providing accurate information.

  Trust in the transaction's completion is built through prompt and accurate fulfillment of orders. Many people purchase at Amazon rather than other Web sites because of its consistently highly rated fulfillment and customer service operations.

Web site design also contributes to satisfying customers. Basic characteristics of the site, such as simplicity, legibility, clarity, and a professional look, are necessities for all Web sites. Strong search engines are especially important for companies with a large number of product offerings.

Information about physical stores, customer service, and delivery and return policies should be easily accessible from the home page. Technology should be a facilitator and not an end in itself, however, and the company should not invest too heavily in design features without being confident of their appeal. Neiman Marcus found that its customers were not interested in viewing luxury products on a high-technology platform. Barnes and Noble discovered that they could not create interest in online parallels to their in-store coffee bars and author visits.

The site should also provide a number of services for customers who need information about the site, the offerings, or products they have purchased. These include comprehensive FAQ (frequently asked questions) sections, easily accessible information on delivery and returns, and rapid email response and technical support, where appropriate.

Numerous delivery options should be available to the customer to allow for both speed and low-cost preferences. Companies such as Nordstrom's, which offers products that need to be examined in person before the sale is complete, have provided particularly generous return policies to overcome the hesitation to purchase online inherent in their product line.

Physical stores can also be used for pick-up of items that are needed immediately in industries such as pharmacies. Customers should also be offered convenient opportunities to return defective or unsatisfactory products, including returning such products to the physical stores.

- *Cross-Channel Coordination: Convenience and Revenue Stimulation.* The Web site and physical stores should not be seen as two separate entities that happen to share a brand name. Cross-marketing is an important component, but ultimately, the online and traditional stores must have complementary roles in the overall corporate strategy. Exploiting the advantages of integration means more than drawing customers to the Web site through promotion in the physical store.

Allowing online customers to pick up and return orders to physical stores provides customers with choices and convenience, bringing more traffic to the physical stores. Initially many traditional companies did not allow online customers to return purchased products to their stores.

Today, virtually everyone allows customers to return undesired items to physical store locations. Numerous studies have shown the propensity of customers to make additional purchases when drawn to the store by online-generated functions. Therefore, the Web site should include an easily accessible store locator function that includes a map to the location, a phone number, and store hours.

The physical store and online operations can each be used to stimulate sales in the other channel. Some products that require high levels of interaction with the product can be introduced to the online customer but sold in the physical locations.

Kiosks that provide a computerized access to the online site, on the other hand, have been a successful mechanism in physical stores to stimulate online traffic. Many retailers have encouraged the use of kiosks to order online products not available in the physical store or when delivery of the products is more convenient. Kiosks are also effective in overcoming concerns about online shopping for less computer literate customers.

The Web site can also provide more convenience for customers who wish to purchase specific items immediately rather than wait for delivery. For example, Office Depot can now direct customers to local stores that currently have the product in inventory. Customers need not call all the local stores and tolerate taped messages and long waits to find a product. Even Internet pure-play companies like Amazon, through its alliance with Borders, for which it provides Web site operations, can direct customers to the nearest Borders store that has a desired product. Customers need only provide a zip code.

Integration of physical stores and online operations can also lead to greater efficiencies. Supply chain advantages that lead to more effective purchasing, inventory control, and logistics management may enhance the company's overall cost structure and result in greater profitability.

SYSTEMS MANAGEMENT

Senior managers must finally ensure that organizational processes are capable of implementing the e-commerce strategy. Information practices, human resources, performance measures, and customer management are all areas in which traditional systems may require adaptation to implement an e-commerce strategy.

- *Modernized Internal Processes: Using Information Effectively.* The cultural transformation described earlier may be enough to make e-commerce possible, but more must be done to maximize its benefits. Information practices must be adapted to promote transparency and availability.

  Changes must ensure that information flows freely throughout the company and is not hampered by artificial organizational boundaries or personal ambitions.
  - Modernized internal processes
  - Incentive-laden HR practices
  - Aligned performance measures
  - Improved customer management

In addition to information sharing, the decision-making processes of the company should be reconsidered. Cross-functional teams and remotely located teams should be assembled with greater frequency, with less emphasis on hierarchical reporting. Decision makers should also have greater self-governance and flexibility.

An important internal process is value chain management. Every company should identify ways to leverage the Internet in each part of the value chain, from procurement to distribution to delivery. In fact, failure to adopt e-commerce-specific cost savings will likely put a company at a serious competitive disadvantage. Strong supply chain management is often the basis for providing superior service.

In the area of procurement, a company can reduce the cost of goods sold by obtaining products through the Internet. Distribution strategies must not only cut costs but also provide the fastest and most convenient customer service. Delivery strategies should maximize convenience and speed for customers, using both the Internet and the company's existing infrastructure to provide these benefits. The best supply-chain practices, however, depend on the type of offering.

- *Incentive-Laden HR Practices: Bringing Your People on Board.* Compensation systems must be aligned with strategy and structure for the e-commerce venture to be a success. The CIO must be compensated as a member of the senior management team to signal the importance and respect shown for the IT function and the centrality and commitment to improved IT and e-commerce.
  At lower organizational levels, compensation systems have additional consequences on alignment. By compensating e-commerce managers the same as managers in traditional commerce, the company sometimes fails to create the necessary incentives for e-commerce success. Though parallel compensation systems can often work, both market forces and the need for speed, creativity, flexibility, innovation, and extra diligence often requires additional incentives and rewards.

Differential compensation, often through stock options, can create an incentive to cannibalize from the company's traditional channels. Such practices can cause conflicts with traditional business units but are often necessary to optimize the use of each channel, especially during the formative years of the e-commerce initiativeÒ Typically, e-commerce compensation should be tied to the overall success of the venture rather than rewarding individual units or channels for performance. This is particularly relevant when the company is seeking full integration, because it helps ensure cooperation and seamlessness between departments. The Internet also provides opportunities to improve the hiring process. Cisco is just one company that has found great benefits from hiring online, including lowered costs, faster filling of positions, and higher competence.

Companies may also want to consider specialized HR practices for their IT departments:

- *Aligned Performance Measures: Planning for the Long-Term.* Strong measurement practices are among the cornerstones of all good systems. Performance measures for e-commerce must overcome the uncertainty and unique dynamics associated with the Internet, and they may be more frequently adjusted in response to real-time information.

With these considerations, it is clear that no company should simply extend its existing performance measures to the e-commerce venture without extensive customization. Still, long-term cost differentials, balanced with a variety of financial, nonfinancial, and leading and lagging indicators, are particularly useful for successful e-commerce implementations.

Some skeptical companies have made unreasonable demands with respect to e-commerce performance. Because they misconceived e-commerce risks and rewards, they had unrealistic expectations of immediate growth and ROI that would not be demanded of any traditional long-term investment. Worse yet, they tied further investment to achievement of these goals, dooming e-commerce before it even could get off the ground.

In most companies, new projects and ventures require short-term ROI, and revenue projections, many of which an e-commerce venture and its related projects may not meet. If the company decides to enter or expand e-commerce, it cannot hamstring the venture by insisting on such short-term requirements throughout. E-commerce has also led many companies to create performance measures other than revenue, ROI, and traditional financial indicators. Some of the new, poorly designed performance measures have had a disastrous effect on strategy implementation.

For example, indiscriminate customer acquisition and attempting to maximize revenue through online advertising often have negative implications for long-term profitability. Single-purchase customers and advertising revenue independent of the company's value proposition are not sustainable strategies. Worse still are nonfinancial measures such as Web page hits and registered users, which may not even be tied to a short-term revenue stream.

In addition to measuring the performance of the business, e-commerce brings added importance to measuring the value and functionality of operations. Most e-commerce strategies will have a strong operational component, including cost savings from value chain management and cuts in labour costs for the online channel. Operational measures should be tracked by some dedicated resource and balanced between financial and nonfinancial assessments of operational performance.

Moreover, companies must create a value capture process to evaluate the success of IT projects associated with the e-commerce venture. Looking at nonfinancial performance measures, the value capture process can help convince skeptical employees of the importance of IT. Even with the value capture process, however, the full benefits of IT investment are often underestimated.

- *Improved Customer Management: Better Service and Better Data.* Companies must also reconsider the internal processes required to provide the high levels of customer service necessary in e-commerce. Online customers need access to some level of customer service at all times.

> There is a trade-off between service that entails a high level of human input and service that is automated and more cost-efficient. Finding the proper balance is a function of the company's offerings, its customer base, and customer feedback.

Customer data is a significant benefit in e-commerce, because of the vast amount that can be learned about customers during a Web site visit in contrast to an in-store visit. Many Web sites, however, have mistakenly focused only on counting hits and visits, while ignoring the more valuable information that can be gathered.

Tracking of customers' interaction with the Web site can be used to identify customers' price sensitivity and information preferences and to gauge satisfaction with the Web site design and accessibility. Gathering and using customer information is important to refine the value proposition and better allocate internal resources. Marketing strategies for the Web site can also be continually refined, using real-time information gathered from customers during their visits, a practice that Staples has used well.

Once a company has established an e-commerce strategy, organizational structure becomes a primary concern in the process of implementing that strategy. In many cases, e-commerce will not initially fit neatly into the existing organizational structure of a traditional company. E-commerce, even to the most technologically savvy company, represents a new channel for procurement, distribution, and sales. E-commerce ventures also put new demands on individuals and business units at every level of the company.

A dynamic model in which strong and supportive leadership and a well-formulated strategy provide the basis for transforming a company through e-commerce. To implement that strategy, structure and systems must be adapted for e-commerce.

Corporate strategy, structure, systems, resources and the external environment are all both inputs and constraints to the determination of e-commerce strategy, structure, and systems. Planning for an e-commerce venture should use the existing structure to determine what existing company strengths can be utilized or enhanced with e-commerce. Implicitly, even some companies that have been unsuccessful in e-commerce have grasped this fact.

But instead of treating existing structure as an input, companies have often treated it as an impediment to e-commerce, deciding to create an entirely new structure outside the organization. They believed that they could not create a new e-commerce structure inside the organization that could effectively implement the e-commerce strategy. They also did not believe they could integrate an e-commerce operation into the corporate strategy, structures, or systems. Sometimes e-commerce was split off as a separate company, sometimes it was separated as a separate functional or business unit, and in a few cases it was fully integrated.

These concerns have been at the core in the debate over structure in e-commerce. Through the late 1990s, companies feared the disruptive nature of e-commerce and were unwilling to make changes in existing company structures and systems. Many companies chose to separate e-commerce from the main company structure.

These separate-structure decisions included establishing separate business units far from company headquarters, creating separate management teams, outsourcing of the entire e-commerce platform, and selling large equity ownership of the e-commerce business to venture capitalists and other outside interests.

Many of these companies have belatedly realized the value of an integrated structure for e-commerce. High-profile failures may have served to convince uncommitted leaders, but the rationale for integration runs much deeper than an analysis of past outcomes. The application of fundamental business principles should also make the benefits of an integrated organizational structure abundantly clear. Some previous discussions on e-commerce have divided the debate of e-commerce structure into a number of separate decision dimensions. Some have encouraged executives to consider integration or separation of equity, brand, management, and operations, while others focused on leveraging two dimensions, the financial and the operational. Although these dimensions are relevant in terms of developing an e-commerce structure, careful choices must be made.

Companies must rely on a well-developed and coordinated implementation of an e-commerce strategy, with aligned e-commerce structure and systems. It would have made little sense, for example, if Wells Fargo had integrated its management structure and operations and then followed in the footsteps of competitors, such as Bank One, by creating a new brand for e-com-merce. Likewise, Office Depot would likely have destroyed most of the benefits of its operational integration if it had sold equity in OfficeDepot.com to a venture capitalist.

In the final analysis, the most fundamental analysis is whether or not to integrate e-commerce, and this choice should direct all the subsequent financial, management, and operational decisions. The implementation of an e-commerce strategy can take different forms, and the structure and speed of implementation are part of the strategic choices. However, companies should make a commitment to long-term full integration. It is the path to that full corporate integration that is an issue. A lack of commitment to e-commerce integration can cause wavering dedication on the part of the company. While Bank of America is currently a leader in online banking, it faced early obstacles because it initially pursued an integrated e-commerce approach. It later moved on to a separate strategic business unit to foster creativity, and then had to switch back to an integrated approach.

Solutions are also described for problems faced when companies lack the internal capabily to fully implement the e-commerce strategies. Finally, the contexts in which external strategic alliances can be a desirable solution are presented.

THE PURPOSE OF LEADERSHIP IS TO REALISE THE MAXIMUM VALUE OF HUMAN POTENTIAL

This is quite a handy definition. It rules out Hitler and Stalin straight away and fits very nicely with JFK's ambition "to go to the moon and do the other things, not because they are easy but because they are hard". It is a very tough standard.

Why would we want anything less from our leaders? It is also a 'societal value' view of leadership. It subscribes to the game theory concept of win-win. 'Leadership' that can only produce gains for some at the expense of others is of no interest to society as a whole. The only problem with this definition is that the key word in it, 'value', is itself notoriously difficult to define. So what exactly does value mean?

As the Leadership Trust version refers to "business performance" let us start by asking what value means in a business context. Should we look at market value as a gauge of leadership? On that measure Jack Welch would score very highly on the leadership scale because GE has a huge market value ($382 billion in April 2005) although he earned his nickname of 'neutron Jack' because of his obsession of getting rid of people and leaving the buildings standing.

He also fired the lowest performing 10% of his managers every year. Does that fit comfortably with our goal of maximising the potential of people? There is also the added complication that share prices can go down as well as up. Bill Gates could be another candidate, not only in view of the enormous market value of Microsoft ($272 billion) but also because of his philanthropic foundation which gives billions of dollars to good causes and his clear aim of trying to eradicate diseases such as malaria. How comfortably does this sit though with Microsoft's strategy of 'killing off' competitors to monopolise their markets or being sued by the EU for abusing their monopolistic position.

Are these really the sort of 'leaders' who we might want to be society's role models? It looks as though just putting a financial figure on value does not necessarily identify great leadership.

So what if we move into the political arena for enlightenment? Who is the better leader Thatcher or Blair (Clinton or Bush)? Who will be judged as having created the most value for society? Is the UK's National Health Service any better under one than the other, for instance? We could also make a direct comparison on their handling of war. The Falklands war resurrected Thatcher's flagging image while the Iraq war might yet prove, ultimately, to be Blair's epitaph. Both assessments, it has to be said, are based on different perspectives of the justification of wars-defence versus pre-emptive action. Both are value judgements and personal perspectives. So not much chance of an objective measurement scale there then.

One final perspective that might aid our thinking is the world of sport. What better environment to discuss leadership and human endeavour:

pushing people to the absolute limit of their potential in the pursuit of excellence? So who is a better leader Alex Ferguson (manager of Manchester United football club), Arsène Wenger (Arsenal) or José Mourinho (Chelsea)? Or is that just another trick question played on us by this elusive thing we call leadership? Are football managers just that-managers?

Surely leaders have to unite people who may have interests that are not that easy to reconcile. Premiership football clubs do not seem to involve any real debate anymore about what its board, its players and its supporters value. No one seems to be too interested in footballers becoming role models of teamsmanship or sportsmanship. Their goal is as clear as a goal is ever going to be-to win the Premiership. The supporters of football clubs must be willing 'followers' and self-selecting. There is no sense here of the real, fundamental challenge of leadership, which is actually to try and get maximum value out of people when some of them do not really want to play ball.

It looks like every attempt to answer a leadership question results in just another more complicated question being posed. So, in a determined effort to produce a better way forward let us take a step back and begin right back at the beginning. What is the purpose of leadership and, more importantly from a practical perspective, what is the basic proposition that drives our interest in leadership development? Then we can ask how better definition and measurement might help.

THE LEADERSHIP MEASUREMENT PROPOSITION

So why are we interested in leadership? Because if we can reproduce or replicate it society will benefit. The microscope analogy has particular relevance here. Whatever apparatus we choose must be able to bring leadership into sharp focus with clear definition. We have to be able to observe leadership and analyse it. This microscope not only has to show us how leadership works at an elemental level but also, more importantly, what makes this organism grow. How does reproduction actually take place? Only then can we hope to spot leadership potential and have any chance of cultivating and nurturing it. Is such a piece of equipment beyond our comprehension? Do we have the technology? If so, what might the main components be?

As someone who has spent the whole of his professional life working in the human resource management (HRM) arena I have always seen the role of HRM as attempting to get the right organisational configuration; with the right people; in the right role and performing at the height of their capabilities. Such an obvious and eminently sensible goal and yet one that is fraught with a multitude of issues, diversions, distractions and downright political subterfuge at every turn. This is particularly true as you move up through organisations to try and ensure the right 'leaders' are in place. The Peter principle of promoting people above their level of competence appears as prevalent today as it has ever been-we only need to consider the average tenure of a CEO, or even a Government minister, to see plenty of evidence of this principle in action. Is this fallout just an inevitable consequence of the Machiavellian attitudes of those clawing their way to the top of the greasy pole or is the answer much more prosaic? Maybe those 'leaders' who profess to having to 'play politics' have really just been using it as a good cover story to hide the fact they were never up to the job in the first place? If so, then we can only blame the methods we use to select and develop effective leadership.

After all, we seem to have arrived at a situation where the most powerful jobs in the country, including the Prime Minister, all MP's and Chief Executives, require no formal qualifications at all. No wonder we still have a serious leadership problem and the only way out of this problem is to have a stab at measuring leadership ability both before and after the fact. Perhaps even a subjective measure of leadership, but based on a commonly agreed scale, is better than no measure at all. Ask any measurement question of any people variable such as height, weight, intelligence and this theory says there will only be a very small number at the top end of the range.

If this holds true for leadership ability then the challenge to society can be expressed simply as 3 options (*):-

1. How can we, in some way, raise this level of leadership ability (shown by the dotted line shift)?
2. How do we ensure that only the best (those with 8 and above) find their way into positions of leadership so that they can make their greatest contribution?
3. What can we do to ensure that the worst candidates (anyone with less than 3) do not get into such positions?

As you are considering these questions it might be worth just reminding ourselves of a particularly irksome but, unfortunately, unalterable fact of life. We can only manage what we measure. So, while such a construct is of great interest, conceptually, there is no way of producing or managing this curve unless we can develop meaningful measures of leadership ability. We have already identified a host of issues that bedevil the subject of leadership definition, and they are all thorny, but a failure to grasp the nettle of measurement will inevitably be the biggest obstacle to progress. It might be problematic but when the only other option is for leadership to happen by chance or default what do we have to lose? Could we not raise the probability of getting better business and political leaders simply by trying? Our recent track record is certainly nothing to be particularly proud of, especially if judged against our prime criterion of societal value.

LEADERSHIP DEVELOPMENT

Leadership development refers to any activity that enhances the quality of leadership within an individual or organization. These activities have ranged from MBA style programmes offered at university business schools to action learning, high-ropes courses and executive retreats.

DEVELOPING INDIVIDUAL LEADERS

Traditionally, leadership development has focused on developing the leadership abilities and attitudes of individuals. Just like people aren't all born with the ability to, say, play football like Zinedine Zidane or sing like Luciano Pavarotti, people aren't all born with the ability to lead. Different personal characteristics can help or hinder a person's leadership effectiveness and require formalized programmes for developing leadership competencies Yet, everyone can develop their leadership effectiveness.

Achieving such development takes focus, practice and persistence more akin to learning a musical instrument than reading a book. Classroom-style training and associated reading is effective in helping leaders to know more about what is involved in leading well. However, knowing what to do and doing what you know are two very different outcomes; management expert Henry Mintzberg is one person to highlight this dilemma. It is estimated that as little as 15 per cent of learning from traditional classroom style training results in sustained behavioral change within the workplace.

The success of leadership development efforts has been linked to three variables:

- Individual learner characteristics
- The quality and nature of the leadership development programme
- Genuine support for behavioural change from the leader's supervisor

Military officer training academies, such as the Royal Military Academy Sandhurst, go to great lengths to only accept candidates who show the highest potential to lead well. Personal characteristics that associated with successful leadership development include leader motivation to learn, a high achievement drive and personality traits such as openness to experience, an internal focus of control, and self-monitoring. Development is also more likely to occur when the design of the development programme:

- Integrates a range of developmental experiences over a set period of time. These experiences may include 360 degree feedback, experiential classroom style programmes, business school style coursework, executive coaching, reflective journaling, mentoring and more.
- Involve goal setting, following an assessment of key developmental needs and then evaluate the achievement of goals after a given time period.

DEVELOPING LEADERSHIP AT A COLLECTIVE LEVEL

More recently, organizations have come to understand that leadership can also be developed by strengthening the connection between, and alignment of, the efforts of individual leaders and the systems through which they influence organizational operations. This has led to a differentiation between leader development and leadership development. Leader development focuses on the development of the leader, such as the personal attributes desired in a leader, desired ways of behaving, ways of thinking or feeling. In contrast, leadership development focuses on the development of leadership as a process. This will include the interpersonal relationships, social influence process, and the team dynamics between the leader and his/her team at the dyad level, the contextual factors surrounding the team such as the perception of the organizational climate and the social network linkages between the team and other groups in the organization.

One practical example of developing leadership specifically so as to influence an organization's safety culture is described by Burman & Evans. Both forms of development may mutually influence each other, as exemplified in the concept of "Deep Change" in Robert E. Quinn 's 1996 book of the same title. Leadership development can build on the development of individuals to become leaders. In addition, it also needs to focus on the interpersonal linkages between the individuals in the team. In the belief that the most important resource that an organization possesses is the people that comprise the organization, some organizations address the development of these resources.

In contrast, the concept of "Employeeship" recognizes that what it takes to be a good leader is not too dissimilar to what it takes to be a good employee. Therefore, bringing the notional leader together with the team to explore these similarities brings positive results. This approach has been particularly successful in Sweden where the power distance between manager and team is small.

SUCCESSION PLANNING

The development of "high potentials" to effectively take over the current leadership when their time comes to exit their positions is known. This type of leadership development usually requires the extensive transfer of an individual between departments. In many multinationals, it usually requires international transfer and experience to build a future leader. Succession planning requires a sharp focus on organization's future and vision, in order to align leadership development with the future the firm aspires to create. Thus successive leadership development is based not only on knowledge and history but also on a dream. For such a plan to be successful, a screening of future leadership should be based not only on "what we know and have" but also on "what we aspire to become". Persons involved in succession planning should be current leadership representing the vision and HR executives having to translate it all into a programme. According to Meir Jacob and Amit Cohen three critical dimensions should be considered:

- Skills and knowledge
- Role perception and degree of acceptance of leading role
- Self-efficacy.

These three dimensions should be a basis of any leadership succession programme.

TYPES OF NETWORK LEADERSHIP ROLES

There are at least eight different kinds of leadership roles in a networked organization. Each of these can be associated with specific network *signatures* consisting of patterns of links and nodes and the social rules governing their interactions. For example, some network leaders, such as visionaries, primarily generate new information and typically do not directly request others to perform tasks for them.

They generally work in conjunction with connector and facilitator leaders who help them get their information out. Connectors, unlike visionaries, may have many symmetric dyadic interactions and act as gateways for a variety of sub-networks, whereas truth-teller leaders may only interact weakly with other members, having strong ties with a relatively small number of peers. Many of these roles can coexist in the same person. However, as networks grow in scale and complexity, these roles often become highly differentiated and expressed as Searle's *institutional* facts.

The Exemplar or "Alpha Member"

Most peer networks, whether they are military, technological, recreational, adolescent, criminal, terrorist, artistic, professional, or athletic, are founded by individuals who exemplify the standards and qualities that characterize the best competencies of the peer network. These are the role models that others imitate. Sometimes their role can be simply symbolic, even ceremonial, but they are nonetheless important in setting the tone and culture of the organization.

Successful and charismatic founders of new organizations, from Bill Gates, Steve Jobs, and Sam Walton to Osama Bin Laden and Aum Shinrikyo, all embody values and personalities that become the values of their organization. These leaders also exemplify the assessment criteria and set the standards for becoming a member of a network. In the military, each Service has its own types of exemplars: pilots and Seals for the Navy; Green Berets, and Rangers for the Army; and fighter pilots for the Air Force. These exemplars embody what is considered the most difficult and admired professional qualities that set that Service apart.

The Gatekeeper

For every network there are membership rules—criteria for being included, retained, elevated, and excluded. The gatekeeper decides who is in and who is out. In Congressional politics, the party leadership plays this role by deciding who gets what committee assignments and whose bills take precedence in a legislative agenda. This is a role that President Johnson as the former majority leader of the Senate understood brilliantly, while President Carter—an outsider, visionary, truth-teller, and moralist—never fully appreciated. In many military organizations, the drill sergeant often plays multiple leadership roles, acting as exemplars, enforcers, and gatekeepers. He weeds out recruits whom he believes fail to meet the standards of his unit. The gatekeeper role is especially important for elite units that seek to achieve a high degree of exclusivity based upon exceptional standards of excellence. Like the doorman to exclusive clubs, the gatekeeper role is a combination of truth-teller, applying the standard for admittance, and enforcer, denying admittance to those parties that fail the test.

The Visionary

The role of the visionary leader is to imagine futures, determine what is limiting about the present, and show what is possible in the future. Visionary leaders such as Steve Jobs, Winston Churchill, Walt Disney, Craig Venter, Billy Mitchell, and Thomas Edison are a constant fount of new ideas and are "at war with the present."

Many high technology startups have been founded by visionaries, but eventually end up being run by operatives or fixers. The visionary leader imagines new possibilities, creating new institutional facts and realities, and therefore plays a critical role in moving networked organizations in new directions.

This is an absolutely critical role in the start-up or crisis phase of an organization. However, it can also be disruptive in circumstances where continuity and execution are critical to success. Visionaries play a vital and sometimes contentious role within the military. They are often the first to see weaknesses in prevalent military doctrine, to espouse new technologies and doctrines, and therefore, to challenge current leadership and entrenched interests.

Consequently, unless they are able to prove themselves within wartime, their ideas can languish for decades. Rare are the individuals such as Lord Nelson or Napoleon, who were both visionaries and the senior commanders. In the case of Billy Mitchell, Col. John Boyd, or even Winston Churchill, it was only later in their careers that their innovations were appreciated. However, as the nature of warfare today is in constant transition with respect both to doctrine and new technologies, the visionary will have increased influence. The visionary role is best coevolved with that of the truth-teller.

The Truth-Teller

In every network organization, someone has to keep the network honest. This entails the very challenging task of identifying free riders and cheaters. In knowledge-based organizations, it is also about ferreting out half-truths, spin, blunders, and lies. Such a leadership role can become easily compromised. Like the accounting function in a corporation or the judicial function in the legal system, truth-tellers can lose their independence, and hence effectiveness. Since these are often the first roles to go in times of stress, successful leadership is exemplified here by independence, transparency, accuracy, and candor in the face of enormous pressure. As Tennyson's ode to Wellington eloquently and astutely expresses, truth telling and resistance to the lure of fame go hand in hand and are a critical and enduring signature of effective leadership.

One of the arguments for modesty in leadership is that the lure of celebrity and its attendant rewards can compromise independence and hence, credibility. Therefore, if a leader is to be an effective truthteller, he or she must also be credible, and even the hint of self-dealing can undermine his effectiveness.

The challenges are especially acute and consequential within military organizations. If credibility breaks down, trust soon becomes the next casualty, and then the overall effectiveness of the chain of command. The admonition "Don't shoot the messenger" is taken from military experience and reflects the high potential cost of reporting unwanted information. In response to such pressures, the military developed the doctrine of "ground truth" after the Vietnam War.

The truth telling goal is to provide authenticated and accurate reporting of the outcomes of missions. It can take enormous courage to resist the inevitable pressures of peers and superiors to report what they want to be known, rather then the truth of the matter. Being a truth-teller can be highly unpopular and a long road to advancement.

Even highly established and previously unchallenged military institutions can come under enormous pressure for truth telling. The armed forces newspaper, *Stars and Stripes*, undertook its own "ground truth investigation" into morale in Iraq in 2003 and was widely censured by some members of Congress and threatened with a reduced budget for its reporting. Similarly, the success and credibility of the enquiry into the alleged tortures within Abu Ghraib and elsewhere within Iraq and Afghanistan will depend upon individuals assuming very strong truth-teller leadership roles.

The Fixer

This is an individual who knows how to get things done and measures him or herself not just by how many people they might know, but rather how they can get things done that others cannot. Such individuals are results oriented. They "know where the bodies are buried" and what "makes people tick." In politics, they are the operatives, the Mr. Fix-its. They are all about opening and closing loops—getting tasks done. In Tennyson's words, they abide by the "rugged maxims hewn from life." They are without illusions and are inherently pragmatic.

They may interact with a range of other network leaders—visionaries, truth-tellers, and connectors—but always with a concrete outcome in mind. Within the military there is the archetype of the "scrounger," an individual who is highly skilled at finding and assembling "found" materials, people, and resources to solve a variety of human and mission needs, from chocolate and silk stockings during WWII, to scrap iron as armor platting for Humvees in Iraq. Fixers are gifted improvisers, what the French call "bricolagers," who take common available materials and repurpose them into something useful. In contrast to those who work through formal channels and depend upon approved procedures, fixers typically are "rule benders" and work through informal networks. Within the British Army during the late Victorian period, the Quartermaster was famous for the orderly but creative acquisition of supplies under the most trying and unpredictable of circumstances.

The Connector

These network leaders participate in multiple social networks, connecting not only with a large number of members, but a highly diverse number of members as well. They are known for having numerous friends, connections, and contacts—for being consummate networkers. Like the visionary leaders, they can introduce variety and options into a network through the diversity of people with whom they interact. They are critical for identifying and accessing new resources and helping to get a message out.

By building links across network boundaries, they can help a networked organization break out of the "lock ins" of scale-free networks and introduce greater diversity, and hence robustness. During WWII, General Eisenhower as the Supreme Allied Commander developed a reputation as a highly accomplished connector leader by virtue of his ability to relate to the different interests and cultural styles of the allied commanders. He was able to make and sustain connections among contending parties in order to keep the alliance together and on course. He was also able to exercise significant control over those whose primary allegiances were to different military organizations.

The Enforcer

In smaller networks, this role is often combined with that of the gatekeeper and even the truth-teller. However, in larger networks it is an independent role. Enforcement can mean physical coercion, but more often entails psychological or peer pressure.

Like the truth-teller function, independence and transparency are critical for overall network effectiveness. Clearly, force and military means are the enforcement methods of last resort, but are necessary in order to buttress other forms of enforcement, which can vary from guilt and shame to legal redress. Most networks have their own forms of redress and enforcement that entail exclusion.

The power of ostracism in Greek city-states, for example, was extremely effective because it not only removed an individual's right of protection but destroyed their social identity as well. An exceptional example of a senior commander acting to enforce discipline across all levels of command was the Duke of Wellington's order during the Peninsular Campaign in 1807. Wellington issued an order that any breach in military discipline towards the treatment of the Spanish civilians and military would result in an immediate flogging and hanging. According to historian Paul Kennedy, this order was enforced with impartiality and force and was instrumental to Wellington's success.

STYLES OF LEADERSHIP

In the past several decades, management experts have undergone a revolution in how they define leadership and what their attitudes are towards it. They have gone from a very classical autocratic approach to a very creative, participative approach.

Somewhere along the line, it was determined that not everything old was bad and not everything new was good. Rather, different styles were needed for different situations and each leader needed to know when to exhibit a particular approach.

Four of the most basic leadership styles are:

- Autocratic
- Bureaucratic
- Laissez-faire
- Democratic

AUTOCRATIC LEADERSHIP STYLE

This is often considered the classical approach. It is one in which the manager retains as much power and decision-making authority as possible. The manager does not consult employees, nor are they allowed to give any input. Employees are expected to obey orders without receiving any explanations.

The motivation environment is produced by creating a structured set of rewards and punishments. This leadership style has been greatly criticized during the past 30 years. Some studies say that organizations with many autocratic leaders have higher turnover and absenteeism than other organizations. Certainly Gen X employees have proven to be highly resistant to this management style.

These studies say that autocratic leaders:

- Rely on threats and punishment to influence employees
- Do not trust employees
- Do not allow for employee input

Yet, autocratic leadership is not all bad. Sometimes it is the most effective style to use. These situations can include:

- New, untrained employees who do not know which tasks to perform or which procedures to follow
- Effective supervision can be provided only through detailed orders and instructions
- Employees do not respond to any other leadership style
- There are high-volume production needs on a daily basis

- There is limited time in which to make a decision
- A manager's power is challenged by an employee
- The area was poorly managed
- Work needs to be coordinated with another department or organization

The autocratic leadership style should not be used when:

- Employees become tense, fearful, or resentful
- Employees expect to have their opinions heard
- Employees begin depending on their manager to make all their decisions
- There is low employee morale, high turnover and absenteeism and work stoppage

BUREAUCRATIC LEADERSHIP STYLE

Bureaucratic leadership is where the manager manages "by the book¨ Everything must be done according to procedure or policy. The manager refers to the next level above him or her. This manager is really more of a police officer than a leader. He or she enforces the rules.

This style can be effective when:

- Employees are performing routine tasks over and over.
- Employees need to understand certain standards or procedures.
- Employees are working with dangerous or delicate equipment that requires a definite set of procedures to operate.
- Safety or security training
- is being conducted.
- Employees are performing tasks that require handling cash.

This style is ineffective when:

- Work habits form that are hard to break, especially if they are no longer useful.
- Employees lose their interest in their jobs and in their fellow workers.
- Employees do only what is expected of them and no more.

DEMOCRATIC LEADERSHIP STYLE

The democratic leadership style is also called the participative style as it encourages employees to be a part of the decision making. The democratic manager keeps his or her employees informed about everything that affects their work and shares decision making and problem solving responsibilities. This style requires the leader to be a coach who has the final say, but gathers information from staff members before making a decision. Democratic leadership can produce high quality and high quantity work for long periods of time. Many employees like the trust they receive and respond with cooperation, team spirit, and high morale.

Typically the democratic leader:

- Develops plans to help employees evaluate their own performance

- Allows employees to establish goals
- Encourages employees to grow on the job and be promoted
- Recognizes and encourages achievement.

Like the other styles, the democratic style is not always appropriate. It is most successful when used with highly skilled or experienced employees or when implementing operational changes or resolving individual or group problems.

The democratic leadership style is most effective when:

- The leader wants to keep employees informed about matters that affect them.
- The leader wants employees to share in decision-making and problem-solving duties.
- The leader wants to provide opportunities for employees to develop a high sense of personal growth and job satisfaction.
- There is a large or complex problem that requires lots of input to solve.
- Changes must be made or problems solved that affect employees or groups of employees.
- You want to encourage team building and participation.

Democratic leadership should not be used when:

- There is not enough time to get everyone's input.
- It's easier and more cost-effective for the manager to make the decision.
- The business can't afford mistakes.
- The manager feels threatened by this type of leadership.
- Employee safety is a critical concern.

LAISSEZ-FAIRE LEADERSHIP STYLE

The laissez-faire leadership style is also known as the "hands-off" style. It is one in which the manager provides little or no direction and gives employees as much freedom as possible.

All authority or power is given to the employees and they must determine goals, make decisions, and resolve problems on their own.

This is an effective style to use when:

- Employees are highly skilled, experienced, and educated.
- Employees have pride in their work and the drive to do it successfully on their own.
- Outside experts, such as staff specialists or consultants are being used
- Employees are trustworthy and experienced.

This style should not be used when:

- It makes employees feel insecure at the unavailability of a manager.
- The manager cannot provide regular feedback to let employees know how well they are doing.

- Managers are unable to thank employees for their good work.
- The manager doesn't understand his or her responsibilities and is hoping the employees can cover for him or her.

VARYING LEADERSHIP STYLE

While the proper leadership style depends on the situation, there are three other factors that also influence which leadership style to use.

- The manager's personal background. What personality, knowledge, values, ethics, and experiences does the manager have. What does he or she think will work?
- The employees being supervised. Employees are individuals with different personalities and backgrounds. The leadership style managers use will vary depending upon the individual employee and what he or she will respond best to.
- The company. The traditions, values, philosophy, and concerns of the company will influence how a manager acts.

6

E-Commerce and E-Business

INTRODUCTION

There are many definitions of e-Commerce. The narrowest refer to it simply as the buying and selling of goods online. Chaffey treats e-Commerce as a subset of e-Business because the former does not include intra-business functions such as the processing of a purchase order. He quotes the following definition of e-Business:

When a business has fully integrated information and communication technologies (ICTs) into its operations, potentially redesigning its business processes around ICT or completely reinventing its business model e-Business, is understood to be the integration of all these activities with the internal processes of a business through ICT.

Zwass defines e-Commerce much more broadly: The sharing of business information, maintaining business relationships, and conducting business transactions by means of telecommunications networks.

In its broadest form, therefore, e-Commerce can be regarded as synonymous with IBM's expression 'e-Business', which is a holistic concept covering the full range of business functions and structures effected by the Internet, and this is the approach taken in this book. Given the marketing perspective of the book, the more general terms 'Internet strategy' and 'Internet marketing' are also used extensively here. Agonizing over definitions is probably a waste of effort, because all these terms are likely to be transitory as the Internet becomes an integral part of business activity. In fact, such terms can be likened to early descriptions of the motor car as a 'horseless carriage'.

Electronic commerce has existed for some years in the form of EDI, but technical problems and restricted functionality contrived to ensure that the system never achieved widespread credibility. The lack of a common standard for document formats meant that companies tended to get locked in to one supplier.

It has taken the growth of the Internet with its universal standard to project electronic trading into mainstream commercial credibility, allowing businesses to connect throughout the value chain, exchange real-time information and streamline business processes both internally and externally. The principal driver for the take-up of e-Commerce is economics. For example, the cost of processing a financial transaction on the Web can be as little as 1 per cent of doing the same at a bank branch using traditional paper methods. So once fixed costs such as equipment and telecommunications lines are covered, the marginal cost of servicing transactions on the Web can be very low. In business-to-business terms, procurement costs can be significantly reduced.

Zwass (1998) devised a hierarchical framework of e-Commerce comprising seven levels to illustrate the interrelationships between its various aspects, and help make sense of the likely impacts of e-Commerce. Zwass regards e-Commerce as comprising three meta-levels:

- *Infrastructure*: the hardware, software, databases and telecommunications that are deployed to deliver such functionality as the WWW over the Internet, or to support EDI and other forms of messaging over the Internet;
- *Services*: messaging and other services enabling the finding and delivery of information, including a search for potential business partners, as well as the negotiation and settlement of a business transaction;
- *Products and structures*: direct provision of commercial information-based goods and services to consumers and business partners, intra- and interorganizational information sharing, and organization of electronic marketplaces and supply chains.

Within these meta-levels are seven distinct levels. The first three make up the technological infrastructure of e-Commerce. Levels 4 and 5 represent the business infrastructure, and levels 6 and 7 cover business-to-business transactions and business-to-consumer transactions through electronic marketplaces and intraorganizational communications through intranets. As these tools encourage the dissemination of information, reducing (and in some cases eliminating) the need for 'privileged points of contacts or gatekeepers in organizations', they are also contributing to 'the move away from centralised, hierarchical approaches and transforming traditional relationships within and between organisations'.

The scope of e-Commerce revenue under headings that can be summarized as the '5Cs':

- *Connection*. AOL, for example, as an ISP, obtains its revenues from connecting customers to the Internet.
- *Commercials*. Some companies obtain revenue from displaying advertisements for other companies. Key sites such as Yahoo! with millions of visitors can charge high fees. Smaller, more specialist Web sites can attract advertisers with relevant products or services to offer; for example, an estate agent's Web site might carry advertisements for removal companies or solicitors.

- *Commerce*. Goods or services are sold directly to customers online.
- *Content*. Some sites can charge for content that can be accessed from the site. For example, a market research firm might offer research reports for sale.
- *Community*. Specialist online community sites may be able to charge a membership fee for access and discussion participation.

TYPES OF E-COMMERCE

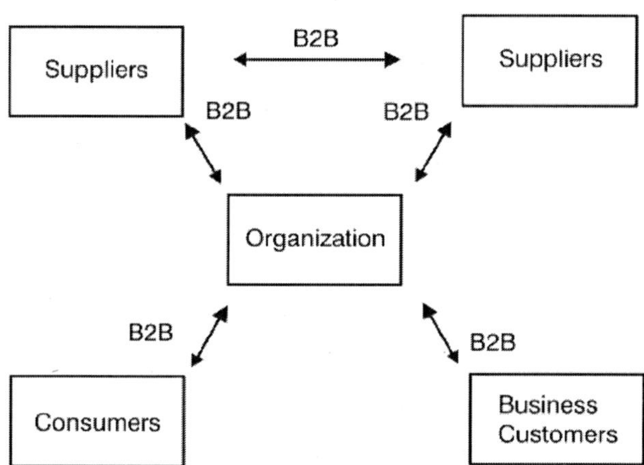

Business to consumer (B2C) refers to the selling of goods and/or services directly to consumers by businesses. The classic example is Amazon which offers in excess of 1.5 million book titles online and has extended its sales into other products, including music CDs, videos and games. Business to business (B2B) refers to the selling of goods and/or services by one company to another as part of their supply chain, and is likely to contribute to at least 80 per cent of the growth of e-Commerce in the next five years.

There are also some more recent arrangements:

- Consumer to consumer (C2C) refers to the selling of goods and/or services between individuals; see, for example, the auction house eBay.
- Consumer to business (C2B) refers to consumers generating trade with businesses. For example, www.letsbuyit.com allows consumers to come together and aggregate their purchasing power to command discounts normally reserved for large organizations. It can also cover individuals such as lawyers or accountants offering their services to businesses.

Business to government (B2G) refers to the trade in goods and services between the private sector and local or national government:

- Peer to peer (P2P) refers to a relationship between two individuals that is electronically mediated but not conducted via any central body. For example, Freenet is a network that promotes the digital exchange of music artefacts on a P2P basis.

Marketing orientation

Table: Online Business Model Typology

Category	Example
e-Shop/e-retailer	Usually with a B2C focus such as www.whsmith.co.uk
e-Procurement	Online business purchasing of goods (B2B) www.rswww.com
e-Malls	A grouping of e-tailers that can be compared with a traditional shopping centre; see, for example, www.indigosquare.com
e-Auctions	B2B or B2C customers bid for goods; for example, www.ebay.com
Virtual communities	Groupings of customers or businesses with similar interests; for example, www.thepetchannel.com
Collaboration platforms	Enable collaboration between customers or businesses; for example, www.egroups.com
Third-party marketplaces	Intermediaries bringing together buyers and sellers; for example, www.esteel.com
Value chain integrators	Offer a range of services across the value chain; for example, the online events booking service www.omniticket.com
Value chain service providers	Provide functions for a specific part of the value chain, for example the logistics company www.ups.com
Information brokerage	Provide information for consumers or businesses, such as price comparisons: www.moneysupermarket.com
Trust and other services	Provide kitemarks authenticating online service quality, www.truste.org, or security, www.verisign.com

A 'marketing orientation' describes a guiding management philosophy or attitude of mind throughout the organization that puts the customer first. This is a much broader view of the role of marketing than is traditionally envisaged - referring just to advertising or sales - and it cuts across a wide range of organizational functions.

Successful adaptation of a marketing orientation also requires effective management of other stakeholder groups such as staff, business partners, shareholders and suppliers. 'The marketing concept should lie at the heart of the organisation, and the actions of directors, managers and employees should be guided by its philosophy.

In fact, it can be argued that in these circumstances a specific marketing department is no longer necessary. This contention is supported by Piercy, who notes that the current emphasis upon the value of cross-functional teams conducting 'pan-company marketing' may obviate the need for marketing departments, especially if such project teams also cross organizational boundaries and blur the distinction between the internal and external environment.

Internet strategy or Internet marketing?

There are significant overlaps between Internet strategy and Internet marketing, particularly if a company adopts a broad perspective of marketing by engendering customer focus throughout the business, as described above. Indeed, the two terms can be regarded as synonymous. Chaffey regards Internet marketing as a subset of Internet strategy that he calls 'sell-side e-commerce', meaning that it focuses on building relationships with customers, in parallel with 'buy-side e-commerce' that focuses on supply chain management.

Chen regards Internet marketing as dealing with operational rather than strategic issues, but includes customer relationship management in the 'operational' category. In this book, we use the term 'Internet marketing' in a broad sense, while still distinguishing strategic aspects and operational aspects.

New business models

Timmers categorizes a number of new types of online business model. In practice, many of these categories overlap, and some are just electronic versions of existing business models as show in table, but the table provides a useful demonstration of the range of e-Commerce activities, some of which are still at an early stage of development. By the time you read this, no doubt there will be more.

CHALLENGES OF E-BUSINESS CHANGE

One of the first challenges companies face when attempting to develop online channels is to consider how such a strategy will impact upon their 'bricks and mortar' organization. Developing a 'clicks and mortar' operation may result in a more 'virtual' form of organization in which traditional ways of working are mixed with electronic communications. It is here that a company encounters its first problem, which is usually one of technology.

The particular difficulty relates to the attempt to evolve 'legacy' systems (i.e. the technical infrastructure that has accumulated to support the business over time) to an infrastructure that will support e-Business. Few businesses find themselves in the position where they can 'throw away' the old and introduce new, customized computer systems. Legacy systems often perform essential activities upon which daily business processes depend. While start-up companies can leapfrog these problems, established ones face some difficult challenges. Effective e-Business solutions demand integrated front-and back-end systems, a process which may demand close co-operation between two groups (or even subcultures) with the organization. As Nigel Waterson of Gemini puts it, 'The front end has quite often been built by guys in ponytails, while the people who understand the back end are often grey haired'. System integration means that when customers interact via the Web, placing orders and purchasing goods, the stock control and financial systems also speak the same language and carry out their part of the transactions.

The problem is that many such back-end systems are unlikely to be based on open Internet protocols and may even have been custom built. Nonetheless, such systems may be critical to a company's business, and include such details as bank account data and stock rotation information. As Conway points out, IT managers are loath to replace them with something new and untested. They may not even fully understand how their legacies work any longer. The people who built the systems may well have left the company, leaving present IT experts reluctant to tinker.

Replacing or upgrading such systems also takes time, which may slow up Web developments critical to speedy e-Commerce innovation.Over and above the technological matters identified above, major *organizational* change issues must be recognized and addressed for online strategies to be realized successfully. This is because of the need to redesign business processes and structures, change organizational culture, and engage in education and training. A wide range of stakeholders may be affected, with many personnel needing to 'buy in' to the change.

There is only one way to do e-Business: fully committed. Everyone in the company must be dedicated to the effort. You can't have ten people for every thousand working on it. You can't delegate it. You have to encourage everyone to jump into the water and support them in teaching each other to swim. I'm asking for the biggest cultural change in your company's history. These issues will now be considered in turn.

Resistance to Change

There are a number of reasons why people may be unwilling to accept organizational change, as summarized below:

- Stability and security are threatened.
- Coping strategies and comfort zones are affected.
- The uncertainty of change creates anxiety.
- Imposed change reduces perceived autonomy and control.
- Job content is changed and new skills are demanded.
- Authority structures and reporting lines are altered.
- Work groups and other relationships are disrupted.
- Established routines and practices are abandoned.
- An individual's power and authority is threatened.

According to Markus (1999), workers' reactions to change vary greatly. She suggests that while some workers readily embrace new technologies, some can be hostile, and the reason for this hostility can often be attributed to poor communication and shifts in organizational power. Effective internal marketing is important here in order to segment employees into 'supporters', 'neutrals' and 'opponents' of change, and then develop appropriately customized communications in order to deal with the differing priorities of each of these groups. Implementation of change involves the disruptive transition from a current state to a future state, as a result individuals or groups can resist change.

They claim that there are three types of problems encountered when an organization goes through a significant change:

- *Power*. Change can be viewed as a threat to existing power structures and it creates uncertainties, so the struggle for power escalates as individuals and groups attempt to control their environment by resisting change.
- *Uncertainty*. Anxiety is created as individuals are not sure where they stand and whether at the end of the change process they will still have a role within the organization. As a result, individuals can act irrationally, as they find it difficult to understand and interpret clearly information related to the change.
- *Control*. During the change period, it becomes difficult to maintain control because goals are changing, as are structures and roles, and certain control systems become irrelevant.

These authors also highlight the important point that within large organizations individuals usually do not openly resist change; instead, they 'subtly or passively' resist. The degree of employee involvement and participation can significantly affect the success of change. Markus claims that workers' reaction to change is dependent on

whether they have had a say in selecting the technology or the way it is introduced and used, how the new technology is communicated, how much training and support are provided, and how carefully the roll out is planned and executed.

Involving employees fully means that they become responsible for the success of the change, becoming 'owners' of the change process. IBM Global Services recommends that in order to build a successful e-Business, organizations need to challenge their employees to:

identify the cultural changes that will also be needed and to shape the processes, the linked education, learning and competency development that will be required to deliver real value in the new ways of doing business that they are proposing.

Another critical point is that organizations are bound to encounter complications in asking individuals to make changes that they are incapable of implementing. Adequate investments in training and development programmes are therefore essential, particularly, for example, if new skills in Web design are required. If individuals do not possess the skills and capability necessary to introduced planned changes, the likelihood of success is significantly reduced.

According to Buchanan and Boddy (1992), the more radical change projects are, the more open they are to organizational disruption and failure. Badham *et al.* (1997) point out that there are two aspects to radical change. The first concerns the issue of 'breadth' - the degree to which change is central to the organization's strategy - and demands radical as opposed to incremental modifications throughout the organization.

The second relates to the degree to which such modifications mark a significant departure from existing ways of doing things. Both of these certainly apply to e-Business. For example, such changes point to business process redesign, the development of cross-functional team working, and the move towards a customer-focused (instead of management-led) culture. These changes are likely to be politically controversial and threaten the interests of a wide range of stakeholders.

Unlike routine change, such initiatives are also likely to be highly complex. As Badham *et al.* note, there may be a high degree of uncertainty as to what to do and how to do it; objectives may be less clear, and resource requirements will be less well known. In addition, it may be less easy to create shared perceptions of goals and build and maintain necessary commitment.

For this reason, these authors suggest that more time will need to be spent ensuring effective communication to encourage flexibility, address perceptions, and generate and regenerate involvement. To illustrate the problems that can ensue in such a situation, the authors describe Merrill Lynch's move into online trading:

At the core of the change process was conflict at many levels within Merrill Lynch. There was conflict between the defenders of the brokers and their commissions and proponents of online investing. There was conflict between Merrill brokers who were concerned about losing customers to online brokers and Merrill brokers who were concerned about losing commissions. There was even conflict among Merrill executives between who favoured setting up a separate online unit to compete with the brokers and those who favoured keeping the online unit under the same executive.

Leadership

Leadership plays a crucial role in effective change management. Hunt (1998) claims that change is a learning process because people have to learn to behave differently, but in order for this process to work and for change to be successful, individuals need to be encouraged, and it is here that leadership becomes very important. Carnall also expresses the need for strong leadership; that is, 'the ability to maintain progress and a facilitative and supportive approach', and suggests that for this to happen, the leader needs to have knowledge of the change area and appropriate skills to encourage learning and change. Some leaders use 'coercive persuasion' to force change; in other words, 'employees have no alternative but to accept the new reality because they have nowhere else to go'.

Although individuals may not like the change, they have no choice, so will accept the change and accommodate the new ideas. He goes on to state that leaders need to be able to 'manipulate people's understandings of what is going on, and who are able to deliver the results quickly'. The role of the leader can be to create conditions under which success can visibly be achieved, even if only in a limited and partial way, and to rationalize and capitalize upon positive events after they have happened.

Managers will instead need to be skilled in the art of leadership and corporate politics. The need to enrol and re-enrol support, neutralize dissent and resistance, and secure resources will demand networking skills and the ability to build consensus and support. They must start by gaining buy-in at the top. As Siegel puts it, 'You can have the world's greatest web strategy, but it won't work unless managers have a stake in the outcome'. To make sure they do, Siegel recommends the formation of a change team, headed by a Chief Net Officer (CNO).

Furthermore, he suggests that businesses should 'Strengthen the team with managers who have good relationships with people in other divisions. The CNO will need a lot of favours, so make sure the team is credible in the eyes of the rest of the company'. If leaders recognize the type of change they are faced with, and are familiar with the sort of skills and tactics that may be employed to deal with it, the management of change is more likely to be successful.

Relationship-building and Communications

The importance of effective internal marketing to engage staff in the change process was emphasized. Increasingly, such communications are a critical aspect of external relationship building too. According to Symonds (1999a), a crucial misconception is that any business is a 'free-standing entity'. For example, in order to participate in a new development such as e-Procurement or customer relationship management, it is essential that companies involve their suppliers, partners and customers in their processes and allow each party to become familiar with each other's processes. This degree of openness and transparency is new to most organizations, and it requires significant change and high levels of trust between participants.

A genuine e-Business strategy provides electronic links in order to 'foster conversations' with staff, customers and partners. Such 'customer-led' approaches involve listening to customers in a strategic way, deepening relationships and loyalty. The importance of engaging in rich customer conversations is underpinned by a number of recent works on e-Business. The highly influential *Cluetrain Manifesto*, for instance, asserts in the first of its ninety-five theses on the new economy that 'markets are conversations'. Newell's *Loyalty.com* (2000) underlines this point, and highlights the way companies must 'leverage customer information' for the effective management of customer relationships on the Internet.

Seybold's *Customers.com* (1998) makes similar points, again focusing on the need for customer-focused strategies that engage customers as parts of a community based around a company's products and personnel. Such strategies suggest something much more radical in terms of change than the mere 'bolt-on' approach of adding an online channel to market, which is often proposed as a straightforward and simple process. It calls for a re-engineering of processes and structures focused around key customer groups, rather than product or service divisions.

It also implies cross-functional, team-based working. As Siegel puts it, The customer-led company has a broad interface across which all employees can get to know their customers. Employees invite customers in to collaborate on new products, support systems, and methodologies. Facilitating those interactions will take new communication skills, new tools, and the ability to move people in and out of product teams easily.

At Dell Computers, for instance, customers are brought into the product planning and manufacturing processes, with all employees encouraged to have contact with customers. Through effective collaboration across boundaries, ideas can be shared about product designs and value propositions. The result is faster and more customer-focused product and service innovation. To produce the capacity for this, considerable attention must be placed on organizational structures, processes, skills and culture - elements that may need a radical overhaul in established companies.

Role of the Change Agent

Buchanan and Boddy emphasize the importance of having an appropriate 'change agent' or 'project champion' in the successful implementation of change. The change agent should be someone who is committed to the success of the project and prepared to 'go the extra mile' in order to motivate, bully or cajole other participants as required.

There is a diverse range of skills associated with performing this role; for example:

- Influencing;
- Negotiating;
- Selling;
- Inspiring;
- Commanding respect;
- Political;
- Magic and miracle working!

It is a tall order for any one individual to have all of these skills, and some will be more important than others at different stages of the project. In practice, therefore, more than one change agent may be required.

Adapting Organizational Culture

There are many ways in which the terms 'culture' and 'organizational culture' can be understood, but for our purposes we have chosen the following: the system of meanings which are shared by members of a human grouping and which define what is good and bad, right and wrong and what are the appropriate ways for members of that group to think and behave.

The pattern of learned basic assumptions that has worked well enough to be considered valid and, therefore, to be taught to new members as the correct way to perceive, think, and feel in relation to the problems of survival and integration.

Schein suggested that employee acceptance of technological change required a change in organizational culture, because practices and values tend to be built around existing technologies that have contributed to the successful development and self image of the organization. One of the strongest elements of culture he identified was the status system attached to these traditions, and the possession by individuals of critical skills. Schein claimed that innovation was a property of culture, and the potential of information technology as a competitive and strategic weapon would not be fulfilled unless innovative cultures were present or developed, enabling the organization to learn and adapt.

This attitude was also noted, whose theory of 'flexible specialization' emerged from their observations that technological progress could be self-blocking, and new products were generally designed to fit existing equipment and procedures. The importance of culture was also emphasized in a study of video disk development by Graham, who found that prevailing cultural values and attitudes in the firm, based upon past experience, were inadequate when it came to dealing with an innovative product in a new market.

Although these studies pre-date the Internet era, they illustrate quite clearly how a change in organizational culture is often necessary for full advantage to be taken of the opportunities presented by new technologies. A vast literature now exists on the subject of how to change culture. As early as 1952, Lewin identified three phases of culture change, namely 'unfreezing', 'change' and 'refreezing'. 'Unfreezing' results from the questioning of norms that have led to a specific failure, thereby sensitizing employees to the need for change, which is then consolidated into new procedures or behaviours during the 'refreezing' phase.

This theory seems overly simplistic and linear in its classification of the technological change process, which in practice appears invariably to be a more dynamic and turbulent series of events. Mintzberg (1979) advocated the development of a culture of 'adhocracy' that is organic and decentralized in structure, thereby avoiding the pitfalls that are usually associated with bureaucracy. He claimed that in search of innovation, such organizations minimize planning, control and the division of labour.

In practice, however, while examples do exist of individual companies, such as British Airways, that have 'created' a new corporate culture, these success stories appear to be few and far between. March and Simon, in their revised edition of a seminal text that introduced the concept of 'bounded rationality' (referring to the limited cognition of organizational members), maintained that their theory still holds true today.

Despite the vastly increased resources available to the modern organization, these authors believed that potential for change would always be constrained by the conflicting agendas of employees. Green also questioned the ability of organizations to manage culture in a prescriptive way: If culture could be levered into shape then, by now, someone would have discovered the method. The metaphors of fine-tuning and fit which abound in much of the literature on culture and strategy are altogether inappropriate for something as complex as human social systems.

He noted that while corporate cultures appear to be stable and static when studied at a particular point in time, applying a longitudinal perspective reveals that they are in fact too multidimensional and dynamic to be susceptible to manipulation by management. The key point about culture change, therefore, is that it is rarely as simple a process as is sometimes suggested when recommended as a tool for implementing projects involving new technology.

THE BUSINESS ENVIRONMENT FOR E-COMMERCE

By the middle of 2001 the business revolution promised by the 'new economy' and the functions of the Internet had come to naught. The promise of a new business model based on e-Commerce or e-Business failed to deliver as the dotcom phenomenon imploded into that of the dot-bomb. Simon Caulkin, management correspondent for the *Observer*, described it as follows:

So, farewell then death of the business cycle, the end of inflation and above all the myth of the New Economy: slain by revisions to US figures that show that, far from lifting the economy permanently to the sunny uplands of unending productivity growth, the great Internet binge has given us levels of improvement that haven't been seen since, er, the 1930s. This quotation brings to mind the cultural revolution promised by punk in the mid-1970s. According to the then manager of the infamous Sex Pistols, Malcolm McClaren, punk would sweep away all hitherto popular culture into the dustbin of history as it represented a new Situationist adventure. In reality, punk was a speeded-up version of good old rock 'n' roll and ironically corresponds to the Pistols' most famous album, *Never Mind the Bollocks.*

Similarly, the Internet, instead of promising a business revolution, speeds up the rate of transactions rather than their primary nature. *Never Mind the Bollocks* seems to be making a comeback, nearly thirty years on, but in a different guise.Where did it all go wrong? Why hasn't the move 'from capitalism to knowledge society', as in the essay title by the management theorist Peter Drucker, become our everyday reality?

According to Drucker, economic history can be divided into three eras:

- The *industrial revolution*. From the late eighteenth century onwards, knowledge was applied to tools, processes and products.
- The *productivity revolution*. From 1880 until World War II knowledge was applied to work.
- The *management revolution*. From World War II onwards, knowledge applied to knowledge itself.

For Drucker, we now effectively live in a 'knowledge society'. For other contemporary theorists we inhabit 'the information society' in which the 'spirit of informationalism' drives all economic and social transactions. There are concepts derived from the same root: the 'weightless economy', the 'thin economy' and the 'weightless society' and the 'death of distance'. The factor common to all these conceptions is the role of technology. In fact, all these accounts can be said to be technologically determinist. That is, it is the technology that is transforming economy and society, rather than the business processes to which technology is put to use. In Drucker's account, technology and the invention of calculating machines, in particular the computer, are central to the progress of society through the three revolutions outlined above. Traditional factors of production - land, capital and labour - have become secondary to knowledge.

As long as there is specialized knowledge these factors can be obtained. In this view, company transactions become weightless. For example, the value of Coca-cola is tied not to the value of production of a fizzy drink, but the power the brand exercises in the market place.

A more salutary account is given by Robert Schiller in his book *Irrational Exuberance* on stock market volatility. He compares the building of the interstate highway system in the United States between 1956 and 1976 and the Internet as innovations. He argues that the Internet is 'notable for its visibility and vividness, and not unprecedented prospects for promoting economic growth and profits'. The interstate and Internet are both network innovations.

The former transformed the economic geography of the United States, promoting lower transport costs, greater market access, outward mobility into the suburbs and the rise of the local shopping mall. Schiller notes that while the Internet offers a wider selection and a greater ability to search, the delivery of goods is not immediate. Consequently, Internet marketing may not be superior to the marketing of the conventional shopping malls. The Internet remains part of the long march of creating innovations, but like all technology it is the nature of human inventiveness that makes them beneficial. The period of building the interstate system coincides with an annual average 1.6 per cent growth in real earnings on the Standard & Poor's 500 index of the financial performance of the top 500 US companies. Despite the enormous impact of the interstate on the economic geography of the United States why were these earnings not higher?

The answer according to Schiller was that the interstate system was just another innovation along the path of inventiveness. Similarly, evidence from McKinsey & Co., the international consultancy, shows that the impact of new technology, including the Internet, on productivity in the United States in the late 1990s was much less than was believed at the time.

The relationship between technological change, economic growth, increased productivity and profits is much more complex and indirect than the easy direct relationship suggested by some popular commentators. In the past decade the service sector has been in the forefront of investment in new technologies in the advanced economies. The benefits of these investments, however, have been decidedly uncertain:

Over the past decade senior managers in banking, insurance, health care, and other services have invested billions of dollars in computers and communications equipment - technology investments that promise to hone operations into an acute competitive weapon. But executives have been deluded: the payoffs have not been fully realized.

The primary reason is that technology alone does not determine corporate performance and profitability. Employee skills and capabilities play a large role, as do the structure of day-to-day operations and the company's policies and procedures. In addition, the organisation must be flexible enough to respond to an increasingly dynamic environment. And products must meet customer requirements.

These observations act as a health warning to the business environment for e-Commerce. This warning is not posted to suggest that Internet-based transactions will fail to deliver *material* benefits to producers and consumers alike.

Rather, they act to signpost the difficulties associated with claims that we now live in a new business, economic and social order. The context in which e-Commerce has developed and the difficulty faced by companies that believe the Internet is the universal solution to all business problems.

First, we examine some definitions and models of e-Commerce, and highlight some of the problems that exist to derive an adequate taxonomy for this emerging area. Next comes an examination of the technological underpinnings of the Internet, and its child, the Web. Following this assessment comes a discussion of issues of trust and governance associated with the Internet, and the fact that there is considerable disquiet in some quarters on leadership.

A brief examination of how to measure the Internet economy is followed by an identification of the drivers and barriers to e-Commerce take-up. We conclude by looking at some of the issues that have arisen from the implosion of the dotcom phenomena into the dot-bomb outcome. By doing so, we suggest that the business environment for e-Commerce has not destroyed the possibilities of a new economy, but is one in which the realities of the business cycle and the role of technological innovation are reasserted.

DEFINITIONS AND MODELS

There are many definitions of e-Commerce, but they all imply some manner of electronic mediation for business transactions. The UK Department of Trade and Industry (DTI) defines e-Commerce as:

The exchange of information across electronic networks, at any stage in the supply chain, whether within an organisation, between businesses, between businesses and consumers, or between the public and private sectors, whether paid or unpaid.

Though the word *commerce* carries with it a sense of activities being undertaken for payment, this definition gives the term *e-Commerce* a broad informational scope to also include activities for which no direct payment is made within a supply chain. A supply chain describes the distribution of goods, services and information flows between market participants within or between industries.

For example, a vehicle manufacturer is at the heart of a variety of supply chains, including parts, raw materials, services, etc., supplied to it by other firms. The optimal management of a supply chain reduces transaction costs. As a result, the competitive advantage of the vehicle manufacturer is enhanced. This explains why many prefer the term *e-Business* rather than *e-Commerce* to describe such electronically mediated activities. The DTI definition does not just place the scope of e-Commerce as being Internet- or Web-mediated, but includes electronically mediated activities undertaken outside the Internet and/or which pre-date the Internet.Earlier forms of e-Commerce, prior to the term being coined, include Electronic Data Interchange (EDI).

This is the exchange of information by trading partners, for example orders, using technically defined templates whose origins go back to 1969. The succeeding decades have seen many large corporations taking up EDI based on value-added networks. Value added is the process whereby each successive stage of production adds more value than the previous stage. Examples include private sector organizations such as IBM and GEIS (part of the US giant General Electric).

Another major sphere is that of Electronic Funds Transfer (EFT) through which the banking system facilitates financial settlements. Prominent amongst EFT systems is SWIFT (Society for Worldwide Interbank Financial Telecommunication), which has handled international inter-bank settlements since the 1960s. The BACS system is one such that handles inter-bank settlement for the UK banking sector. Finally other industries have created their own forms of EDI such as the airline reservation system, SABRE.There is a distinct difference between the Internet and these other forms of electronic transactions:

- The Internet uses protocols that are *open* and *non-proprietary*. That is, these protocols are published so that theoretically any user can use them to hook up to the Internet

- EDI systems are *closed* or *proprietary* systems, which are open only to paying participants.

The fact that systems are closed means a greater guarantee of security for all transactors. Open systems are by definition open to potential fraudulent activity. So though the economic transactions may be alluring, the potential threat to the integrity of global payment systems is too great at present for the major international banks to shift towards Web-enabled systems. One of the major challenges to examining, analysing and explaining the business environment for e-Commerce is the confusion of terms. Perhaps more importantly, the lack of appropriate models by which to examine, analyse and explain it inhibits clarity of thought and interpretation.

Central to any market transaction, whether in a geographical or virtual location, is the exchange of information. In a market economy, prices signal information about transactions between consumers and producers and between producers themselves. The equivalent in e-Commerce is Business-to-Consumers (B2C) and Business-to-Business (B2B). The advantage of e-Commerce to consumers is greater access to fuller information on prices of goods and services. The advantage to producers is they can directly access a greater market potential for their goods and services.

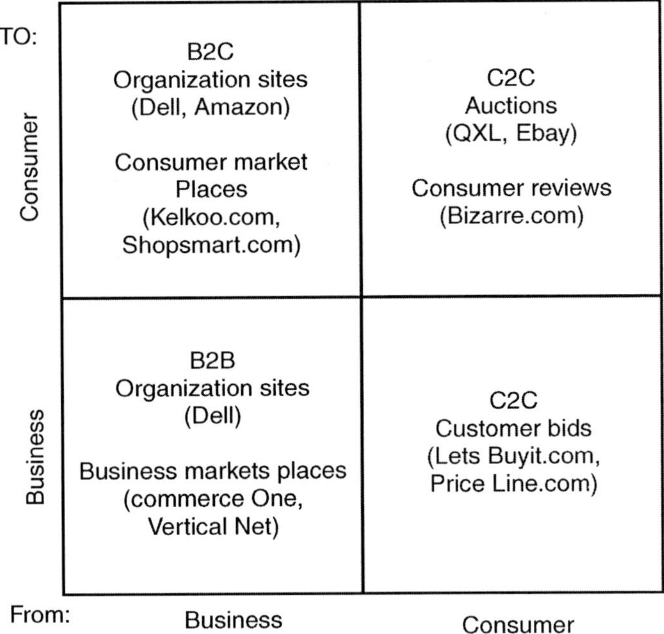

Fig. Taxonomy of Transactions Between Businesses and Consumers

However, e-Commerce does not overcome the problem of transaction costs (particularly transport costs) and immediacy in purchasing goods and services at designated locations, although it may reduce search costs in some general instances and shift them from producers to consumers in others. Essentially, e-Commerce does not alter the nature of exchange and transactions in a market economy.

Moreover, given the relatively low level of Internet commerce in most advanced economies, the heroic assumption that the Internet is now the universal market transactor is not vindicated by evidence. Given the United States had first-mover advantage, and the size of its economy (which is only slightly less than the whole of the European Union), it may come as no surprise that e-Commerce revenue in the United States in 2000 was twenty-three times that of the United Kingdom, thirty-three times that of France and seventeen times that of Germany.

The ratio of B2B to B2C for the same year in the United Kingdom, France and Germany was 7.04, 7.06 and 7.09 respectively, compared with 7.07 for the United States. If one looks at the contribution of total e-Commerce to national income, measured by Gross Domestic Product (GDP), the results do not stand up to many of the hyped claims.

Notwithstanding the rise and then fall in e-Commerce revenues in 2000 and 2001, and allowing for the size of the US economy, e-Commerce represents a small proportion of all economic transactions. The essential issue is that the dominant virtual medium is television and is likely to remain so for a long time, so that adaptations of this technology to the demands of e-Commerce are more likely to generate longer-term benefits and greater market access. There is also a tendency to conflate goods and services that can be downloaded via a modem, for example software and music, with more physical goods that have to be delivered to the home or pick-up point. In other words, there is as much variability in e-Commerce transactions as there is in conventional ones.

Examples of B2C include Amazon.com, the on-line retailer of books, music and games. Amazon started achieving profitability ($5 million) only in the last quarter of 2001 after having invested $3 billion in its short life, much of which has been spent establishing itself as an on-line brand and creating a fulfilment system. The disadvantage for many B2C companies dealing in tangible goods is the lack of a distribution system that is reliable and economically efficient. These firms to date have difficulty obtaining the economies of scale and scope derived by large retail outlets in conventional shopping malls.

Much of B2B activity is associated with the operation and management of supply chains. Advances in information and communications technology (ICT) have facilitated the development of real-time supply chains, that is, orders for goods and services that are activated immediately. For example, the Ford Motor Company had proposed to link its suppliers of car parts to Ford's production sites through their Web sites so that adjustments in demand for parts could occur instantaneously. However, rather like Just-in-Time (JIT) inventory systems, instantaneous delivery of large items of inventory from anywhere in the globe was not realizable owing to size and cost restraints.

The technology does speed up the turnover time of production through instant receipt and processing of orders. What these changes produce is an electronic continuum along which supply chains find themselves in terms of the two types of flow:

- Those which use electronic mediation to organize their supply chains, but whose tangible goods require physical transportation, and whose payment is handled using traditional inter-company means.
- Products whose entire supply chain can be mediated by electronic means, in terms of product, payment and its mediation. So digital artefacts, for example computer programs can be developed, and then searched for, ordered, invoiced, paid for and delivered to customers using wholly electronic means.

Chaffey's taxonomy includes other less well cited e-Commerce models such as C2C and C2B. Consumer-to-Consumer (C2C) implies the sale of goods and services between individuals, often via auction sites such as eBay. Consumer-to-Business (C2B) implies individuals selling goods and services to companies. Examples include the sale of cars by individuals to companies. Conceptually in these cases, it is difficult to define who is the consumer and who is the producer. By definition, a consumer does not sell. Such models persist even though the semantic irregularities demand otherwise, partly because no better descriptions currently exist, and that these are part of marketing strategies and ploys by particular companies.

A more concrete model is Business-to-Public Institution, or, more commonly in the United Kingdom, Business-to-Government (B2G). This relates to the trade in goods and services between the private sector and the different forms of government, whether local, regional or national. This particular description is gaining greater resonance as governments in the advanced economies seek to promote the concept of e-Government. A final model is the User-to-User or Peer-to-Peer, which is styled P2P. This implies a relationship between two individuals that is electronically mediated but not via any central body. Freenet is an example of a network that promotes the digital exchange of music artefacts on a P2P basis.

THE CONCEPT OF BUSINESS ETHICS

Ethics is about understanding right and wrong. Business ethics is an increasingly acknowledged part of business life, and this is no less true for e-Business. The concept of business ethics and looks particularly at how they relate to e-Business. It will discuss the extent to which ethical e-Business issues are distinctive, how they result in particularly challenging dilemmas because of the need to rely on computers and evolving debates about ethics in cyberspace. In theoretical perspectives on business decision making, the dominant discourse is often focused on maximizing profit for company shareholders alone.

This perspective is increasingly proving to be inadequate. In practice, profit maximization in the long term may best be achieved by making sustainable decisions that take the consequences for trust between stakeholders (including employees, competitors, suppliers, customers, the local community and shareholders) into account. This is called 'enlightened self-interest' - where business managers take 'ethical' decisions because of the positive impact on the financial bottom line.

It is far from being the only reason for the increasing acknowledgement of business ethics. Some business people see the primary role of business as being other than profit maximization. Owner-managers of small firms, for example, have been found to be particularly concerned about the financial and personal welfare of their employees. Business and managers have increasing power as a result of their activities, and with it comes responsibility for their actions.

While there are common understandings of right and wrong in business life which we use every day and see in newspaper headlines, a detailed consideration of ethics in business cannot rely on shallow statements of how we ought to behave. It is necessary to draw on well established theories of ethics. Here the briefest of introductions will be given to some of the key ethical perspectives. Further reading on ethics is strongly recommended.

Ethical theories offer frameworks by which individuals can reflect on the acceptability of actions taken and evaluate moral judgements and moral character. The theories are normative, and outline ways of assessing good and bad behaviour, usually on the basis that decisions about moral practices can be cognitively arrived at. The purpose of the application of ethical theory is *not* to make blanket judgements about the rights or wrongs of the actions observed. The theory enables a systematic analysis using established structures for analysing behaviour from the perspective of moral philosophy. Ethical egoism, utilitarianism, Kantianism, discourse ethics theory and virtue theory.

Ethical egoism and utilitarianism are consequentialist theories. This means that, when considering whether an act is right or wrong, the actor considers the likely outcome of that act. Both theories suffer from the fact that outcomes can be difficult to predict and they also ignore the individual rights of others.The ethical egoist acts in a way which furthers his or her own self-interest (although it may be 'enlightened' self-interest). Faced with the possibility, for example, of copying a competitor's Web page design, the ethical egoist will weigh up what the likely outcomes will be if he or she does so.

If caught out and labelled with a bad reputation by employers, possibly even facing legal charges of violating copyright, the ethical egoist will not copy other people's work. If the egoist will not be found out and will save him or herself time and trouble while still fulfilling work obligations, then the outcome is positive for the egoist and he or she should act in order to further their own self-interest. The theory suffers from inconsistency, since the egoist simultaneously must expect that everyone else will further their own self-interests too, which may well conflict with their own advancement. Utilitarianism promotes the notion of achieving maximum happiness for society (or avoidance of pain and pursuit of pleasure).

The person acting ethically according to utilitarianism will weigh up carefully which act will result in the most positive outcomes for those individuals who will be affected by it, a kind of cost-benefit analysis for happiness. When deciding, for example, whether to undercut the prices of high-street booksellers, an Internet-based business that bases the ethics of its activities on utilitarianism would consider all the positive and negative impacts on individuals of not making their books cheaper, and all the positive and negative impacts on individuals of undercutting.

In such an example, although a price cut might result in some job losses and reduced dividends for shareholders, the weight of advantage for many customers is likely to be widespread, hence utilitarianism might see price undercutting on the Web as ethical.Kantianism is a very important ethical theory.

Kant argued that every individual must seek to do his or her duty. He defined 'duty' very precisely as obedience to the 'categorical imperative', which is what an individual would consider to be the rational, universal, ethical action.

The act is the focus of attention in Kantian ethics and an ethical act is one which complies with the categorical imperative, i.e.:

- It is universalizable - if it is right in one situation for one person, it must be right in every situation for everyone.
- It respects other people and never uses them as a means to the actor's end.

This approach is clearly quite different from the consequentialist perspectives. For Kant the consequences of an act do not matter. It follows that it is our ethical duty not to lie, cheat or steal, to keep promises and not to use others. Discourse ethics theory focuses on the process by which a decision is reached. Ethical actions are those which are reached by full, open discussion including all those who are connected in any way with a decision. For a business this means including all stakeholders actively in decision making. This is impracticable in some instances, and is not always culturally readily achievable, since some groups are more disposed to work towards consensus than others.

The Chinese government, for example, seeks to block access by its citizens to Web sites containing material deemed inimical to the Chinese Communist Party. They do so by blocking access to two Californian search engines, Google and Altavista, via Chinese internet service providers. This action, while no doubt well intentioned, also blocks the autonomy and free choice of the citizens. They have no opportunity to voice their preference, negotiate or discuss the issue. Power is held by one party, unless individuals have the technical ability to overcome the restrictions, for example by using a numerical address.

Table. Summary of Ethical Theories

Theory	Basis	Characteristics
Ethical egoism	Consequence-based: maximize own selfinterest	Promote own well-being above everyone else's
Utilitarianism	Consequence-based: maximize utility	Greatest good of the greatest number
Kantianism	Act-based	Act in a way which is universalizable Treat people as ends in themselves, never means to ends
Discourse ethics theory	Process-based	Consensus by full, open discussion
Virtue theory	Character-based	What sort of person should I be?

Virtue theory considers the character of the individual who acts. A virtuous person is one who classically possesses characteristics of justice, wisdom, temperance and courage. Modern-day virtues include co-operation, loyalty, friendliness and trustworthiness. However, there is no definitive list of virtues, and they may be culturally distinctive.

In the realms of e-Business, many of the issues are still finding legal precedent. Most of the ethical theories incorporate reference to legal perspectives, for example Kantians will on the whole follow the law, as will ethical egoists, since it is likely to be in their own self-interest so to do. In the global context of e-Commerce, the law simply does not provide sufficient, worldwide guidance on how e-Business managers should behave. Ethics can help fill that gap.

ARE THERE DISTINCT ETHICAL ISSUES IN E-BUSINESS?

e-Business enthusiasts will be well aware of the technical and financial advantages of e-Commerce. There are also ethical benefits. These include the potential to remove prejudice and barriers, as transactions are carried out via disembodied computer screens.

The lack of need for a physical presence in a particular place, as long as computer access is available, opens up all kinds of possibilities for freedom of mobility and inclusion of those with physical needs which make working in an office environment difficult (ranging from physical disability to a distinct preference for working on a beach!). Internet-based business activities are opening up markets, improving information provision about different products, including non-corporate information. (For example, typing 'Nike' into a search engine finds company pages as well as sites about Nike products alleging human rights abuses by the company.) The Internet allows consumers much greater access to information, opening up the market and undermining monopolies. Such impacts are highly ethical according to a utilitarian perspective.

Freedom of speech is often cited as one of the benefits of cyberspace. Freedom of speech is a fundamental human right, yet it is not enjoyed by all. The Internet can be a means of increasing freedom of speech. Technology and law have been unsuccessful as a means of controlling what is on the Web. This means, at one extreme, that abhorrent pornography is available and that inaccurate claims made in relation to e-Business products or services are equally difficult to control.

We generally become aware of ethical issues through dilemmas, conflicts and discomfort with situations, behaviours and acts. The more challenging aspects of e-Business, particularly the implications for workplaces reliant on ICTs and the new issues prevalent to cyberspace.

COMPUTERS IN THE WORKPLACE

The expansion of e-Business goes hand in hand with reliance on computers in the workplace. Organizations have become information technology-intensive in their operations, and this in itself has significant implications for employees.

Advantages and Changes

Anyone who works in an office will have noticed some of the great advantages of workplace computerization. Among other advantages, the new communication medium eases the sharing of information. For instance, UK customers of www. Amazon.co.uk will find that they are 'known' to the German www.

Amazon.de Web site when they log on there for the first time. There is no need to re-register even though a new retail Web site has been accessed. Customer records kept on an electronic database mean that more and more data can be gathered and marketing targeted at individuals. The computerization of many activities results in at least the potential for reducing paper files and archives.

In fact the 'paperless office' turns out to be mythical, as some aspects of computerization result in an increase of paper production (for example, the ease of producing several edited versions of a report rather than one completed one), and individuals do not have sufficient confidence that an electronic file can be held with the same security as a paper one. Despite the evident advantages of computers, the fallibility of computers and computer systems and the fragility of electronic data do not lend credibility to reliance on strictly electronic records.

Disadvantages

Prolonged computer use without a break can result in eyestrain and serious problems from repetitive strain injury (RSI), for example from constant use of the same muscles in manipulating the mouse. Back problems are increasingly common in the workplace as individuals maintain constant, inappropriate positions while sitting at a desk to use a computer. Ergonomic solutions to these problems are available but not widely used.

Damage to the environment as a result of computer use is unknown, but the speed of technological updates results in a very short life cycle of computers as two- or three-year-old' machines are discarded as being out of date. In addition of course, computers require constant electricity supply. Some suggest that teleworking and the reduced need for face-to-face interaction may have negative psychological effects on individuals, who experience isolation and the loss of 'social glue'. Others argue that computerization enables social freedom for the shy and the removal of potential prejudice, as race, age and disability cannot be seen through a computer screen of text.

COMPUTER-MEDIATED COMMUNICATION

One of the key questions confronted by business ethicists is whether computer-mediated communication (CMC) requires fundamentally different ethical considerations than have gone before. Those who argue that there is a difference cite areas such as the following for their reasoning: the changed relationship between humans, the fragility and ownership of electronic data, use and abuse of workplace facilities, and monitoring and privacy. While none of these factors is in itself unique, the combination of new perspectives, and the rapidity with which new technologies are becoming the norm in the workplace, do establish a heightening of certain issues in a unique combination in relation to ethical use. Here the focus is particularly on electronic mail and Internet technology and use.

The Changing Nature of Human Relationships

A key characteristic of the computerized workplace is the changing nature of relationships between humans that ICTs have enabled. There can be a lack of 'social glue' in a highly computerized world, where there is no natural space for casual conversation.

The extent to which e-mails are really different from previous technologies such as communication by fax machine or disembodied telephone is unclear. There *is* a difference: we say things in e-mail that we might never say in hard copy or verbally, and different rules of grammar, punctuation, and even honest representation and use of crude language, seem to apply.

In a UK context, personal relationships are an important bond in managing business and organizations. This is achieved even where communication technologies enable increased personal distance between those communicating. Just as a 'business' telephone call may begin with some social conversation, an e-mail too can combine the social and strictly functional business for which it is composed. Electronic communication may even support 'social glue' by enabling naturally shy people to take part in communication fully without the psychological pressure of face-to-face contact.

The removal of the immediate proximity of sender and receiver of messages may have Equal Opportunity implications. While telephone helps prevent some prejudicial judgements such as those based on skin colour, age or dress, dialect and manner of speaking may still be discerned. The typewritten script of an e-mail, although not guaranteeing grammatical accuracy, offers everyone the opportunity of an equally professional status. Interestingly some interpret this as 'coldness' and use symbols to convey emotions such as happiness (), thereby personalizing their message.

CMC also allows the leaving of messages for respondents to pick up as and when is convenient for the respondent, and potentially avoids the need for individuals to waste time chasing up absent colleagues. Telephone answer machines can operate on the same principle, but an e-mail can cope with a rather more complex message. This sophistication does not prevent individuals ignoring their messages, but that is a human rather than electronic frailty! CMC commonly allows asynchronous 'discussion', where there is a time gap between normally text-based messages being sent and responses received.

Finally, a key point here must be the combination of communication media. Where a sensitive point is being made about which the response of the receiver cannot be predicted, the messenger may choose face-to-face or telephone communication in order that the response can be read *as the message is delivered,* and the tone of delivery adjusted simultaneously. In fact, just as with other communications methods, there is still a need for 'interpersonal skills' in choosing the medium and the mode of delivery.

CMC can be seen as a liberating social force, offering an additional means of communication, and empowering those who are less comfortable with other methods. While it might be a mistake to consider it as a replacement for other means of communication, it can certainly act as a complement and, used sensibly, enables communication rather than disabling it.

Fragility and Ownership of Electronic Data

The apparent fragility of electronic data, for example the fact that important data tables can be altered with almost no trace, adds additional responsibility to the conveyors of electronic information. Issues of responsibility for accuracy and the protection of information become paramount. This, it could be argued, is one of the distinctive features of electronic communication, since systems of protection for intellectual works (such as patenting and copyright) were designed for tangible products. At the moment there is neither clear protection for electronic data nor understanding of the limits of ownership and responsibility for accuracy. Such issues are compounded by the potential for mass dissemination via the Internet and by means of electronic mail. Given that even accidental inaccuracy by experienced keyboard operators occurs at a rate of one inaccurate keystroke per 100, the potential for incorrect information dissemination is great. Similarly the ownership of electronic data, accurate or otherwise, is unclear and could have critical implications for the user and subject of information.

Even if we accept that employers own the data that is sent on their systems (that is, e-mail content sent by employees), interpretation of the data may be incorrectly handled by employers, particularly since e-mails are commonly written in shorthand and abbreviated form.

Use, Dual use and Abuse

The increasing prevalence of computer-mediated communication in the work-place has focused the minds of employers on the use of organizational equipment for non-organizational tasks. This is not of course a new phenomenon. The blurred lines between work and personal life are to be found in the use of work stationery for personal tasks, the use of private telephones for 'work' calls, the use of work telephones for 'private' calls, the reading of newspapers in work time, unpaid overtime, and so on.

Such issues are particularly relevant in office environments. Some occupations, such as factory production line work and call centre operators, are indeed more strictly controlled and delineated in the timing of their activities. There are no clear lines to be drawn in any of these cases. The introduction of widely available ICTs has again broadened the spectrum of possibilities by offering a powerful tool of information access and distribution to many employees.

A distinction can be made here between use, dual use and abuse of ICTs in the workplace. Brown (1996) distinguishes between the realms of business necessity and of individual personhood and suggests that their intersection covers the domain of workplace privacy. A link has been made between Brown's notions of 'business necessity', 'workplace privacy' and 'individual personhood' and the employment of ICTs for 'business use', 'dual use' and 'abuse'. The associations in the diagram are not absolute but they may provide a useful framework for considering the issues of the use of workplace CMC, such as e-mail and Internet access, common to any e-business.

Using the available CMC resources for business necessity is the easiest to identify. Where e-mail or the Internet are employed for purposes directly related to the functional role of the individual in the organization, there is no immediate problem.

Where e-mail or the Internet is used for purposes which have nothing whatsoever to do with the organizational business, or the well-being of the individual in doing his or her task, it might be said that there has been an abuse of the access to CMC facilities. 'Abuse' of a firm's resources can be defined as the use of e-mail by the employee to further personal rather than organizational objectives. This might include illegal activities such as hacking into national security databases, but is not restricted to them. Examples might be the circulation of offensive materials, the setting up of a personal private business on work equipment or the accessing of indecent Web sites. With few exceptions such actions amount to abuse of the organization's resources.

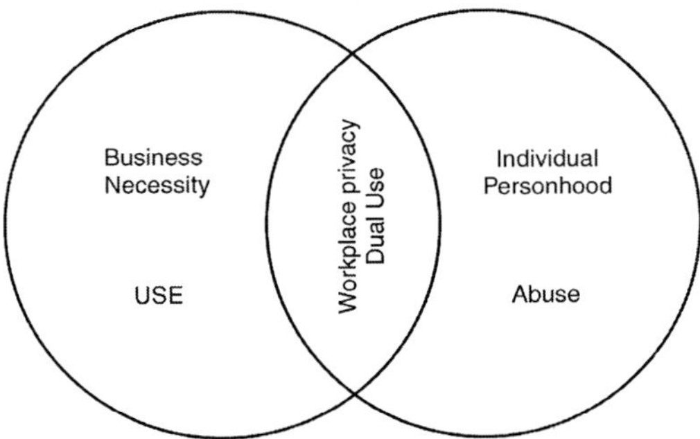

Fig. Locating the use and Abuse of ICTs in the Workplace

The most difficult area to discern is the intersection between use and abuse, the area where personal use may have some positive workplace implications, and work use may benefit the individual personally. Internet surfing for hobby interests will hone the IT skills of employees who use those same skills for work tasks. Non-work friends may enable problem solving that would otherwise cost time and resources in-house, whether they be through the resolving of ICT queries or personal counselling.

The ability of employees to resolve individual issues such as the renewal of car insurance over the Internet allows them to concentrate on work tasks. Furthermore it is natural, even desirable, that employees become friendly with colleagues, and the combining of social and work discussions within e-mails is a clear example of 'dual use'. Individuals do not leave their personal lives at home entirely, and employers should not expect them to do so. Employers might keep in mind that employees will often take work home with them, either literally or mentally.

It seems a fair reciprocal exchange to be tolerant of home life making an appearance in the workplace. Accepting employees as whole human beings, with all the benefits and some of the drawbacks this may bring, is likely to be beneficial to all in the longer term. No differentiation has been made in the discussion so far between use of workplace CMC and use of work time. This, again, is a difficult distinction. On the one hand utilization of organizational software and hardware may not in itself be considered problematic by employers. The equipment has been purchased for work reasons and once installed the incremental costs of its use are likely to be negligible. However, the work time which employees use in the pursuit of personal goals may well be an issue.

Surfing the Internet proves to be a surprisingly time-consuming activity, and responding to personal e-mails may well distract individuals from their work tasks. The relevance of time lost must to some extent depend on the type of work done. Where individuals are doing tasks strictly limited to particular hours, or even paid by the hour, time lost during the working day will be of significance.

On the other hand, for professionals who are measured by their output rather than their (intellectual or actual) presence nine to five, time lost might be considered as merely a reallocation of time use. The management of household matters in work time is inevitable in a social environment in which workdays are longer and household management responsibilities are shared between multiple earners with careers. Important in the consideration of the use and abuse of work time is the fact that the technology is readily available to monitor Internet and e-mail use of networked employees remotely.

Monitoring and Privacy

In the context of ICT development, electronic monitoring of employees - in and outside the workplace - has enormous potential for infringing the privacy of employees and customers. ICT archiving and particularly computer-mediated communication mean that employees in the workplace can be monitored to unprecedented levels. Electronic monitoring can be defined as the capture and analysis of 'data' to measure the work (not) performed by employees. These data may show Web sites accessed, e-mail traffic, e-mail content or the use of video and audio facilities. Electronic monitoring is sometimes seen as a sinister 'Big Brother is watching you' perspective on our lives.

Reasons put forward to defend the use of electronic monitoring in the workplace include the following:

- *Security.* Closed Circuit Television (CCTV) can protect against theft and violence.
- Employers pay employees to do a particular job. It could be argued that employers have a *contractual right* to check that employees are doing what they are paid to do.
- Monitoring of employees stops abuse of work time and *increases productivity*.
- Electronic monitoring is simply an electronic version of *'managing by walking about'*, which saves management time.
- Electronic means of measurement mean that performance appraisal of employees is backed up by precise statistics and is *unbiased*.
- Electronic monitoring provides data *quickly and frequently*.
- It ensures *realistic targets* are set.

Electronic monitoring may be used as a deterrent to stop inappropriate work-place behaviour, rather than being used to penalize those caught not working 100 per cent of the time. This can be likened to Jeremy Bentham's

Panopticon. The Panopticon was a circular prison with no bars. All the cells were arranged around a tower with a single guard in it. From the tower the guard could see into all the cells. However, the prisoners could not see whether they were being observed. Their behaviour was thus controlled by the fact that they *might* be being monitored. In the same way that a speed camera without a film in it can still influence motorists to keep to the legal speed limit, the fact that employees or customers know that they may be being watched means that they act as they would if they *were* being watched.On the other hand, like watching rats in a cage, constant monitoring can have uneasy effects on individuals. Those against electronic monitoring argue that:

- It constitutes an *invasion of privacy*. Being paid by an organization does not mean that it owns you.
- Monitoring implies suspicion of misbehaviour. This *undermines the trust, goodwill and loyalty* of employees toward the employer.
- Monitoring results in the setting of *unrealistic targets,* because employees cannot keep up the fastest rate constantly. The result is increasing stress, absenteeism and ultimately employee turnover.
- In a climate of increasing empowerment, monitoring erodes the independence of the individual to work in a way which suits him or her (e.g. chat to a friend between 9:30 and 10:00 but work over lunchtime) and *disempowers* the individual's control.
- Electronic monitoring is more suited to *measuring quantitative* factors than qualitative ones, hence number of phone calls rather than relationship building with potential clients is most likely to be measured in a call centre.

In most countries, legally there is generally no reason why employers should not monitor employee e-mails, yet it is unlikely to be in the employer's self-interest to exercise the right. Monitoring employees to check whether they are abusing company resources may be justified if the system is being overloaded, although setting limits would achieve the same ends. Being an employer does not mean having the right to monitor private conversations.

CAMPUS E-BUSINESS

The unprecedented flow of information across networks and between organizations, coupled with the power of computers to extract, compile, organize, and republish information, has made e-business possible. These same capabilities are also raising significant concerns and issues related to the appropriate use of institutional information and the protection of information originating or residing in college and university information systems. The developmental phase facing colleges and universities today on the road to enabling e-business as one of integration. Our progress in adopting e-business in higher education will be enabled or constrained by institutions' abilities to develop, implement, enforce, and automate complex rules that authorize these consumers to partake of university services—for example:

- What rights will distant learners have regarding access to licensed university information resources?
- How can colleges and universities protect usage logs that record student and faculty library consumption activity for materials licensed from third parties?

The privacy, access, ownership, and security issues posed by e-business are extraordinarily complex and represent as much a set of cultural, behavioral, and policy issues as technical ones. Colleges and universities have long—and correctly—been described as self-governing anarchies or adhocracies. Higher education's hallowed and well-established traditions of self-governance and shared governance are responsible for our remarkable history of achievement, service, and innovation. These traditions also make integration hard. In many ways, achieving the necessary level of technical integration to enable e-business is the least complex aspect of preparing the institution for e-business.

Many campus chief information officers (CIOs) understand what it means to reorient systems from their current functional office views to the end-user views (student, parent, alumni, inter-enterprise) that e-business will demand. In most cases, the technical tools to achieve this kind of integration exist. In short, technical integration is a significant issue that can be addressed by vision, talent, and money. The thornier integration challenges are cultural and relate to role definitions, authority and power, and values. These issues will define the boundaries of an institution's approach to, and its likelihood of success in, implementing e-business.

THE NEED FOR A POLICY FRAMEWORK TO SUPPORT E-BUSINESS

In a farsighted article, Graves, Jenkins, and Parker at the University of North Carolina described the development of an electronic information policy framework. As e-business drives the Internet and Web from an infrastructure for storing static information to one over which much of the institutional mission is delivered, the need for such a policy framework becomes overwhelming. Although sound information policies will not guarantee entry into the world of e-business, lack of these policies will bar the door. Colleges and universities will need to develop a cohesive and consistent set of policies to guide the members of their community in a number of areas, including the following:

- Digital identity and the access to institutional technology and information resources
- Use of the institution's name and trademarks
- Acquisition, retention, and disposition of information resources
- Ownership of information in institutional systems and the management of intellectual property rights

Each of these issues is enormously complex, and colleges and universities worldwide have struggled with them for years. Digital Identity and Access to Institutional Technology

AND INFORMATION RESOURCES

In the technical context, colleges and universities must develop the means to authenticate an individual as himself or herself, recognize the individual as a member of the institutional community, and confer on or deny this individual different rights and authorities as a community citizen. In physical reality, these activities are transacted in a variety of complex formal or informal ways. We can demand photo ID cards, check signature files, or wave to the familiar librarian who regulates access to the closed stacks.

The regulation of access to institutional resources in the physical context is governed by a tapestry of policies, procedures, customs, norms, and historical happenstance that computers are not yet intelligent enough to deal with. Instead, computers depend on precise information that derives absolute answers to the following questions: (1) are you who you claim to be, and (2) are you allowed to ... [consume this service, enter this building, use this parking lot]?

Not only is this a technical challenge of enormous proportions, it is a policy quagmire that requires colleges and universities to make explicit and public distinctions about the rights and privileges that accrue to different members of the academy. What rights does the president's spouse really have? What rights do lecturers have, relative to career-ladder faculty? These policy issues will become more complex as colleges and universities move into distance education and implement cradle-to-grave strategies to create relationships with promising applicants, lifelong learners, and potential donors. Of course, it is important to note that for public institutions, managing access to institutional information must be situated in the context of public records laws, which themselves are hard to reduce to simple rules that can be automated.

USE OF THE INSTITUTION'S NAME AND TRADEMARKS

The Internet and the World Wide Web are, among other things, a publishing infrastructure. Web browser technology is relatively simple to programme as well as to use, allowing "a thousand flowers to bloom." At nearly every college and university, a myriad of operational and dead Web pages make volumes of campus information and misinformation available to anyone with an Internet connection.

Many institutions provide incoming students with sufficient disk storage to encourage their development of personal Web sites. Of course, into every flower garden will come the occasional weed, snail, or other predator. From a policy perspective, the challenge posed by the Internet and the Web is the challenge of cultural integration. Colleges and universities must specify policies that regulate the appropriate use of these very public resources. At stake in this extraordinarily complex area to govern are a variety of serious legal and public relations issues, including these:

- Pornographic materials on official institutional sites
- Sale of advertising on pages containing campus trademarks
- Creation of fraudulent sites
- Commercial use of campus resources for personal gain
- Trademark infringement
- Neglect of sites that make inaccurate, anachronistic, and obsolete information available to legislators, trustees, donors, auditors, and others

All of these issues can and will emerge within the broader policy contexts that typically respect and encourage free expression by members of the institution's community. As Graves, Jenkins, and Parker advise, "Any policy will need to balance the institution's role in protecting access to sensitive or potentially objectionable information and its role in supporting an individual's right of free expression". This difficult balancing act is hardly new, but is complicated by the levels of integration anticipated by e-business applications.

ACQUISITION, RETENTION, AND DISPOSITION OF INFORMATION RESOURCES

E-business, in much of the popular literature, begins with something called "e-tailing": the marketing of the enterprise to its existing or prospective clients. In one context, higher education institutions have been doing this for years. Each year, colleges and universities acquire the files of high school students who achieve high scores on the PSAT and shower these college-bound tenth and eleventh graders with literature extolling the virtues of their campus.

In an e-business context, smart and aggressive institutions will acquire more and more information in the competition for the "best" students. These institutions will likely develop robust profiles of students to match against the target profiles of successful applicants. Similarly, the pathologies of university hospital patients will be profiled for matching against promising experimental drugs and therapies for possible targeting of such patients for clinical trials.

These practices are entrepreneurial, effective (relative to their goals), and probably beneficial; certainly college-bound students want to be discovered and patients want access to the best modes of treatment available. However, the unprecedented ability of institutions to acquire personal information, combine this information in unique ways, and store massive amounts of this information on individuals who may, or may not, be part of the institutional community will raise significant privacy and security issues.

New policies regarding what kind of information is to be collected, how this information is to be used, and how long it is to be retained will become increasingly important. The failure to develop new standards of practice in this area will invite new regulation of this area of institutional activity. The issue of individual and institutional access to this kind of information will also rise in importance and must be dealt with explicitly in campus information policy. In addition to developing the technologies and policies to ensure privacy and secure and protect information under institutional management, colleges and universities will need to devise and implement new policies to describe, manage, and protect related classes of information. Such classes of information include confidential information (tenure and promotion files), proprietary information (patents, trademarks, copyrights), privileged information (attorneyclient communications, counseling files), and trade information (public and private research activities).

E-business, among other things, assumes an unprecedented level of interoperation among the systems and data resources of "trading partners." In the future, campus suppliers will have access to institutional procurement systems, as will publishers, high schools, consortium partners, and others. This integration of systems and information will demand that policies and contracts regulate the acquisition, use, retention, and disposition by others in the newly extending community. This has already become a complex area of policy development at research universities, where the university values of open sharing of research findings clash with desires of private clinical research sponsors to protect information as proprietary.

A final area of concern under this broad umbrella is the management of licensed software and information resources. Campus information policy must respect the rights of authors and distributors. Evolving technologies and law will likely enhance authors' and distributors' ability to track the use of their licensed property and perhaps even to implement campuswide penalties when infringements are identified.

OWNERSHIP OF INFORMATION AND INTELLECTUAL PROPERTY RIGHTS

Information policy must seek to distinguish the ownership status of information embodied in institutionally owned digital storage and transport media from the responsibilities for managing this information. Information policies should strive to define the standards and care with which information resources must be managed, while recognizing the inherently decentralizing tendencies of networked information and resources. Most information policy frameworks that address networked information define and articulate a concept of information stewardship that allows the web of campus-related information to evolve in a fashion that balances the needs of individuals and local campus units with those of the institution as a whole.

Perhaps the most complex aspect of preparing the campus information policy environment for e-business is the set of policy issues surrounding the ownership and management of intellectual property generated on the campus. Colleges and universities have developed robust policies for the ownership and management of intellectual property protected by patents, but the rights to intellectual property developed by faculty and protected by copyright have traditionally remained with individual faculty. In fact, the total economic value of published college and university intellectual property has been small historically, and the institutional investment in the creation of this property has also been small.

The application of Internet, Web, and other information technologies to the core educational mission of higher education is changing all of this. Today, pioneering faculty are investing considerable time and energy to Web-enable their courses. Institutions in many cases are partnering with these faculty by providing grants to purchase release time from other obligations and by placing a variety of technical tools at the faculty's disposal.

For the first time, faculty course materials organized in this fashion can reach beyond the confines of the classroom, hence changing simultaneously the cost structure, the investment model, and the economic value of traditional course materials. Courses created in this fashion become courseware and begin to accrue many of the attributes of books, which also are evolving to become more interactive.

As the e-learning aspect of the e-business revolution evolves, institutions, their faculty, and publishers are looking at course materials as scalable economic goods that can be modularized. New pedagogical standards are evolving in concert with new neuroscientific findings about the learning process.

Institutions such as the University of Phoenix and Great Britain's Open University are investing millions of dollars in curricula for networked delivery. Faculty course notes on the Web are being reportedly pirated and repackaged for distribution by new proprietary e-business enterprises.

Clearly the new potentials posed by the integrated technologies of e-business suggest the need for new policies regarding the ownership and management of rights to faculty course materials. Such changes are, however, countercultural and could also lead to new divisions on the campus. e-business is likely to change the way institutions operate. It is a mission-critical undertaking that will challenge longstanding institutional policies and will therefore demand the careful application of change management techniques and processes.

ELEMENTS OF AN INTEGRATED POLICY FRAMEWORK

Although each institution will develop a policy that best reflects its priorities, strategies, values, and history, a framework should contain some common elements. The list that follows is offered as a starting point.

Critical Assumptions

The institution will balance the rights of individuals with the institution's responsibility to make information available to support the mission. The role of the central campus is to articulate the standards of data access and integrity and to differentiate user rights and privileges so as to achieve such balance. The following key assumption will need to be articulated:

- Under what conditions (responsibilities of resource users) and for what members of the community are access to the network, network-based services, and networked information a basic right of the campus community?

OPERATING PRINCIPLES

Policies are by definition value laden. Institutions can be well served by considering bounding the framework by principles. At the University of North Carolina (UNC), information policy is bounded by principles that do the following:

- Identify the responsibility for making information available
- Limit the institution's regulatory responsibility for information for which it is not responsible
- Assume institutional responsibility for defining access privileges to its information for classes of users

The UNC policy framework and those of other leading institutions also outline in broad terms legal, ethical, technical, governance, and economic issues for the purpose of acculturating the policy reader to the complexity of the issues and the basic values of the institution.

Information Access and Security

It will be important to establish the notion that institutional electronic information resources—including data, applications, systems, "We don't want just anyone coming in here and making toast. Type in your password." hardware, software, and networks—are valuable. Institutional assets, including electronic information resources, must be protected according to the nature of the risk and to the sensitivity and criticality of the resource being protected.

Information policy should endeavor to identify major classes of information assets requiring protection and assigning to them differential levels of protection. Information classes might include privileged information, personal information, personnel information, and public records.Areas in which security-related policies need to be addressed include the following, paraphrased from the University of California's "Business and Finance Bulletin IS-3: Electronic Information Security":

- Logical security. The policy should identify security measures to be enforced through software, network, or procedural controls (version management, and so forth), as well as communications security and reduction of risk from intrusive computer software. Various measures include end-user access controls, system administration access controls, applications software development and change control, and controls on data backup, retention, data privacy, and data transfers and downloads. Encryption policies will also need to be developed as these capabilities become ubiquitous, as will policies that specify which applications and resources must be protected by firewalls.

- Physical security. Even in an e-business environment, there are physical disaster controls and access controls (for example, check stock and other financial instruments) that must be covered by institutional policy.
- Managerial security. Although there are unique risks inherent in the management of electronic and particularly networked information resources, many of the risks remain people related. An information policy framework should attempt to integrate institutional policy related to bonding and background checking for personnel with access to sensitive and critical information. Procedures to implement such policies should also identify the processes for altering authorities when changes in duties or employment status occur.
- Responsibilities. An information policy framework must identify both those responsible for maintaining the policy and those responsible for its implementation. Ideally, policy compliance escalation procedures should be specified.
- Definitions and authorities. A policy framework should define key terms such as authorized user, disaster, and security. Information management roles such as stewardship and proprietorship should also be defined. Regulations and laws that govern an institution's access and security policies should be referenced, including public records law.
- Digital certificates. An emerging technology to meet the needs of electronic security in the networked context is the use of public key infrastructure and digital certificates. Institutions that implement certificate authorities and digital certificates also will need to develop congruent policies that identify processes for approving authorities, standards for certificates, and identification of certificates. Policies will have to be enacted that govern whether certificates are issued to individuals, servers, or certificate authorities; what the responsibilities of these authorities
- Are; and what the expiry dates of these certificates will be. Finally, policy in this evolving arena will need to describe the processes for registering and issuing certificates, maintaining a repository of certificates and public keys, revoking or renewing certificates, and managing the certificate authority's private key.

Disaster Protection

The information policy framework should describe the institution's plans, policies, and procedures for ensuring business continuity, including plans for testing critical systems periodically.The disaster recovery plan should identify emergency response procedures and specify teams of personnel responsible for responding to emergency situations.

E-MAIL

Although e-mail is not specifically a tool of e-business, its governance as a critical element of the overall campus information policy framework is critical. Institutions are advised to develop specific policies related to e-mail that establish the following elements:

- E-mail accounts as institutional property
- The institution's service commitments regarding e-mail
- The ownership of information produced and received using institutional mail accounts
- Institutional access to information in mail accounts under normal or extraordinary (emergency, investigative, and so forth) conditions
- Allowable use, including use for individual commercial gain, representations, and false identity
- Security and confidentiality of information in institutional mail accounts
- Individual and institutional responsibilities and authorities for ensuring compliance with policy

INTELLECTUAL PROPERTY

Policy related to the management and ownership of intellectual property is highly complex. For intellectual property not developed on campus and covered by copyrights, patents, licenses, or other contracts, the policy parameters tend to be straightforward:

- Software resident on institutional hardware must be used according to the terms specified under the appropriate software license agreement.
- The institution is responsible for compliance with licenses entered into by the institution on behalf of members of its community. It should maintain the right to revoke licensed privileges in cases where violations have been identified. Substantial violations of license conditions should be specified under policy, as should the process for investigating alleged misuse and for implementing remedial action.
- Information resources such as databases, books, and journal articles are governed by copyright law or by license agreements with their publisher. Institutional policy should affirm the rights of authors, publishers, and distributors to their intellectual property; define what constitutes fair use in the context of law and licenses; and identify the processes for investigating alleged misuse and for implementing remedial action.

For intellectual property developed on campus, the institution must distinguish between so-called works for hire and other works produced in the discharge of an employee's work-related roles:

- The ownership of a work for hire is generally assumed to be the property of the institution. The information policy framework should make explicit reference to the institution's assumptions about what works are considered to be works for hire and what ownership rights the institution wishes to assert. This policy should also specify what rights individuals who are creating works for hire may have (publication of a work report in a professional journal) and what the process is for securing individual access to such works.
- The ownership of other intellectual property produced by members of the campus community is more likely to fall under an institution's faculty handbook, or in policy covering patents, or even conflict of interest and commitment. As the boundaries between course materials and published materials begin to blur, institutions will need to revisit the ownership issues as part of an integrated information policy framework.

Policy by its nature is soft, squishy, and difficult. Policy development and the policy environment are inherently value laden, and therefore there are no detailed instructions for policy formulation. Policies are for the most part context specific. A Bible college's definition of appropriate use of technology will likely differ from that of a public research university.

Policy can be integrative, and integration is the mandate that looms ahead for institutions seeking to implement e-business solutions. Colleges and universities anticipating the move to e-business must recall that e-business in many areas is not merely the application of new technology to old processes. E-business applications will open new vistas and create new risks. Extending the name and reach of your college and university can and will swell the ranks of members of your communities. As communities grow, opportunities grow. And along with opportunities come fraud, abuse, and misuse. An integrated information policy framework will be hard to institute. On the other hand, an integrated, e-business environment without a supporting policy framework will be nearly impossible to manage.

THE PURPOSE OF A BUSINESS-LEVEL STRATEGY

The purpose of a business-level strategy is to create differences between the firm's position and those of its competitors. To position itself differently from competitors, a firm must decide whether it intends to *perform activities differently* or to *perform different activities*. In fact, "choosing to perform activities differently or to perform different activities than rivals" is the essence of business-level strategy. Thus, the firm's business-level strategy is a deliberate choice about how it will perform the value chain's primary and support activities in ways that create unique value.

Indeed, in the complex 21st-century competitive land-scape, successful use of a business-level strategy results only when the firm learns how to integrate the activities it performs in ways that create competitive advantages that can be used to create value for customers. Firms develop an activity map to show how they integrate the activities they perform. The manner in which Southwest has integrated its activities is the foundation for the successful use of its inte-grated cost leadership/differentiation strategy. We describe how Southwest Airlines is *killing* its competitors. The tight integration among Southwest's activities is a key source of the firm's ability to operate more profitably than its competitors.

Southwest Airlines has configured the activities it performs such that there are six strategic themes—limited passenger service; frequent, reliable departures; lean, highly productive ground and gate crews; high aircraft utilization; very low ticket prices; and short-haul, point-to-point routes between midsized cities and secondary airports. Individual clusters of tightly linked activities make it possible for the outcome of a strategic theme to be achieved. For example, no meals, no seat assignments, and no baggage transfers form a cluster of individual activities that support the strategic theme of limited passenger service. Southwest's tightly integrated activities make it difficult for competitors to imitate the firm's integrated cost leadership/differentiation strategy.

The firm's culture influences these activities and their integration and contributes to the firm's ability to continuously identify additional ways to differentiate Southwest's service from its competitors' as well as to lower its costs. In fact, the firm's unique culture and customer service, both of which are sources of differentiated customer features, are competitive advantages rivals have not been able to imitate, although some have tried. US Airways' Metro-Jet subsidiary, United Airlines' United Shuttle, and Continental Airlines' Continental Lite all failed in attempts to imitate Southwest's strategy. Hindsight shows that these competitors offered low prices to customers, but weren't able to operate at costs close to those of Southwest or to provide customers with any notable sources of differentiation, such as a unique experience while in the air. Fit among activities is a key to the sustainability of competitive advantage for all firms, including Southwest Airlines.

As Michael Porter comments, "Strategic fit among many activities is fundamental not only to competitive advantage but also to the sustainability of that advantage. It is harder for a rival to match an array of interlocked activities than it is merely to imitate a particular sales-force approach, match a process technology, or replicate a set of product features. Positions built on systems of activities are far more sustainable than those built on individual activities."

TYPES OF BUSINESS-LEVEL STRATEGIES

Firms choose from among five business-level strategies to establish and defend their desired strategic position against competitors: *cost leadership, differentiation, focused cost leadership, focused differentiation,* and *integrated cost leadership/differentiate.* Each business-level strategy helps the firm to establish and exploit a particular *competitive advantage* within a particular *competitive scope.* How firms integrate the activities they perform within each different business-level strategy demonstrates how they differ from one another. Thus, firms have different activity maps, meaning, for example, that Southwest Airlines' activity map differs from those of competitors Jet- Blue, Continental, American Airlines, and so forth.

Superior integration of activities increases the likelihood of being able to outperform competitors and to earn aboveaverage returns as a result of doing so. When selecting a business-level strategy, firms evaluate two types of potential competitive advantage: "lower cost than rivals, or the ability to differentiate and command a premium price that exceeds the extra cost of doing so." Having lower cost derives from the firm's ability to perform activities differently than rivals; being able to differentiate indicates the firm's capacity to perform different activities.

Thus, based on the nature and quality of its internal resources, capabilities, and core competencies, a firm seeks to form either a cost competitive advantage or a uniqueness competitive advantage as the basis for implementing a particular business-level strategy. There are two types of competitive scope—broad target and narrow target. Firms serving a broad target market seek to use their competitive advantage on an industry-wide basis. A narrow competitive scope means that the firm intends to serve the needs of a narrow target customer group. With focus strategies, the firm "selects a segment or group of segments in the industry and tailors its strategy to serving them to the exclusion of others." Buyers with particular needs and buyers located in specific geographic regions are examples of narrow target customer groups.

A firm could also strive to develop a combined cost/uniqueness competitive advantage as the foundation for serving a target customer group that is larger than a narrow segment but not as comprehensive as a broad customer group. In this instance, the firm uses the integrated cost leadership/ differentiation strategy. None of the five business-level strategies is inherently or universally superior to the others.

The effectiveness of each strategy is contingent both on the opportunities and threats in a firm's external environment and on the possibilities provided by the firm's unique resources, capabilities, and core competencies. It is critical, therefore, for the firm to select a business-level strategy that is based on a match between the opportunities and threats in its external environment and the strengths of its internal environ-ment as shown by its core competencies.

COST LEADERSHIP STRATEGY

The cost leadership strategy is an integrated set of actions taken to produce goods or services with features that are acceptable to customers at the lowest cost, relative to that of competitors. Firms using the cost leadership strategy sell no-frills, standardized goods or services to the industry's most typical customers.

Cost leaders' goods and services must have competitive levels of differentiation in terms of features that create value for customers. Indeed, emphasizing cost reductions while ignoring competitive levels of differentiation is ineffective. At the extreme, concentrating only on reducing costs could find the firm very efficiently producing products that no customer wants to purchase. The firm using the cost leadership strategy targets a broad customer segment or group. Cost leaders concentrate on finding ways to lower their costs relative to those of their competitors by constantly rethinking how to complete their primary and support activities to reduce costs still further while maintaining competitive levels of differentiation. Cost leader Greyhound Lines Inc. , for example, continuously seeks ways to reduce the costs it incurs to provide bus service while offering customers an acceptable experience.

Recently Greyhound sought to improve the quality of the experience customers have when paying the firm's low prices for its services by "refurbishing buses, updating terminals, adding greeters and improving customer service training." As primary activities, inbound logistics and outbound logistics often account for significant portions of the total cost to produce some goods and services.

Research suggests that having a competitive advantage in terms of logistics creates more value when using the cost leadership strategy than when using the differentiation strategy. Thus, cost leaders seeking competitively valuable ways to reduce costs may want to concentrate on the primary activities of inbound logistics and outbound logistics.

Cost leaders also carefully examine all support activities to find additional sources of potential cost reductions. Developing new systems for finding the optimal combination of low cost and acceptable quality in the raw materials required to produce the firm's goods or services is an example of how the procurement support activity can facilitate successful use of the cost leadership strategy.

Big Lots Inc. uses the cost leadership strategy. With its vision of being "The World's Best Bargain Place, " Big Lots is the largest broadline closeout discount chain in the United States. Operating under the format names of Big Lots, Big Lots Furniture, Wisconsin Toy, Consolidated International, Big Lots Capital, and Big Lots Wholesale, the firm strives constantly to drive its costs lower by relying on what some analysts see as a highly disciplined merchandise cost and inventory management system.

The firm's stores sell name-brand products at prices that are 15 to 35 per cent below those of discount retailers and roughly 70 per cent below those of traditional retailers. Big Lots' buyers travel the country looking through manufacturer overruns and discontinued styles, finding goods priced well below wholesale prices. In addition, the firm buys from overseas suppliers. Big Lots thinks of itself as the undertaker of the retailing business, purchasing merchandise that others can't sell or don't want.

The target customer is one seeking what Big Lots calls the "closeout moment, " which is the feeling customers have after they recognize their significant savings from buying a brand name item at a steeply discounted price.

The customer need that Big Lots satisfies is to access the differentiated features and capabilities of brand-name products, but at a fraction of their initial cost. The tight integration of purchasing and inventory management activities across its full set of stores is the main core competence Big Lots uses to satisfy its customers' needs. Firms use value-chain analysis to determine the parts of the company's operations that create value and those that do not.

The primary and support activities that allow a firm to create value through the cost leadership strategy. Companies unable to link the activities through the activity map they form typically lack the core competencies needed to successfully use the cost leadership strategy. Effective use of the cost leadership strategy allows a firm to earn above-average returns in spite of the presence of strong competitive forces.

Rivalry with Existing Competitors

Having the low-cost position is a valuable defence against rivals. Because of the cost leader's advantageous position, rivals hesitate to compete on the basis of price, especially before evaluating the potential outcomes of such competition. Wal-Mart is known for its ability to both control and reduce costs, making it difficult for firms to compete against it on the basis of costs. The discount retailer achieves strict cost control in several ways: "Wal-Mart's 660, 000-square-foot main headquarters, with its drab gray interiors and frayed carpets, looks more like a government building than the home of one of the world's largest corporations. Business often is done in the no-frills cafeteria, and suppliers meet with managers in stark, cramped rooms. Employees have to throw out their own garbage at the end of the day and double up in hotel rooms on business trips."

The former Kmart's decision to compete against Wal-Mart on the basis of cost contributed to the firm's failure and subsequent bankruptcy filing. Its competitively inferior distribution system—an inefficient and high-cost system compared with Wal-Mart's— is one of the factors that prevented Kmart from having a competitive cost structure. Although Wal-Mart is favorably positioned in terms of rivalry with its competitors, there are actions firms can take to successfully compete against this retailing giant. We discuss these actions in the Strategic Focus. Notice that in each instance, competitors able to outperform Wal-Mart complete one or more activities that create value for customers better or differently than Wal-Mart.

Bargaining Power of Buyers

Powerful customers can force a cost leader to reduce its prices, but not below the level at which the cost leader's next-most-efficient industry competitor can earn average returns. Although powerful customers might be able to force the cost leader to reduce prices even below this level, they probably would not choose to do so. Prices that are low enough to prevent the next-most-efficient competitor from earning average returns would force that firm to exit the market, leaving the cost leader with less competition and in an even stronger position.

Customers would thus lose their power and pay higher prices if they were forced to purchase from a single firm operating in an industry without rivals. Consider Wal-Mart in this regard. Part of the reason this firm's prices continue to be the lowest available is that to successfully compete against competitors that are also trying to implement a cost leadership strategy, Wal-Mart continuously searches for ways to reduce its costs relative to competitors'. Thus, customers benefit by Wal -Mart having to compete against others trying to use the cost leadership strategy and lowering its prices in the course of engaging in competitive battles.

Bargaining Power of Suppliers

The cost leader operates with margins greater than those of competitors. Among other benefits, higher margins relative to those of competitors make it possible for the cost leader to absorb its suppliers' price increases. When an industry faces substantial increases in the cost of its supplies, only the cost leader may be able to pay the higher prices and continue to earn either average or above-average returns. Alternatively, a powerful cost leader may be able to force its suppliers to hold down their prices, which would reduce the suppliers' margins in the process. Wal-Mart uses its power with suppliers to extract lower prices from them. These savings are then passed on to customers in the form of lower prices, which further strengthens Wal-Mart's position relative to competitors lacking the power to extract lower prices from suppliers.

Potential Entrants

Through continuous efforts to reduce costs to levels that are lower than competitors', a cost leader becomes highly efficient. Because ever-improving levels of efficiency enhance profit margins, they serve as a significant entry barrier to potential competitors. New entrants must be willing and able to accept no-better-than-average returns until they gain the experience required to approach the cost leader's efficiency. To earn even average returns, new entrants must have the competencies required to match the cost levels of competitors other than the cost leader. The low profit margins make it necessary for the cost leader to sell large volumes of its product to earn above-average returns. However, firms striving to be the cost leader must avoid pricing their products so low that their ability to operate profitably is reduced, even though volume increases.

Product Substitutes

Compared with its industry rivals, the cost leader also holds an attractive position in terms of product substitutes. A product substitute becomes an issue for the cost leader when its features and characteristics, in terms of cost and differentiated features, are potentially attractive to the firm's customers. When faced with possible substitutes, the cost leader has more flexibility than its competitors. To retain customers, it can reduce the price of its good or service. With still lower prices and competitive levels of differentiation, the cost leader increases the probability that customers will prefer its product rather than a substitute.

Competitive Risks of the Cost Leadership Strategy

The cost leadership strategy is not risk free. One risk is that the processes used by the cost leader to produce and distribute its good or service could become obsolete because of competitors' innovations. These innovations may allow rivals to produce at costs lower than those of the original cost leader, or to provide additional differentiated features without increasing the product's price to customers.

A second risk is that too much focus by the cost leader on cost reductions may occur at the expense of trying to understand customers' perceptions of "competitive levels of differentiation." As noted earlier, Wal-Mart is well known for constantly and aggressively reducing its costs. At the same time, however, the firm must understand when a cost-reducing decision to eliminate differentiated features would create a loss of value for customers.

A final risk of the cost leadership strategy concerns imitation. Using their own core competencies, competitors sometimes learn how to successfully imitate the cost leader's strategy. When this occurs, the cost leader must increase the value that its good or service provides to customers. Commonly, value is increased by selling the current product at an even lower price or by adding differentiated features that customers value while maintaining price.

DIFFERENTIATION STRATEGY

The differentiation strategy is an integrated set of actions taken to produce goods or services that customers perceive as being different in ways that are important to them. While cost leaders serve an industry's typical customer, differentiators target customers who perceive that value is created for them by the manner in which the firm's products differ from those produced and marketed by competitors. Firms must be able to produce differentiated products at competitive costs to reduce upward pressure on the price customers pay for them. When a product's differentiated features are produced with noncompetitive costs, the price for the product can exceed what the firm's target customers are willing to pay. When the firm has a thorough understanding of what its target customers value, the relative importance they attach to the satisfaction of different needs, and for what they are willing to pay a premium, the differentiation strategy can be successfully used.

Through the differentiation strategy, the firm produces nonstandardized products for customers who value differentiated features more than they value low cost. For example, superior product reliability and durability and high-performance sound systems are among the differentiated features of Toyota Motor Corporation's Lexus products. The Lexus promotional statement—"We pursue perfection, so you can pursue living"—suggests a strong commitment to overall product quality as a source of differentiation. However, Lexus offers its vehicles to customers at a competitive purchase price.

As with Lexus products, a good's or service's unique attributes, rather than its purchase price, provide the value for which customers are willing to pay. Although it is currently experiencing difficulties, including ongoing investigations of the firm's finances, specialty retailer Krispy Kreme uses a differentiation strategy to produce premium-quality doughnuts. A unique recipe to produce its products and The Doughnut Theatre are sources of differentiation for Krispy Kreme. Continuous success with the differentiation strategy results when the firm consistently upgrades differentiated features that customers value, without significant cost increases. Because a differentiated product satisfies customers' unique needs, firms following the differentiation strategy are able to charge premium prices.

For customers to be willing to pay a premium price, however, a "firm must truly be unique at something or be perceived as unique." The ability to sell a good or service at a price that substantially exceeds the cost of creating its differentiated features allows the firm to outperform rivals and earn above-average returns. For example, shirt and neckwear manufacturer Robert Talbott follows stringent standards of craftsmanship and pays meticulous attention to every detail of production.

The firm imports exclusive fabrics from the world's finest mills to make men's dress shirts and neckwear. Single-needle tailoring is used, and precise collar cuts are made to produce shirts. According to the company, customers purchasing one of its products can be assured that they are being provided with the finest fabrics available. Thus, Robert Talbott's success rests on the firm's ability to produce and sell its differentiated products at a price significantly higher than the costs of imported fabrics and its unique manufacturing processes. Rather than costs, a firm using the differentiation strategy always concentrates on investing in and developing features that differentiate a good or service in ways that customers value.

Robert Talbott, for example, uses the finest silks from Europe and Asia to produce its "Best of Class" collection of ties. Overall, a firm using the differentiation strategy seeks to be different from its competitors on as many dimensions as possible. The less similarity between a firm's goods or services and those of competitors, the more buffered it is from rivals' actions. Commonly recognized differentiated goods include Toyota's Lexus, Ralph Lauren's wide array of product lines, and Caterpillar's heavy-duty earth-moving equipment. Thought by some to be the world's most expensive and prestigious consulting firm, McKinsey and Co. is a well-known example of a firm that offers differentiated services. A good or service can be differentiated in many ways. Unusual features, responsive customer service, rapid product innovations and technological leadership, perceived prestige and status, different tastes, and engineering design and performance are examples of approaches to differentiation. There may be a limited number of ways to reduce costs. In contrast, virtually anything a firm can do to create real or perceived value is a basis for differentiation.

Consider product design as a case in point. Because it can create a positive experience for customers, design is becoming an increasingly important source of differentiation and hopefully for firms emphasizing it, of competitive advantage. Indeed, product design may be a competitive dimension that will help GM get out of the 1970s mind-set in which the firm appears to remain grounded. Some analysts believe that newly formed, interactive collaborations between GM designers and engineers are contributing to the development of car designs that are more stylish and visually appealing. Firms using a differentiation strategy should remember that the work being completed in terms of all competitive dimensions should be oriented to satisfying customers' needs. A firm's value chain can be Analysed to determine whether the firm is able to link the activities required to create value by using the differentiation strategy. Examples of primary and support activities that are commonly used to differentiate a good or service.

Companies without the skills needed to link these activities cannot expect to successfully use the differentiation strategy. Next, we explain how firms using the differentiation strategy can successfully position themselves in terms of the five forces of competition to earn above-average returns.

Rivalry with Existing Competitors

Customers tend to be loyal purchasers of products that are differentiated in ways that are meaningful to them. As their loyalty to a brand increases, customers' sensitivity to price increases is reduced.

The relationship between brand loyalty and price sensitivity insulates a firm from competitive rivalry. Thus, Robert Talbott's "Best of Class" neckwear line is insulated from competition, even on the basis of price, as long as the company continues to satisfy the differentiated needs of its customer group. Likewise, Bose is insulated from intense rivalry as long as customers continue to perceive that its stereo equipment offers superior sound quality at a competitive purchase price.

Bargaining Power of Buyers

The uniqueness of differentiated goods or services reduces customers' sensitivity to price increases. Customers are willing to accept a price increase when a product still satisfies their perceived unique needs better than a competitor's offering can. Thus, the golfer whose needs are uniquely satisfied by Callaway golf clubs will likely continue buying those products even if their cost increases. Similarly, the customer who has been highly satisfied with a 10-year-old Louis Vuitton wallet will probably replace that wallet with another one made by the same company even though the purchase price is higher than the original one.

Purchasers of brand-name food items will accept price increases in those products as long as they continue to perceive that the product satisfies their unique needs at an acceptable cost. Loyal customers of Abercrombie and Fitch Co. 's "preppy but edgy casual clothing at high prices" continue to buy the products even as they become more expensive. In all of these instances, the customers are relatively insensitive to price increases because they do not think that an acceptable product alternative exists.

Bargaining Power of Suppliers

Because the firm using the differentiation strategy charges a premium price for its products, suppliers must provide high-quality components, driving up the firm's costs. However, the high margins the firm earns in these cases partially insulate it from the influence of suppliers in that higher supplier costs can be paid through these margins. Alternatively, because of buyers' relative insensitivity to price increases, the differen-tiated firm might choose to pass the additional cost of supplies on to the customer by increasing the price of its unique product.

Potential Entrants

Customer loyalty and the need to overcome the uniqueness of a differentiated product present substantial barriers to potential entrants. Entering an industry under these conditions typically demands significant investments of resources and patience while seeking customers' loyalty.

Product Substitutes

Firms selling brand-name goods and services to loyal customers are positioned effectively against product substitutes. In contrast, companies without brand loyalty face a higher probability of their customers switching either to products that offer differentiated features that serve the same function or to products that offer more features and perform more attractive functions.

Competitive Risks of the Differentiation Strategy

As with the other business-level strategies, the differentiation strategy is not risk free. One risk is that customers might decide that the price differential between the differentiator's product and the cost leader's product is too large. In this instance, a firm may be offering differentiated features that exceed target customers' needs. The firm then becomes vulnerable to competitors that are able to offer customers a combination of features and price that is more consistent with their needs. Another risk of the differentiation strategy is that a firm's means of differentiation may cease to provide value for which customers are willing to pay.

A differentiated product becomes less valuable if imitation by rivals causes customers to perceive that competitors offer essentially the same good or service, but at a lower price. For example, Walt Disney Company operates different theme parks, including The Magic Kingdom, Epcot Center, and the newly developed Animal Kingdom. Each park offers entertainment and educational opportunities. However, Disney's competitors, such as Six Flags Corporation, also offer entertainment and educational experiences similar to those available at Disney's locations. To ensure that its facilities create value for which customers will be willing to pay, Disney continuously reinvests in its operations to more crisply differentiate them from those of its rivals.

A third risk of the differentiation strategy is that experience can narrow customers' perceptions of the value of a product's differentiated features. For example, customers having positive experiences with generic tissues may decide that the differentiated features of the Kleenex product are not worth the extra cost. Similarly, while a customer may be impressed with the quality of a Robert Talbott "Best of Class" tie, positive experiences with less expensive ties may lead to a conclusion that the price of the "Best of Class" tie exceeds the benefit. To counter this risk, firms must continue to meaningfully differentiate their product for customers at a price they are willing to pay.

Counterfeiting is the differentiation strategy's fourth risk. Makers of counterfeit goods—products that attempt to convey a firm's differentiated features to customers at significantly reduced prices—are a concern for many firms using the differentiation strategy. For example, Callaway Golf Company's success at producing differentiated products that create value, coupled with golf 's increasing global popularity, has created great demand for counterfeited Callaway equipment.

Through the U. S. Customs Service's "Project Teed Off " programme, agents seized over 110 shipments with a total of more than 100, 000 counterfeit Callaway golf club components over a three-year period. Altria Group's domestic tobacco division, Philip Morris USA, files lawsuits against retailers selling counterfeit versions of its cigarettes, such as Marlboro. Judgments Philip Morris has won in these suits include immediate discontinuance of selling the counterfeit products as well as significant financial penalties for any future violations. Pfizer is placing radio tags on bottles of Viagra. The small computer-like chips allow Pfizer to track each bottle of Viagra and confirm its legitimacy.

THEORETICAL ISSUES IN BUSINESS ETHICS

CONFLICTING INTERESTS

Business ethics can be examined from various new perspectives, including the perspective of the employee, the commercial enterprise, and society as a whole. Very often, situations arise in which there is conflict between one or more of the parties, such that serving the interest of one party is a detriment to the other(s). For example, a particular outcome might be good for the employee, whereas, it would be bad for the company, society, or vice versa. Some ethicists (e.g., Henry Sidgwick) see the principal role of ethics as the harmonization and reconciliation of conflicting interests.

ETHICAL ISSUES AND APPROACHES

Philosophers and others disagree about the purpose of a business ethic in society. For example, some suggest that the principal purpose of a business is to maximize returns to its owners, or in the case of a publicly-traded concern, its shareholders. Thus, under this view, only those activities that increase profitability and shareholder value should be encouraged, because any others function as a tax on profits.

Some believe that the only companies that are likely to survive in a competitive marketplace are those that place profit maximization above everything else. However, some point out that self-interest would still require a business to obey the law and adhere to basic moral rules, because the consequences of failing to do so could be very costly in fines, loss of licensure, or company reputation. The noted economist Milton Friedman was a leading proponent of this view.

Some take the position that organizations are not capable of moral agency. Under this, ethical behaviour is required of individual human beings, but not of the business or corporation.

Other theorists contend that a business has moral duties that extend well beyond serving the interests of its owners or stockholders, and that these duties consist of more than simply obeying the law. They believe a business has moral responsibilities to so-called stakeholders, people who have an interest in the conduct of the business, which might include employees, customers, vendors, the local community, or even society as a whole.

Stakeholders can also be broken down into primary and secondary stakeholders. Primary stakeholders are people that are affected directly such as stockholders, where secondary stakeholders are people who are not affected directly such as the government. They would say that stakeholders have certain rights with regard to how the business operates, and some would suggest that this includes even rights of governance.

Some theorists have adapted social contract theory to business, whereby companies become quasi-democratic associations, and employees and other stakeholders are given voice over a company's operations. This approach has become especially popular subsequent to the revival of contract theory in political philosophy, which is largely due to John Rawls' *A Theory of Justice*, and the advent of the consensus-oriented approach to solving business problems, an aspect of the "quality movement" that emerged in the 1980s. Professors Thomas Donaldson and Thomas Dunfee proposed a version of contract theory for business, which they call Integrative Social Contracts Theory.

They posit that conflicting interests are best resolved by formulating a "fair agreement" between the parties, using a combination of i) macro-principles that all rational people would agree upon as universal principles, and, ii) micro-principles formulated by actual agreements among the interested parties. Critics say the proponents of contract theories miss a central point, namely, that a business is someone's property and not a mini-state or a means of distributing social justice.

Ethical issues can arise when companies must comply with multiple and sometimes conflicting legal or cultural standards, as in the case of multinational companies that operate in countries with varying practices. The question arises, for example, ought a company to obey the laws of its home country, or should it follow the less stringent laws of the developing country in which it does business? To illustrate, United States law forbids companies from paying bribes either domestically or overseas; however, in other parts of the world, bribery is a customary, accepted way of doing business. Similar problems can occur with regard to child labour, employee safety, work hours, wages, discrimination, and environmental protection laws.

It is sometimes claimed that a Gresham's law of ethics applies in which bad ethical practices drive out good ethical practices. It is claimed that in a competitive business environment, those companies that survive are the ones that recognize that their only role is to maximize profits.

CORPORATE ETHICS POLICIES

As part of more comprehensive compliance and ethics programs, many companies have formulated internal policies pertaining to the ethical conduct of employees. These policies can be simple exhortations in broad, highly-generalized language (typically called a corporate ethics statement), or they can be more detailed policies, containing specific behavioural requirements (typically called corporate ethics codes). They are generally meant to identify the company's expectations of workers and to offer guidance on handling some of the more common ethical problems that might arise in the course of doing business. It is hoped that having such a policy will lead to greater ethical awareness, consistency in application, and the avoidance of ethical disasters.

An increasing number of companies also requires employees to attend seminars regarding business conduct, which often include discussion of the company's policies, specific case studies, and legal requirements. Some companies even require their employees to sign agreements stating that they will abide by the company's rules of conduct. Many companies are assessing the environmental factors that can lead employees to engage in unethical conduct. A competitive business environment may call for unethical behaviour. Lying has become expected in fields such as trading. An example of this are the issues surrounding the unethical actions of the Saloman Brothers.

Not everyone supports corporate policies that govern ethical conduct. Some claim that ethical problems are better dealt with by depending upon employees to use their own judgment. Others believe that corporate ethics policies are primarily rooted in utilitarian concerns, and that they are mainly to limit the company's legal liability, or to curry public favour by giving the appearance of being a good corporate citizen.

Ideally, the company will avoid a lawsuit because its employees will follow the rules. Should a lawsuit occur, the company can claim that the problem would not have arisen if the employee had only followed the code properly. Sometimes there is disconnection between the company's code of ethics and the company's actual practices. Thus, whether or not such conduct is explicitly sanctioned by management, at worst, this makes the policy duplicitous, and, at best, it is merely a marketing tool.

To be successful, most ethicists would suggest that an ethics policy should be:

- Given the unequivocal support of top management, by both word and example.
- Explained in writing and orally, with periodic reinforcement.
- Doable....something employees can both understand and perform.
- Monitored by top management, with routine inspections for compliance and improvement.
- Backed up by clearly stated consequences in the case of disobedience.
- Remain neutral and nonsexist.

Ethics Officers

Ethics officers (sometimes called "compliance" or "business conduct officers") have been appointed formally by organizations since the mid-1980s. One of the catalysts for the creation of this new role was a series of fraud, corruption and abuse scandals that afflicted the U.S. defence industry at that time. This led to the creation of the Defence Industry Initiative (DII), a pan-industry initiative to promote and ensure ethical business practices.

The DII set an early benchmark for ethics management in corporations. In 1991, the Ethics & Compliance Officer Association (ECOA) — originally the Ethics Officer Association (EOA)— was founded at the Centre for Business Ethics (at Bentley College, Waltham, MA) as a professional association for those responsible for managing organizations' efforts to achieve ethical best practices. The membership grew rapidly (the ECOA now has over 1,100 members) and was soon established as an independent organization. Another critical factor in the decisions of companies to appoint ethics/compliance officers was the passing of the Federal Sentencing Guidelines for Organizations in 1991, which set standards that organizations (large or small, commercial and non-commercial) had to follow to obtain a reduction in sentence if they should be convicted of a federal offence. Although intended to assist judges with sentencing, the influence in helping to establish best practices has been far-reaching.

In the wake of numerous corporate scandals between 2001-04 (affecting large corporations like Enron, WorldCom and Tyco), even small and medium-sized companies have begun to appoint ethics officers. They often report to the Chief Executive Officer and are responsible for assessing the ethical implications of the company's activities, making recommendations regarding the company's ethical policies, and disseminating information to employees. They are particularly interested in uncovering or preventing unethical and illegal actions. This trend is partly due to the Sarbanes-Oxley Act in the United States, which was enacted in reaction to the above scandals. A related trend is the introduction of risk assessment officers that monitor how shareholders' investments might be affected by the company's decisions.

The effectiveness of ethics officers in the marketplace is not clear. If the appointment is made primarily as a reaction to legislative requirements, one might expect the efficacy to be minimal, at least, over the short term. In part, this is because ethical business practices result from a corporate culture that consistently places value on ethical behaviour, a culture and climate that usually emanates from the top of the organization. The mere establishment of a position to oversee ethics will most likely be insufficient to inculcate ethical behaviour: a more systemic programme with consistent support from general management will be necessary. The foundation for ethical behaviour goes well beyond corporate culture and the policies of any given company, for it also depends greatly upon an individual's early moral training, the other institutions that affect an individual, the competitive business environment the company is in and, indeed, society as a whole.

BUSINESS ETHICS AS AN ACADEMIC DISCIPLINE

As an academic discipline, business ethics emerged in the 1970s. Since no academic business ethics journals or conferences existed, researchers published their papers in general management outlets, and attended general conferences, such as the Academy of Management. Over time, several peer-reviewed journals appeared, and more researchers entered the field. Especially, higher interest in business topics among academics was observed after several corporate scandals in the earlier 2000s. As of 2009, sixteen academic journals devoted to various business ethics issues existed, with Journal of Business Ethics and Business Ethics Quarterly being considered the leading A+ outlets.

RELIGIOUS VIEWS ON BUSINESS ETHICS

The historical and global importance of religious views on business ethics is sometimes underestimated in standard introductions to business ethics.

Particularly in Asia and the Middle East, religious and cultural perspectives have a strong influence on the conduct of business and the creation of business values.

Examples include:

- Islamic banking, associated with the avoidance of charging interest on loans.
- Traditional Confucian disapproval of the profit-seeking motive.
- Quaker testimony on fair dealing.

Related Disciplines

Business ethics should be distinguished from the philosophy of business, the branch of philosophy that deals with the philosophical, political, and ethical underpinnings of business and economics. Business ethics operates on the premise, for example, that the ethical operation of a private business is possible — those who dispute that premise, such as libertarian socialists, (who contend that "business ethics" is an oxymoron) do so by definition outside of the domain of business ethics proper.

The philosophy of business also deals with questions such as what, if any, are the social responsibilities of a business; management theory; theories of individualism vs. collectivism; free will among participants in the marketplace; the role of self interest; invisible hand theories; the requirements of social justice; and natural rights, especially property rights, in relation to the business enterprise.

Business ethics is also related to political economy, which is economic analysis from political and historical perspectives. Political economy deals with the distributive consequences of economic actions. It asks who gains and who loses from economic activity, and is the resultant distribution fair or just, which are central ethical issues.

Multinational Corporation

A multinational corporation (MNC) or transnational corporation (TNC), also called multinational enterprise (MNE), is a corporation or enterprise that manages production or delivers services in more than one country. It can also be referred to as an *international corporation*.

The first modern MNC is generally thought to be the Poor Knights of Christ and the Temple of Solomon, first endorsed by the pope in 1129. The key element of transnational corporations was present even back then: the British East India Company and Dutch East India Company were operating in different countries than the ones where they had their headquarters.

Nowadays many corporations have offices, branches or manufacturing plants in different countries than where their original and main headquarter is located. This is the very definition of a transnational corporation. Having multiple operation points that all respond to one headquarter. This often results in very powerful corporations that have budgets that exceed some national GDPs. Multinational corporations can have a powerful influence in local economies as well as the world economy and play an important role in international relations and globalization. The presence of such powerful players in the world economy is reason for much controversy.

Market Imperfections

It may seem strange that a corporation can decide to do business in a different country, where it doesn't know the laws, local customs or business practices. Why is it not more efficient to combine assets of value overseas with local factors of production at lower costs by renting or selling them to local investors?

One reason is that the use of the market for coordinating the behaviour of agents located in different countries is less efficient than coordinating them by a multinational enterprise as an institution The additional costs caused by the entrance in foreign markets are of less interest for the local enterprise. According to Hymer, Kindleberger and Caves, the existence of MNEs is reasoned by structural market imperfections for final products. In Hymer's example, there are considered two firms as monopolists in their own market and isolated from competition by transportation costs and other tariff and non-tariff barriers. If these costs decrease, both are forced to competition; which will reduce their profits. The firms can maximize their joint income by a merger or acquisition which will lower the competition in the shared market. Due to the transformation of two separated companies into one MNE the pecuniary externalities are going to be internalized. However, this doesn't mean that there is an improvement for the society.

This could also be the case if there are few substitutes or limited licenses in a foreign market. The consolidation is often established by acquisition, merger or the vertical integration of the potential licensee into overseas manufacturing. This makes it easy for the MNE to enforce price discrimination schemes in various countries. Therefore Humyer considered the emergence of multinational firms as "an (negative) instrument for restraining competition between firms of different nations".

Market imperfections had been considered by Hymer as structural and caused by the deviations from perfect competition in the final product markets. Further reasons are originated from the control of proprietary technology and distribution systems, scale economies, privileged access to inputs and product differentiation. In the absence of these factors, market are fully efficient. The transaction costs theories of MNEs had been developed simultaneously and independently by McManus (1972), Buckley & Casson (1976) Brown (1976) and Hennart (1977, 1982). All these authors claimed that market imperfections are inherent conditions in markets and MNEs are institutions which try to bypass these imperfections. The imperfections in markets are natural as the neoclassical assumptions like full knowledge and enforcement don't exist in real markets.

BUSINESSES AND STAKEHOLDERS

A business is owned by its shareholders. A traditional view is that the behaviour of the business is nobody's business but the owners', the shareholders who are interested in profit. A more modern view is to consider all the groups of people that are affected by a business' behaviour – employees, customers, suppliers, the local community – and not just the shareholders.

The word 'stakeholders' is used to describe this wider community of interests. Some investment funds and pension companies refuse to invest in businesses whose behaviour they disapprove of eg arms manufacturers.

BUSINESS AND ETHICS

Ethical behaviour is morally 'good' behaviour. Businesses have always been ethical to the extent that their owners and managers have been interested in ethical behaviour (sometimes very little). There is now a new and strong interest from a growing number of businesses in ethical behaviour, especially in large MNCs which operate in different societies with different ethical standards. Some businesses even employ professional philosophers to help them understand the ethical consequences of their behaviour.

The main reason for this is that society at large takes more of an interest in ethical behaviour, and society has much bigger expectations of businesses. There are Different Reasons Given for This Development.

1. Employees (including managers) are better educated than they used to be, and so understand these issues better than they used to.
2. We have a less deferential society where 'ordinary' people are more willing to questions and challenge the decisions of their 'elders and betters'.
3. Competition for customers is fiercer, and any possible reason for losing customers has to be taken seriously.
4. The same issue is developing in employment, with employers increasingly dependent on attracting high quality staff who, with more choice than they used to have, are less willing to work for morally 'iffy' businesses.
5. The media have become very good at exposing questionable behaviour. Allied to this is that information is now so easy to get hold of, and the Internet makes it easier again.
6. Business decisions can be much more complex than they used to be., especially where very advanced technology is involved, and not all the consequences are known.
7. Businesses are entering new and morally more debatable areas. A good example of this is medical businesses where new knowledge about eg genes raises the possibility of products that pose fundamental moral questions; these were simply irrelevant until recently because no-one knew how to do it.

External environment of a business refers to all those factors that directly influence the working of the business. However, these factors are outside the control of the business.

External environment shapes the kind of business activity you can have. That is why it is extremely important for business. The factors that constitute the external environment include:

- Political and Legal factors
- Economic factors
- Social and Cultural Factors
- Technological Factors
- Competitors
- Demographics of consumers.

Now whatever the business might do, it can not control all the above factors. It can only plan its business by studying the trends in these factors closely. The Political and Legal factors define the government policies. These policies determine what kind of relaxation the business has. The Economy defines that kind of economic or business activity it can have. The Social and cultural factors along with the demographics of the society defines the acceptability and sales of that product. The technological factors define the technology and its affects on business. Lastly, competitors are also one of the influential factors.

All businesses and organisations operate in a changing world and are subject to forces which are more powerful than they are, and which are beyond their control. No business can survive without continued interaction with the external environment, just as a ship at sea is subject to powerful natural forces of which it needs to be aware and deal with, organisations are influenced by forces in their external business environment. Any business strategy needs to take account of all these forces so that opportunities and threats can be identified and the organisation can navigate its way to success by matching its internal strengths to external opportunities. (A SWOT Analysis can help here.) As an aid to identifying all these external forces, a couple of acronyms come in handy.

7

Internet and Marketing Management

INTRODUCTION

In a broad sense, is becoming increasingly central to marketing strategy. Think of the trend towards mass customization, in which customers can specify their exact requirements and the production process is customized accordingly. Detailed knowledge of customer needs is essential here if the goods are to be produced on an individual basis.

Another example concerns permission marketing where specific services are provided to customers based entirely on 'permission' that the customer has given the company. This means that a travel company may be given permission by a customer to send them promotions that relate only to self-catering holidays in Florida in the month of October - and nothing else.

The company will need to be able to process and act upon this information (which of course is research data about customer preferences) and not just send the customer a general brochure that includes all of the company's holidays.

Loyalty, and hence customer retention, is based upon a thorough understanding of customer needs that can be established and maintained only by research. The economic benefits of customer retention are obvious: revenues and market share grow through repeat business and referrals, while costs fall through economies of scale and the reduced amount of effort that needs to be spent on customer acquisition and the servicing of familiar customers. McDaniel and Gates (2002) describe the example of British Airways, which researched the preferences of first-class passengers and found them to be - sleep. So, as an alternative to receiving a series of intrusive services during the flight, such passengers can now have dinner in the lounge before take-off and then enjoy an uninterrupted flight.

The Internet is becoming an increasingly important *source* of research data (known as secondary data) as well as providing a cost-effective new *medium* for the research process itself, for example as an alternative means of collecting data by completion of an online questionnaire rather than from telephone or face-to-face interviewing (known as primary data).

THE INTERNET AS A SOURCE OF SECONDARY DATA

The best way to find information on the Internet is to key in the unique Uniform Resource Locator (URL) which will take you directly to the page required, without the need to rely upon search engines. Organizations can promote their URL address on company stationery, on the side of vehicles or buildings, or in other increasingly innovative ways.

If you are looking for information without knowing the exact source, then a key word search on one of the many search engines is the best strategy to adopt.

The exponential growth of the Web is making the task of search engines increasingly difficult because of the sheer volume of new sites and information being placed on the Web. McDaniel and Gates (2002) provide a comprehensive table of their book explaining the features of the major search engines, as well as a list of sites that are of specific relevance to market researchers. You might also like to try www.netskills.ac.uk for an online tutorial guide to searching the Internet, or www.researchbuzz.com, which has news on new information sources and search engines, or www.searchenginewatch.com, which explains how search engines work.Information available online is increasingly diverse. For example, exporters now have the opportunity to resolve historical information gaps when contemplating trading internationally that previously may have dissuaded firms from pursuing such strategies.

Details of market access, exchange control regulations, costs of import duties, etc. are now much more transparent on the Web. Some organizations are competing to offer quality content online, thereby enhancing their brand image and encouraging repeat visits and recommendations for research purposes. Many of the traditional sources of market information are now available online, for example annual reports, large-scale market surveys, government reports and economic data. While there are valuable data freely available, care needs to be taken because the Internet also carries vast amounts of poor-quality data. As with traditional market research, appropriate questions to ask are:

- Are the data relevant?
- Are the data accurate?
- Are they up to date?
- What sampling techniques have been used to collect the data?

The Internet as a means of collecting primary data

There are a number of primary research tasks that can be effectively carried out online; for example:

- Measuring the effectiveness of a firm's Internet strategy;
- Measuring customer satisfaction levels;
- Obtaining customer feedback on new product/service ideas;
- Polling consumers for information about any subject.

Undertaking primary research to measure the effectiveness of a company's Web site is a critical aspect of the evaluation of online marketing strategy. A brief overview is provided here. The following questions may be asked:

- Are the objectives of the site being met?
- Is the corporate message getting across?
- How effective are the various promotional techniques used to attract visitors to the site?
- What changes need to be made to improve the quality of customer service offered?
- Is the site easy to use?
- How many sales are resulting from online contacts?
- How many visitors are coming back to the site?
- How much new business has resulted from the Web site (as opposed to its merely offering an additional channel to existing customers)?
- How does the site compare with those of competitors?
- Channel promotion measures assess why customers visit a site:
- Which sites have they been referred from? (What was the electronic link?)
- Which offline adverts did they see?

From this analysis it should be possible to measure the percentage of customers whose enquiry was prompted by online and offline means respectively, thereby guiding the nature of future promotional campaigns.

- Channel buyer behaviour measures assess which aspects of the Web site content are visited, the times of day and the duration of the visit. This analysis enables 'stickiness' to be measured, for example the average length of a visit, and the proportion of first-time to repeat visitors. It can also suggest changes to site structure and content.
- Channel satisfaction measures evaluate customers' perception of online service quality issues such as email response times. It is also possible to use services such as Gomez to benchmark service quality against the competition.
- Channel outcome measures compare the number of site visitors to the number of actual purchases made; in other words, how many visitors leave the site without buying anything. For example, if 10 purchases result from 100 visits, the conversion rate is 10 per cent.
- Channel profitability measures are a critical test of success. How much does the online channel contribute to business profit after taking account of the costs incurred?

In addition to evaluating existing marketing strategy, research can also play a more proactive role through identifying changes in the market and customer needs, thereby suggesting future strategic directions for the firm. Asking customers what they expect from a company's site and obtaining feedback on current promotions can provide important information to aid market segmentation and other marketing applications. For example, Honda now has different sites for male and female customers, following a research exercise that established how men preferred detailed graphics emphasizing different aspects of car performance, while women preferred brief factual information.Company intranets can also be used effectively to gather research data from staff, a key group of stakeholders whose importance is now increasingly recognized by the designation 'internal customers. Staff opinions are a valuable source of research data that can be sought and collated through an online questionnaire.

INTERNAL MARKETING

The basic premise behind *internal marketing* is that a company's communications with its customers and other external stakeholders are unlikely to be effective unless employees within the firm are aware of (and prepared to buy into) the message that the firm is trying to put across. It is fashionable to refer to employees as 'internal customers'.

If all employees are clear about the company's mission, objectives and strategy then there is a much better chance that customers will get the same message. Research has shown that firms where employees understand organizational goals had considerably higher returns on capital than those where employees felt excluded or uninformed. It has been estimated that more than 20 per cent of a firm's communications are actually with itself rather than with external stakeholders.

Yet internal communications are rarely accorded the same degree of attention and resources as external communications. Sometimes very basic errors are made. For example, if the person responsible for mailing out corporate brochures is not told that a facility for customers to e-mail such requests to the firm has been implemented, incoming messages may well be ignored by that person in the mistaken assumption that someone else is dealing with them. It should now be evident that the principles of internal marketing mirror those of human resource management.

Organizational structure was once the way in which companies could control the flow of information within the firm. Clear hierarchies of responsibility meant that information flowed slowly up and down functional areas, but was often not made available to other parts of the organization, or could be excluded from certain individuals. Individuals' position in the management hierarchy could be ascertained by the degree of access they had to important information.

Powerful fiefdoms could be established by individuals who controlled access to such information. With the development of internal company intranets, it is possible (in theory at least) for such information access barriers to be transcended. Real-time access to information can be available to any employee with Internet access, and the activities of diverse functional areas may become transparent to employees at all hierarchical levels. In practice, of course, decision makers can still choose to restrict access through passwords or firewalls. There are obvious benefits here to a marketer analysing market conditions or customer behaviour, but the sheer volume of information now available to organizations can create problems of its own.

For established firms looking to add online channels to their existing marketing activities, many of the marketing challenges are internal. Significant organizational change may be involved and effective communication within the firm of the need for change and the role of each employee in effecting it is essential to ensure staff commitment. Internal customers can be segmented into supporters, neutrals and opponents of change and communications with each group phrased appropriately. It is particularly vital to ensure 'buy-in' from key decision makers with the authority to enforce change, as well as from potential *champions* (sometimes referred to as 'rainmakers') who will drive the project forwards and communicate their enthusiasm to others.

Inappropriate cultural norms can militate against successful relationship building. Too often, customer care programmes are instigated as a 'quick fix', without making any changes in management behaviour, or attempts to evaluate the success of the programme. While press attention has focused on the achievements (and, more recently, the struggles) of Internet entrepreneurs, little mention has been made of the service workers who make up the bulk of the demand for labour in new technology industries. Many work in call centres that have been dubbed 'the new sweatshops'. In service-intensive organizations the power is in the hands of lower-level, front-line employees, upon whose handling of service encounters managers must depend for the achievement of organizational objectives.

As Piercy notes: 'Too many employees who deal directly with customers are damaging the product, service or corporate brand every time they open their mouths. ' For example, the technique of 'mystery shopping', where researchers anonymously check out the quality of service provided by staff, may well be feared and resented. Dissatisfied or demotivated staff can try to sabotage enforced 'smiling' policies or even wear their name badges upside down.

One major UK DIY retailer implemented a customer care programme that required shop floor staff to be much more proactive in serving customers and suggesting suitable products. What management failed to note was the limited extent of employee commitment and willingness to accept the extra pressures associated with such responsibility. Instead of feeling empowered and motivated by the 'upgrading' of their jobs, many staff resented the interference and preferred the security and predictability of sitting at the till all day.

Although 'clicks and mortar' organizations might be expected to struggle with integrating online relationship building, it is interesting that the 'dotcom' brigade does not seem to be immune to the problem. Leibovich, in an article appropriately entitled 'Service workers without a smile', provides an interesting account of employment conditions at Amazon, world-famous for its ground-breaking policies of online customer relationship building. Staff are pressured to work as quickly as possible in order to achieve customer satisfaction targets, particularly those who earn low wages packing books at the firm's distribution centres or answering e-mails from customers. The author notes: 'Customer service employees work in a patchwork of cubicles scattered over three downtown Seattle buildings.

The quarters have an old industrial feel, with gritty exteriors that belie the company's sleek online identity'.As mentioned earlier, the principles of internal marketing can also be extended to prospective employees with the notion of *employer branding*, in recognition that employees are a significant source of competitive advantage in a market place where products and services are easily copied. Employer branding involves treating staff and potential staff as internal customers.

The aim is to acquire a reputation as a good firm to work for, thereby attracting and retaining the brightest and most dedicated employees, enabling the firm to stand out from its competitors. In an age where people expect to work for a number of firms (or indeed for themselves) during the course of their career, retaining key staff is becoming more and more difficult. Some firms are experimenting with paternity leave, flexible work arrangements and empowerment of staff or open communications through simplified management hierarchies in order to be seen as a 'good employer'. 'Forward-looking companies are working on the assumption that they have to do a continuous selling job on the employee'.

The relationship between internal marketing and relationship marketing. In what may be regarded as the ultimate integration of internal marketing and customer relationship marketing, Ulrich (1989) advises giving customers a major role in staff recruitment, promotion and development, appraisal and reward systems.

While this policy may be too radical for many organizations, it can be seen from this discussion that a suitable internal climate is a necessary first step in the development of a customer orientation, rarely a simple task for an established organization. In much of the human resources literature, relationships between employees have received far less attention than relationships between employees and managers. Even discussions of team working often focus on what the team can deliver for the manager, the company or the customer. This is a pity.

Employee-employee relationships are extremely important for organizations for many reasons, as they can:

- Help to create a positive and constructive company climate and culture.
- Provide an important source of allegiance to the company through commitment to colleagues.
- Create channels for knowledge exchange, particularly informal or tacit knowledge, vital for product and service delivery and quality.

- Provide a vital basis for internal marketing, particularly through building 'internal customers' and internal customer relations, for example, between departments. Although formal internal service-level agreements can help, it is often informal personal relations and agreements that get the job done more efficiently and effectively, and improve a company's service quality overall.

Perhaps one of the most over-hyped assertions made by organizations is the desire to have motivated staff committed to the company. In reality, there are numerous examples of organizations in which such statements are mere rhetoric not backed up by action. What are the sources of employee commitment?

In practice, this can be achieved through a variety of means that have to be very carefully tailored to specific types of work and whether or not employees are working individually or within groups. Very broadly, we can think of the ways in which motivation - making employees more willing to undertake their work for the good of themselves and the company as a result of personal drive and commitment, making them identify more strongly with, and be more loyal to, their work, their work teams and the company - is generated as follows:

'Hard' Reward Strategies

These might include:

- Reward for performance above the standards or targets set, such as financial bonuses, or forms of remuneration over and above the basic wage, which can be offered on a regular basis (e.g. daily, monthly or yearly).
- One-off rewards such as all-expenses-paid holidays, meals, shopping vouchers, etc., for good performance. Such rewards are often used for staff performance that is well regarded by customers as a signal of what kind of care is valued by customers and, in turn, by the organization.
- Share options are an excellent way of getting employees literally to 'buy into' the company's business performance. It also helps to draw employees' attention to aspects of a company's performance that lie outside their immediate job (e.g. changes and opportunities in the competitive environment).

'Soft' Formal Reward Strategies

These might include deciding on and then publicizing 'Employee of the Month/ Year' winners, where the winners are made known to the organization in newsletters, posters or on the company intranet. A 'hard' reward may be given, but a primary objective is to publicize good performance and to share knowledge about how that good performance was achieved with both employees and, of course, customers.

'Soft' Informal Reward Strategies

- *Team meetings.* Time for reflection is difficult in a busy environment, but 'time out' not only to seek improvements but also to share success can provide positive and constructive feedback on individual and team performance.
- *Regular positive feedback.* How can employees know if they are doing a good job or not? The good colleague, supervisor or manager will not just wait until the annual appraisal but can provide such feedback as frequently as they wish. Informal feedback and praise for a job well done are a primary source of maintaining motivation among staff, often referred to as the *organizational climate.* A strong motivational climate is very important at any time, but can be vital at times of crisis and change, in order to maintain focus when things may become uncertain or difficult.

INVOLVEMENT AND PARTICIPATION

Again, it would be easy to be cynical about gaining employee commitment. It could be argued that commitment is often thought about as a one-way street where the employee is expected to commit heavily to the company but the company expects to put in the minimum of effort.

Some of the rewards listed earlier can provide commitment, but more can also be done. The most effective mechanisms operate through involvement and participation processes. Blackburn and Cornelius (2001) have suggested that involvement and participation can add value to workplace organizations, certainly by generating employee commitment but also by encouraging workplace learning.

So, for example, problem-solving meetings can help information exchange about actual and potential problems and their solutions. The key is really how 'participative' are participation processes?In unionized firms there may be joint consultation between management and unions on matters such as pay and conditions. In non-unionized firms, involvement and participation are often achieved through the following:

- *Team briefings* where managers brief employees on actual or possible changes, and feedback and suggestions are sought.
- *Problem-solving and quality circles* in which front-line issues are discussed and suggestions for improvement and change made.
- *Empowerment interventions* where employees are given the autonomy to make decisions about specific aspects of their work without having to consult with their supervisors or managers.

The company culture and organizational climate play a vital role in determining the willingness of both managers and employees to pursue these approaches. Further, the more exploitative the culture and demotivating the climate, the less likely such approaches will be taken seriously or succeed.

The Value-added of e-HRM

Perhaps one of the most exciting developments that all organizations can exploit is e-HRM. e-HRM concerns the use of electronic means for managing key aspects of HRM. Once again, a note of caution: the technology may be the means but it is not the end: the value of e-HRM is highly dependent upon a number of factors, including:

- The basic quality and relevance of the e-HRM systems in use.
- Whether employees, managers and HR professionals are adequately trained to use e-HRM systems.
- How effectively e-HRM is integrated with other more conventional systems of HRM, including strategic HRM.
- Identification of the most appropriate Internet and intranet systems that meet the organization's needs.

THE ROLE OF THE MARKETING DATABASE

A database may be defined as a comprehensive collection of interrelated data, which can be accurately manipulated or retrieved. A marketing database will typically contain details of customers and the transactional or behavioural histories associated with those customers and can benefit all the elements of the marketing mix, whether in broadcast or direct communications or in sales promotion or PR.

There is a role for the database in supporting advertising, market research, product development, sales force management and motivation and sales promotion. Hence the concept of Database Marketing should not be confused with Direct Marketing, nor should it be considered a medium in itself, competing with others in the marketing mix, but rather as a tool to improve performance, efficiency and effectiveness in marketing communications.

The marketing database helps develop a clear, *actionable* understanding of customers and develop a dialogue that ideally should always be relevant, timely and focused on qualified opportunities.

Database Marketing of the 1980s and 1990s strove for *one-to-one* relationships and its success has been commendable *within the context of the available techniques*. New concepts, tools and expertise will now help deliver an outcome that is closer to the vision. The increased awareness and availability of data within organizations has coincided with the appearance of new, intuitive data analysis tools. This combination allows the derivation of information and interpretation of trends within time frames conducive to achieving the required dynamics.

As companies seek to integrate their suppliers, their customers and their marketing partners in complex relationship structures, new quantities of data are becoming accessible for exchange and sharing and the value of the data as a corporate asset is increasing. The existence and growth of the World Wide Web and the increasing exponents of the medium have implications on both sides of the data-driven communications equation. On the one hand, the Web provides a novel, exciting and convenient medium for delivering a message to customers and prospective customers. On the other, it presents a channel for data collection that makes possible concepts that were only hypothetical in the past.

WORKING WITH DATA

Data are things that are given, facts that when combined with other facts can constitute information. Jenkinson (1995) identified four types of explicit data, referred to as Primary Research, Secondary, Performance and External. Whilst these types remain valid, some broadening of the definitions is required to gain a better understanding of how they link and are complementary:

- *Basic data.* Rather than being just primary research data received directly from the customer, basic data may be viewed generically as the most fundamental elements, acquired usually as part of a standard business process. These will include a customer's name and address, e-mail address, definitions of the company's products or services, its URL, pricing, campaign definitions, branches and channels of distribution, sales force or dealer network.
- *Qualifying data.* Qualifying data are data from any source that in any way add description to the basic data. For example, a company may wish to collect the demographics of its customers (age, sex, income, occupation), their lifestyle information or geographical profiles.
- *Behavioural or transactional data.* These are data that record how customers have reacted, what they have bought or enquired about and all the transactional information a company may hold.
- *Externally sourced data.* External data cover everything that augments, qualifies or enhances the basic data that are acquired from outside the business and outside the relationship with customers or suppliers. For example, companies may rent or buy lists of prospects to add to their database or may acquire additional data to enhance their existing records such as correcting the postcode or adding qualifying data elements.

There is a fifth type of data. It is not explicit but is known as *tacit* data. These are data that are normally held in the minds of the people using the database.

The data represent their understanding of their relationship with their customers or suppliers; they are the low-level view acquired through experience or local knowledge and are intuitive, intimate and topical. Their inclusion enables the explicit data to be put into context and interpreted and helps convert information into manageable knowledge, itself a combination of data and information-processing technology with human creativity and innovation.

SOURCES OF DATA

There are a variety of methods for acquiring data into the business. Some are a function of the business processes such as completing a sale or taking an enquiry. Others may be contrived tactics with the main objective of collecting a particular item of data for the database.

Essentially, data can be acquired from six types of source:

- Leveraging current business processes,
- Tactical activity,
- Purchase lists,
- Marketing partners,
- Enhancement from external sources,
- Business information vendors.

Leveraging Current Business Processes

Business processes can be amended so that new information is acquired as part of regular activities; for example, adding questions to an application form, having a telesales agent ask additional questions or having a sales person qualify a prospect prior to making a sales call. Companies must satisfy themselves that they are acquiring all the data they can from the encounter with the customer or prospect (or even supplier).

Most common data sources are:

- *Sales.* Does the company collect details for each sale? Is the basis of the customer database to be found in the accounts department?
- *Web site registrations.* Customer registrations are a reliable source of information so long as the precautions for data quality have been applied. Companies often take this opportunity to ask some additional questions to acquire qualifying information for the database.
- *Enquiries/help line.* When customers and prospects call in or complete an enquiry screen on the Web site there is an opportunity for the company to acquire additional information or qualify or verify data already held.
- *Complaints.* This may be the first occasion a company has to acquire even primary data about this customer - perhaps also take the opportunity to acquire some additional information. Record the complaint on the database; classify it and its outcome so that this can be used in later relationship management. A properly handled complaint can mean a more satisfied customer. Often a customer whose major complaint was handled well becomes a better customer than one who experienced a number of minor complaints.
- *Redemptions.* Sales promotion campaigns or consumer competitions can yield valuable data if one or two relevant questions are added to the entry form.

- *Marketing research and surveys.* Such surveys can provide high-level data that can be extrapolated across the database.
- *Accounts.* Ascertain spend levels, returns and credit control issues, all of which may be used as segmentation or selection criteria for marketing initiatives.
- *Third parties and marketing partners.* Companies may identify non-competitive marketers whose target markets are similar to their own; there may be opportunities for piggy-back activities or cross-marketing or joint venture initiatives.
- *Branches and channels.* Companies with front-line contact with their customer base will identify opportunities for data gathering.
- *Servicing.* Do customers have to come back to have their product serviced? This provides an opportunity both for data gathering and timelyverification.

Tactical Activity

Companies may launch specific tactical promotional campaigns, the object of which is to augment the database or acquire additional data. They could include:

- *Sales promotions, prize draws and competitions.* These all provide the opportunity to collect entrants' details. The techniques can be used tactically to gather primary information (e.g. prospecting or customer identification) or for data enhancement, by requiring entrants to proffer new information about themselves or their household.
- *PR events.* Those who attend company events, product launches, etc., demonstrate an affinity with the brand. Primary and qualifying data can be captured as qualification of entry or through sales promotion or prize draw techniques at the event.

The increasing use of the Internet for customer data acquisition has introduced a key benefit to database marketers. The wide acceptance of customers to use registration or query form screens obviates the cost of data capture and potentially increases the accuracy of input. With all other media the hard copy captured data have to be punched in, either by a company employee or more usually by a data entry bureau that may be on the other side of the world, and this can impose a considerable cost on the exercise.

Purchase or Rent lists

Companies can acquire lists from external sources to augment their database, expanding the volume of prospects or qualifying or updating existing records. Some will be available for purchase, others on a lease basis, allowing a pre-defined number of uses or unlimited use within a specified time period. Most lists are available on a one-use rental basis. Leased and rented lists will be seeded with names of contacts to guard against illicit use of the data. Reputable list managers or brokers should be able to furnish this detail and will provide a data mandate confirming the origin and ownership of the data and any data protection implications. The British List Brokers' Association or the Institute of Direct Marketing can give advice on choosing a list supplier.

CASE STUDY: MISTAKEN IDENTITIES

An estate agent dealing in very expensive properties wished to acquire a list of householders in the smartest areas of England. It went to the trouble of selecting those neighbourhoods with the highest Council Tax bandings and translating them into the specific postcodes it felt defined the geographical areas it desired. The agent then merely requested names and addresses in those areas from a list broker supplying data from the electoral roll. By requesting data purely by postcode, and with no other qualifying data, the selection it received comprised a list of people living in those areas which included chauffeurs, cooks and household staff. Given the type of householders in those areas, many were not on the electoral roll, since they were overseas nationals, or people for whom these properties were second or third homes.

Marketing Partners

Data can also be acquired through data swaps with other organizations with which there is an affinity. There are some industries that have formally created data pools used by members who may even be competing (e.g. charities). Formal marketing partnerships can also yield data from a number of contributors and partners will have predetermined access and use. All these must of course comply with data protection best practice and legislation.

Data Enhancement from External Sources

Additional qualification data can be sourced externally. Postcodes and postal address structuring can be applied either by specialist bureaux or by using software that has as its reference the postal address files of the countries in which the company is marketing. There are around 200 national postal administrations around the world providing this data.

This rapid addressing concept has been widely adopted by call centres that need to ensure swift and accurate address entry; entering the postcode drives the automatic population of most of the address. Web site registration is being made easier and more accurate by providing a similar function using the postal address files. The site visitor merely has to enter his postcode for the majority of the address to be populated in the appropriate fields.

It should be noted, however, that this process provides such results only in territories where the postcode can be linked to a discrete selection of addresses, as in the United Kingdom. The move towards the 5+4 format in the United States will help to some degree, but those countries using the standard European four- or five-digit code or clones of the US-originated 5-digit zip code can proceed only as far as confirmation of city. Some countries, for example the Republic of Ireland, have no postal codes at all.

Adding Qualifying Data

Companies that specialize in qualified databases can match a subject company's data to theirs and provide the missing information. Companies such as Claritas, Consumer Surveys, Consodata and Experian have established databases of millions of households in the United Kingdom and continental Europe. Each record is qualified by an extensive array of research factors that can provide demographic and lifestyle information for consumer databases, and social value grouping information can be acquired and added in, thereby adding both explicit and aspirational/ attitudinal (psychographic) elements for profiling. Some data companies can also provide purchase intention for specific types of products or services.

The psychographic aspect can be a major influence on segmentation. Psychographics is not, as some believe, synonymous with lifestyles. Two households may have identical demographics and be differentiated by their lifestyle preferences, but further differentiation may be achieved by understanding their aspirations and attitudes towards the product, the brand or their own profile.

CASE STUDY: ROVER

Rover, the motor manufacturer, needed to identify prospects for a new mid-range car. Having used demographic and lifestyle questionnaires across its new car owner database, it had a robust profile of the prospects it sought. Mailing lists were recommended that met this profile, and one particular list seemed especially apt. To be certain, a selection of names was tested by telephone research. Whilst the demographics and lifestyles were accurate, the psychographics were not. These people were so concerned with their personal image that they preferred to have a pre-owned, larger prestige car with perhaps a personalized licence plate on their driveway rather than a brand-new but smaller car. The list was a list of second-hand car snobs and not of any great use to Rover's new car sales task, and hence Rover's proposition would be irrelevant to a prospect on that list.

For business-to-business, similarly, business demographic criteria (turnover, number of employees, type of premises, sector, etc.) can be added, as can the job titles of business contacts and the names of people in specific job functions. Arrangements can be put in place for changes of important elements, like key personnel, to be provided on a proactive basis so that the quality of the data can be readily maintained.

Business Information Vendors

Business information vendors can also provide information on sectors or performance within certain markets, specific company information, competitor activities and even information on weather, travel and currency fluctuations can be provided on a 'constant awareness' basis and can be integrated into the data strategy.

Adding Research Data

Research data can be both discrete and general. If research is discrete then it can be matched back to the subject, providing specific qualification criteria for those who respond. Information can then be extrapolated across other similar subjects to provide selection criteria, expanded profiles or segmentation.

Other Data Elements

Some data elements may be 'organically generated' within the database. Such data are referred to as *derived* data and may be acquired as a result of analysis or applying specific calculations. A simple example may be the automatic calculation of customers' age from their date of birth or the creation of banded values such as age groups (twenty-one to thirty-five, fifty-plus, etc.) from discrete personal data. More complex algorithms can be applied to generate scores or propensity quotients that can be used as additional selection or segmentation criteria.

There is overhead attached to holding data in terms of storage, disk space and the implication on hardware and software. There is also a management overhead - the greater the amount of data held, the more management time will be required in data checking, handling data problems and administering the database. There is also a data protection implication: are you acquiring and holding data that really you have no use for and should not be collecting as it is irrelevant to your business?

DATA QUALITY

The value of the data in the database will relate directly to its quality and integrity. It is possible to achieve meaningful results without sophisticated modelling, so long as you have high-quality, robust and reliable data. The better the quality of the data, the more reliable the answers will be to queries run against the database.

Validation processes help with quality and integrity, making sure that the data being added to the database is valid. Business rules manage the validation process, and reference tables ensure conformity and adherence to standards and should be applied in all aspects of data acquisition and use. When designing a data capture device, like an entry form or application screen on a Web site, or when capturing data either using in-house data entry resources or an external data punching bureau, the brief should be the same, with all referring to the same set of rules.

The analytical or selectivity applications of the database rely on conformity; hence the table of references ensures that only values within the predetermined set may be entered into the database. For example, a Web site registration form may request details of how the customer first accessed the site. Normally termed the source code, or media code, this is an important piece of data, since not only does it provide feedback on marketing response but it also establishes a criterion on which customers could be selected for future contact. If left to their own devices to complete a free text field, customers may enter, a free text string complete with typographical errors. Using a reference table of acceptable responses, conformity is assured and the quality of the data is maintained. Bear in mind also the data storage overhead: the free text string has to be held verbatim, whilst the selected value in a table need only be held as a code reference.

Key Issues to Manage

Data acquisition - are all marketing initiatives sharing the same data goals, are the needs of other departments being taken into consideration?

Decay

Data will decay over time. Business data tend to decay at a greater rate, since people move jobs, companies move premises or reorganize, acquire or are acquired by other companies or go out of business more often than individuals move house. Estimates suggest that 30 per cent of management and professional staff change positions annually.

Data Appraisal

In order to assess the quality of the data, an audit should be carried out. View the data on screen or in hard copy - most databases will allow the user to export data into a more familiar environment, like Microsoft Excel, where you can either view the data or print out the spreadsheets if more convenient, checking for key indicators regarding the reliability of the data.

DYNAMICS OF DATA-LED MARKETING

Commercial intelligence and knowledge management are being addressed on varying levels of sophistication, often usually emanating from IT departments. Instead they need to be a key process in the definition, implementation and ongoing measurement of the commercial strategy.

Information gathering has emerged as a natural activity of the sales force, research and development, purchasing and marketing functions by nature of their regular external contacts. Until now this has been a disparate activity suffering from, on the one hand, the natural tendency to contain information within departmental boundaries or, on the other, exhibiting reluctance to share information within the business.

e-Commerce has imposed new, reduced time scales in direct marketing activity. Previously the direct marketer could anticipate when a mailing or phone call was effected and, within some degree of control, when a response would be generated. Access to the Web has reduced this element of control. A marketer can no longer engineer when a contact may wish to encounter his message, proposition or brand, or, indeed, come across it. As companies move seamlessly across borders, this process will become increasingly involved. A complex struggle will take place. Enlightened multinational corporations may gain advantage over leaner and fitter small and medium-size enterprises (SMEs) through the tactical use of information, whilst empowered SMEs may outsmart those larger competitors that remain with the traditional methods.

There is a need to establish valid methods of acquiring data from customers and visitors to e-Commerce Web sites and applying the resultant information and knowledge to drive variations in Web site content and appearance and to determine commercial propositions and further data acquisition. Customers and prospects presented with the same Web pages on each visit and being expected to reactively search for relevant products and offers will soon tire of e-Commerce and the marketer will lose the opportunity to develop a true relationship with the customer. Similarly, a visitor to a site presented with a vast array of qualification questions would be equally turned off. Tailoring the view of the site to the visitor will mean that qualification questions can be posed on an incremental basis, to populate the database using a hierarchy of importance to drive the questionnaire.

The development of the Web has coincided with the appearance of new, intuitive data analysis tools employing techniques that provide for the delivery of information and the definition and interpretation of patterns within that information, within time frames conducive to achieving the required dynamics.

CASE STUDY

The company had a large corporate account-based database on an IBM AS400 platform (addressing different transactional or customer service needs), plus a number of small department-owned databases run on PCs that included a Marketing database that was held externally and a system for managing events and conferences.*The problem*No links existed between the Marketing and Events databases or between the Events database and the AS400 systems. This meant that there were duplicate records but nowhere could the company achieve a total view of the contacts.

Nor were there any business intelligence (BI) tools; the Marketing Department was relying on pre-set reports. Each time a marketing campaign was planned, selections had to be made from each of the databases and discrete extracts run; these were then provided to the mailing house, which undertook a de-duplication process subject to predetermined selection hierarchies, to provide the final mailing file.The objective was to provide:

- A single, comprehensive view of a customer's dealings.
- Improvement in the quality of management information.
- A means to acquire and retain useful client information in a database.

The CRM issues demanded a central data repository. The recommendations were for the company to audit its data and pass it through a cleansing and enhancement process, prior to matching the duplicate records and merging data according to preset business rules. The central AS400 system was augmented, with all additional data and each contact flagged by status (e.g. customer, prospect, enquirer, etc.). Regularly refreshed extracts were exported into a data mart (analysis universe), which was further augmented with qualifying data that the central system could not hold or for which development on the AS400 system was not economic and summarized or aggregated transactional histories. Business intelligence tools were introduced alongside the universe to facilitate querying, *ad hoc* analyses and campaign planning and management.

In this way the company was able to leverage the investment in the transactional system, could close down the satellite databases in the departments and introduce additional purpose-specific data without the need for costly redevelopment of the central system. For the first time the company would have a total customer view and could begin to maximize the opportunities from customer-centric CRM.

As the knowledge culture grows, so the interest in data throughout the enterprise also grows. The benefits of combining information from different departments, from different regions, even from different businesses, are being realized. Software tools such as intelligent agents search for meaningful additions to the knowledge base and data marts with business intelligence software facilitate the analysis of extensive data sets from disparate sources right on the desktops, within hours rather than months and without the mammoth budgets normally associated with corporate data warehouses.

This overall concept, taking the basic principles of data-driven marketing so successfully implemented in direct mail and telemarketing, aims to establish a process for creating the 'back back-end' of e-Commerce, its link to both internal and external marketing data and knowledge bases and the implementation of customer relationship management.

The existence and growth of the Web and the increasing exponents of the medium have implications on both sides of the data-driven communications equation. On the one hand, the Web provides a novel, exciting and convenient medium for delivering a message to customers and prospective customers. On the other, it presents a channel for data collection that makes possible concepts that were only hypothetical in the past.

The beginning of the 1990s saw the introduction of data driving a variety of media beyond the traditional direct mail. For instance, computers were inter-faced with telecommunications equipment to derive applications to assist in the management of customer relationships, enabling call centre agents to prepare themselves for calls, access customers' records and have repeat calls from a customer always channelled through to one agent. Or data being used to drive variations in customer magazines and newsletters, with such notable examples as Rover's internationally acclaimed *Catalyst* magazine bringing lifestyle versionalization and reader personalization to the realm of contract publishing. However, in all these cases the systems that drove them relied upon pre-selection and qualification of the data.

The industry even talked about unqualified contacts as being *suspects* rather than prospects. The sheer wealth of information available on the Web, the ability to identify and acquire it and the tools now available to manage it in all its varying formats and structures all mean that disparate data, wherever they may reside, could be made available to add qualification, enhancement or verification to a marketer's database. The natural corollary to that is a keener degree of customer profiling and targeting and a greater level of personalization of message, proposition and presentation.

Previously the data process was often presented as a funnel to depict a channel for information that is open to as much as possible at the top, but which needs a process of filtering and selection to be applied to that information so that the best is allowed to pass through into the business process. The down side was that controls had to be in place at the top to guard against overflow, which could mean the loss of both bad and good potential information.

The new information channel is less of a funnel and more of a wide conduit. It still allows as much as possible in at the top, but there is less need for those controls since the value of the data cannot be predetermined. Valid, but unstructured, data can be fed in from a multitude of sources, both internal and external, and their value determined once any links are identified. The information can then be attributed to the records on the database and parameters to drive the relationship established.

These new concepts also have implications for clustering and segmentation. Combinations of demographic and behavioural criteria have traditionally defined clusters. Once defined, these have been used to drive product development and marketing activity. Cluster sets change their content and their direction; individuals join and leave as new information is learned about them and as the importance of the business rules inherent in the data relationships is recognized. This means that the clusters are volatile and dynamic. Their dynamism must be tracked and the changes identified in order to keep the marketing strategy and communications schedule on track.

Marketers can find that markets for their products are dwindling, readership for their magazines is flagging and response to their once attractive offers reduced.

This may not be because the product is any lower in quality or the price has leapt; it can be that the customer profile once associated with that product or marker has changed shape and has moved out of the target zone for that marketer. As considered above, has the customer turned thirty-one and so is no longer eligible for a Club 18-30 vacation? Has the child reached an age where his parents are no longer interested in nappies?

These changes and new viable targets must be recognized to effect and maintain product and communications strategies. Early warning of changes in customer profiles can be provided from constant data feeds with triggers identified to drive proposition, communication channel and delivery.

THE MARKETING MIX

The idea of the marketing mix has been around for many years - well before an 'e-' came in front of Marketing or anything else. As far back as the first half of the twentieth century, the job of the marketer was described as a 'mixer of ingredients'. Marketers devise strategies and tactics aimed at providing satisfaction and adding value for customers. The various elements are blended into a 'marketing mix' - a phrase first coined by Neil Borden (1964) of Harvard Business School.

The marketing mix can be defined as the blend of tools and techniques that marketers use to provide value for customers. It is most widely known as E. Jerome McCarthy's (1960) '4Ps': Place, Product, Price and Promotion. 'Place' is not quite self-explanatory, but refers to the routes organizations take to get the benefits of the product or service to the intended customers - channels of distribution. 'Product' means both tangible product and also 'service' and all the ways in which an organization adds value. 'Price' means not just the price charged, but also all aspects of pricing policy, including, for example, distributor margins. 'Promotion' is not just the more specialized 'sales promotion', but also every way in which a product is promoted to customers - from print advertising to Web sites.

The 4Ps are used as an approach to marketing planning that, according to later editions of McCarthy's still-popular *Basic Marketing*, has worked for millions of students and teachers. The prominence of the 4Ps derives largely from Kotler's and colleagues' focus on these as central to marketing strategy (*Marketing Management* and *Principles of Marketing* texts - the early US editions of which were widely accepted as the basis of marketing teaching).

In recent decades, there have been numerous attempts to update and revise the marketing mix. For example, Jefkins (1993:37) pointed out that the concept of 4Ps is no more than a simplifying convention that 'loses sight of the chronological sequence'. He devised a more realistic twenty-element mix that attempted to describe the marketing process sequentially, starting from conception, through pricing, product, distribution and sales to maintaining customer interest and loyalty.

Some marketers assert that there are '5Ps' of marketing, with the fifth being 'People'. 'People' has two meanings in this context. First, customers are people, often buying according to emotion and whim. Without these fickle customers, we have no business. Second, people make it happen. Without people to put marketing plans into operation, nothing happens. Booms and Bitner (1982) proposed that for marketing services, the marketing mix should be extended to seven, by adding 'Process' and 'Physical evidence' in addition to 'People'. For a service, where there is no tangible product, the process of providing the service is all-important. Similarly, a service cannot be sampled. The provider needs to present evidence of the quality of the process.

With an increasing 'service' element in the added value of most production activities, the '7Ps' approach is becoming more widely accepted. The e-Retailing book in this series will return to the '7' approach. For simplicity we shall use the better-known '4' here as a framework for examining online marketing operations. The operational aspects of the other three will be incorporated where relevant.

In recent years, what marketers actually do has changed radically. Some authors have questioned whether the old idea of the marketing mix can still be valid. The challenge is based on a shift of emphasis towards relationship marketing and customer relationship management (CRM), aspects which are fundamental to marketing the e-Business. The CRM approach has many advantages, we focus on the well-tried 4Ps as an aid to classifying marketing tactics, e- or otherwise.

One development has merit as being descriptive of the way marketers think about the customer. The '4Cs' (Lauterborn 1990) imply more emphasis on customer wants and concerns than do the Ps. 'Place', rather than implying managements' methods of placing products where they want them to be, can be thought of as 'Convenience for the customer', recognizing the customers' choices for buying in ways convenient to them. 'Product', rather than being something that a company makes, which then has to be sold, can be thought of as a 'Customer benefit' - meaning satisfactions wanted by customers. 'Price' may be what companies decide to charge for their products, but 'Cost to the customer' represents the real cost that customers will pay, including, for example, their own transport costs. Finally, 'Promotion' suggests ways in which companies persuade people to buy, whereas 'Communication' is a two-way process also involving feedback from customers to suppliers. In the sections that follow, we consider the operational aspects of marketing the e-Business. While using the better-known 4Ps for our headings, we draw attention to differences in approach implied by the 4Cs.

PLACE

'Place' (Convenience in the 4 Cs) means the elements of the marketing mix that marketers use to enable customers to access the benefits of a product or service. Traditionally, this has meant 'channels of distribution' through (e.g.) various wholesaler and retailer combinations. Viewing from the 'convenience for the customer' (4Cs) perspective gives a more customer-orientated focus. This is a vital decision area for the e-Business for three reasons. First, relatively small local companies can widen their market and even export. Second, many e-Businesses aim to gain competitive advantage by using e-Systems to de-layer the distribution chain. For example, Dell (www.dell.co.uk) supplies customers directly, rather than through distributors, wholesalers or retailers.

Third, distribution is an area where some e-Businesses have been severely criticized for failing to deliver customer service.

Place elements of the marketing mix have been changing rapidly over recent decades, and these changes impact in many ways on the marketing operations of the e-Business. First, the growth of retailer power has involved major retailers taking more control of their supply chains. The involvement of wholesalers has been reduced, tending to give way to contract logistics (under retailer control). At the same time, supply chains have become more efficient, with computer network links between suppliers and retailers - many still based on EDI. Predating the Internet, EDI is based on privately owned third-party computer networks. Stock levels have been reduced using techniques such as JIT and Enterprise Resource Planning (ERP). Control of the physical distribution, ordering, invoicing and payment systems, particularly for major retailers, is often still carried out using EDI networks such as Tradanet (www.gegxs.com/gxs/products/product/traser). Increasingly, though, retailers such as Tesco are allowing Internet access to their suppliers for real-time electronic point-of-sale (EPOS) data. Trusted supplier partners can thus respond more quickly to changes in customer demand.

PRODUCT

'Product' is equivalent to Customer benefit in the 4Cs. In fact, people do not buy 'products' as such, but rather solutions to problems, or good feelings. The oft-quoted example is of a company selling the 'product' of an 8-mm drill bit. What the customer actually buys, though, is 8-mm holes. The customer is not interested in features of the drill such as the grade of steel used, only in whether it will solve the particular problem: drilling through plaster, mortar and brick, for example. Online catalogues selling B2B might well describe this as 'tungsten carbide tipped' in the realistic expectation that trade customers will fully understand the purpose. When selling B2C, a description more in line with customer wants should be used, say 'for drilling masonry for wall plugs and similar'. When buying online, customers are far less likely to request help than they are in the store, cash-and-carry, buying via telesales or even when placing a formal written order. Rather, when buying online, customers who need help in understanding a product are more likely to abandon the transaction and find an alternative supplier, or even buy through a different channel. e-Businesses, therefore, need to be particularly careful about describing products clearly in customer benefit terms.

The second reason why customers buy products - to get good feelings - is also apt for the e-Business. Other channels such as the retail store or the face-to-face salesperson are often much better at identifying and satisfying customers' emotional needs and wants. The physical store uses atmospherics in the attempt to change mood and give shoppers a pleasant emotional experience when buying. Emotional cues may include visual (decor), olfactory (perfume), touch (smooth and cool or soft and cuddly) and oral (music) cues.

Similarly, the sales representative selling face to face has the opportunity of using verbal and non-verbal (body language) communication to build personal relationships with customers, enhancing the emotional value of products.

In trying to replicate the physical buying experience, the e-Business is at a disadvantage. On the other hand, with transaction data ready-digitized, the e-Business is well placed to enhance product value using CRM techniques. For example, data-mining can be used to build a picture of products most likely to be wanted by individual customers. Products tailored specifically can be offered proactively. Amazon (www.amazon.co.uk), for instance, uses such a system to match new books to existing customers likely to be interested in them.

The Internet, though, has the advantage in selling information-based products, including market information, business application and games software. For example, to find information on size and trends of consumer markets, there is no need to purchase a heavy paper-based report; the information can be downloaded from suppliers such as Mintel (sinatra2.mintel.com).

PRICE

'Price' is equivalent to cost to the customer in the 4Cs. Pricing decisions generate revenue, whereas the rest of the marketing mix involves costs. Pricing decisions are particularly critical for the e-Business as there is a customer perception that prices should be lower online than otherwise. Many organizations (e.g. Eurotunnel; www.Eurotunnel.com for car crossings from England to France) apply a standard discount for online purchase.

In some cases, customers can make much bigger savings buying online. For instance, to buy tickets from a travel agent in the UK for the Calgary Stampede rodeo in Canada (www.calgarystampede.com/stampede) is likely to be expensive, as the agent will probably sell these only as part of a package. Tickets can be booked directly via the Internet at a substantial saving. Some e-Businesses sell almost solely on the basis of price. For example, emagazineshop (www. emagazine shop.com) sells a wide range of the magazines normally available at newsagents'. Subscription prices are normally lower than newsagents, but emagazineshop offers lower prices still. The most popular magazines are discounted by at least 20 per cent, more specialist ones 10 per cent. This is a rare example of a pure-play dotcom, founded in 1997, that has survived the dotcom crash and is growing steadily, now employing 25 people.

Despite the Internet facilitating de-layering of intermediaries, it is still not automatic that costs will be less for selling online. Someone still has to carry out functions such as breaking bulk and physical delivery - and for online sales these can be even higher than for offline (many small orders delivered to individual customers rather than fewer, larger deliveries to a store), with consequent loss of advantages of economies of scale. Hence, many suppliers selling on the basis of cheap prices, even successful ones like Amazon (www.amazon.co.uk), struggle to make a profit on their e-Operations. Again, this is an area where the success of emagazineshop is an exception.

Not all prices are lower on the Internet. As already mentioned, the cost to the customer includes not just the selling price, but all the costs of buying. To buy from a (bricks) grocery supermarket incurs transport costs, and also the notional cost of the value of a customer's travel time. Tesco (www.tesco.com) is able to make a charge for home delivery, which its many e-Customers must consider represents good value.

The Internet is an ideal medium for operating a mechanistic market. For the customers, this means quick and easy access to the 'best' deals. For sellers, this should in theory mean a level playing field, where products offered at a competitive price sell, regardless of issues such as the size of the organization; hence the suitability of the Internet for electronic trading exchange.

The level playing field idea, though, has hit some snags when translated to practice, and price-based services have achieved no more than modest success to date. A number of buying services are available such as Shopsmart (uk.shopsmart.com), the leading consumer price comparison site, and ComputerPrices (www. ComputerPrices .co.uk), which finds the cheapest computer kit in the UK. Priceline (www.priceline.com) is an alternative price-based service that creates a market or reverse auction.

Enter the price you want to pay for a wide range of services like flights or hire cars and the system searches for suppliers willing to sell at that price - but the customer cannot choose the (say) airline for their flight. The company does, however, guarantee that it will be one of the top airlines. Most UK customers, though, prefer to have more control over what they get, rather than buying purely on price. For most e-Businesses, pricing remains as for non-electronic strategies; that is, based on the complex interaction of all elements of the marketing mix and value.

Marketing pricing is still what it was, the price that customers are willing to pay, based on considerations such as the company, brand, reputation and product. The difference that e-Commerce makes is that pricing and competitor information is faster and more transparent, meaning that market forces also tend to act faster and perhaps more efficiently. There is thus a tendency for prices to converge at lower levels.

PROMOTION

'Promotion' is equivalent to Communication in the 4Cs. First thoughts on promoting the e-Business must be that it is unnecessary - the business can rely on its super Web site. Having built that Web site, it can sit back and wait for customers. Of course, we quickly realise that there is more to it than that. Why should visitors come to our Web site? If surfers do find it, are they our potential customers? In practice, it is likely that we will have to be more proactive in promotion, integrating e- with other communications channels.

For many businesses, selling predominantly both on- and offline, the Internet is just one of a wide range of communication channels. The 'process' of integrating the communication tools is vital.

'People' play a vital part in the marketing communication process, even (or perhaps especially) for the e-Business. Customers want human contact, and those businesses that can provide a real human to interact with a customer quickly - whether online, via email, over the telephone or even face to face - are more likely to succeed than some of the faceless, e-only operations that have been getting a reputation for poor service. Similarly, though, those e-Businesses with customer-friendly systems that effectively mimic human interaction (www.google.com) and Amazon (www.amazon.com)) tend to be more popular than the more mechanistic sites. The People aspect is also important for e-Businesses in tailoring offers to the individual customer. For example, Amazon emails details of new books to customers whose profile makes them likely customers.

MAKING BANNERS WORK

Recently, a perception has arisen in the marketing world that banner ads are not cost-effective. Despite this, online advertising expenditure is still growing, and has now reached well over £150 million per year (£30 million more than cinema advertising, for example).

The interstitial, a pop-up that interrupts browsing to show an ad, is a much more active form of advertising. Some people using the Web for a specific purpose find these irritating, though. Online advertising company RealMedia (www.uk.realmedia.com) is using a less intrusive system called adPointer. This generates an ad when the cursor has not moved for a specific time.

Schemes that provide users with incentives to look at advertisements have been around for some years, but in the UK, Bananalotto.com (www.bananalotto.com) has raised the stakes by offering the chance to win £1 million as you click the banner ad. KPE, the media and entertainment consultancy, developed around ten games for its clients. Managing Director Paul Zwillberg says, 'So much of the Internet has been characterized by repurposing things that worked well in print or on TV. "Advergaming" is ... a new combination that's made for the medium.... You take one of the most popular uses of interactive content and marry it with tried and tested advertising models like brand association, trial or data capture and you get something really wonderful.'

8

Electronic Retailing

CUSTOMER VALUE AND PROFITABILITY IN GROCERY E-RETAILING

- Customer density
- Loyalty
- Buying power
- Ordering efficiency and customer information
- Operational efficiency and customer service level
- Large range of products
- Price level
- Shopping convenience

Tanskanen *et al.* (2002) reported on 'six lessons learned' for profitable grocery e-retailing and Anckar *et al.* (2002) identified 'four sources of customer value'. As the UK's leading supermarket, Tesco has the advantage in loyalty, buying power and range of products. Economies of scale should also give the market-leader a potential advantage in good-value selling prices.

In theory, therefore, the other players need to try to gain their competitive advantage from the remaining factors: shopping convenience, operational efficiency, customer service, the ordering interface and product information. These can be addressed by, for example, making the website informative, quick and easy to use, supplying exactly (or with a minimum of substitutes) what is ordered and providing accurately timed delivery slots.

CLOTHING AND FOOTWEAR

Clothing is not an obvious product for e-retailing. First, of course, clothing is normally bought by look, feel and fit, all of which are difficult for the e-shopper to evaluate on the Web. Second, clothing is bought not just for warmth and modesty, but also to express our self-image. Any purchase errors in (e.g.) style, therefore, carry a particularly high perceived risk. Indeed, de Kare-Silver's ES test rates basic clothing at 19 (out of 50), well behind books (38), DVD movies and groceries (27). (For a product to be suitable for e-retailing, de Kare-Silver recommends a minimum score of 20.) Nevertheless, clothing represents one of the major categories in UK e-retail (although worldwide it is one of the slowest-growing categories). One reason may be that clothing has historically been one of the major mail-order categories in the UK. Both shoppers and suppliers are used to home delivery channels for clothing. The clothing e-retail market leader Next has been supplying fashion clothing by mail order since 1988.

Surprisingly, lingerie and hosiery is one of the most popular product categories for e-retailing, perhaps driven by the success of the leader, The same way that Tesco has driven the expansion of grocery e-retailing. Leaves has a winning approach both in the creative permission-based marketing and the novel online bra measuring system. In particular e-shopping for lingerie appeals to men, who may often be embarrassed to buy these products in-store.

Look and feel' goods tend to be compared and evaluated before buying - i.e. they are high involvement purchases. For example, a survey reported in the *New Straits Times* in 2001 found that 85 per cent of respondents would not buy clothes online because they prefer to try them on before purchase. Enjoyment is often a motivation for in-store clothes shopping (and other comparison shopping). In the bricks retail store, 'atmospherics' are often used to increase enjoyment and hence sales. The effectiveness of such techniques is well known in-store, we argue that equivalent considerations are also important for the e-retailer.

Emotional aspects such as enjoyment strongly predict shoppers' attitudes towards e-shopping. According to Chicksand and Knowles (2002), equivalent features can be identified to help in overcoming the difficulties of selling 'look and feel' goods like clothing online. The equivalent stimuli for the clicks store include: sound, personalization/customization, usability of the website, visuals and text. *Web atmospherics* can help compensate for the lack of sensory experience in e-shopping. Nevertheless, the indications are that shoppers' needs for enjoyment (rather than just utilitarian) benefits are not being satisfied by e-retailers. Even clothing market leader Next makes little attempt at the use of web atmospherics on the e-retail site.

Personalization is a key element of web atmospherics, but most clothing e-retailers personalize very little. Developments aimed at helping to overcome this drawback include the Eddie Bauer (US clothing retailer) 'virtual closet' which allows shoppers to match up items with a 'Style Builder'. With Virtual Model (www.virtualmodel.com - one of the '100 best websites' from *Internet Magazine*) you can create a 3-D virtual model of yourself online and dress yourself with clothing from top suppliers such as Lands End - claimed to increase the likelihood of a sale by 19 per cent.

These e-retailers keep a database of sizes and items bought that is available on your next visit, personalizing the experience and saving purchase time. The potential for clothing includes the body scan.

For example, shoppers can visit selected Levi stores for the scan, which is then held on a database. In theory, this could then be used for e-shopping, incorporating the scan data into a 3-D virtual closet such as Virtual Model. Shoppers could be confident that the clothes would fit. Unfortunately, Levi does not actually offer the body scan data for e-retailing on the Virtual Model/Kohls (www.kohls.com) site.

Customization is another key element of web atmospherics for clothing. Mass customization refers to self-designed products. Shopper involvement in the design of the products adds considerably to the personal feel of the shopping experience.

Shopper satisfaction can be enhanced by more closely matching exact needs. In the case of Nike, shoppers can customise shoes, not just with colours and styles, but also, for example, with a name or message.

A potential drawback of this system, though, is concern over what happens if the customer wants to return the product for any reason? Fanbuzz e-retails clothes, allowing shoppers to decide their own styles, colours, graphics and sizes. These custom items are 10-20 per cent more expensive than non-custom ones, but many customers are prepared to pay more for customized products.

Although the market for e-retailing clothes is growing only slowly, if the mass-market e-retailers such as Next and Marks & Spencer were to improve web atmospherics, e.g. more attractive, interactive site design and layout, more personalization and customization incorporating features used by specialists such as Lands End and Nike, there should be considerable scope for further growth.

CLASSIFICATION OF RETAIL STORES

The same term, retail store, is used to refer to the vast R. H. Macy and Company department store in New York City and to the smallest cigar and newsstand operated in the lobby of a public building. Such a varied structure of retail institutions limits the extent to which it is possible to generalize about the totality. For proper understanding and evaluation of this structure and changes therein, it is essential to break it down into significant components through meaningful classifications, each of which may be studied by itself and in comparison with other segments with which it comes into competitive conflict or which may be deemed as socially or economically desirable alternatives.

It is possible to classify retail stores in an almost unlimited variety of ways. All of these classes are meaningful for some purposes, but it would be an endless and repetitious task to discuss all of them in detail. A limited number of classification bases which have been selected with care to reveal the more significant characteristics of the retailing structure and to point up the major competitive, social, and economic problems and implications resulting there from.

Ownership Classes

Analysis of retail stores in terms of ownership classes has long been of great interest because this approach involves numerous competitive and other implications. Such a breakdown reveals what groups have an entrepreneurial interest in retailing and which tend to dominate the institutional structure. Certain legislative and tax questions are involved. Certain regulatory and tax legislation tends to preserve or fortify the status of some ownership classes while placing handicaps or limitations on others. Type of ownership often reflects differences in operation, especially with respect to financial structure, method of procuring merchandise, and the degree to which retail store operations are integrated with the performance of wholesaling and manufacturing functions.

Single-Unit Independent Stores

Over a long period of years, the independent retailer who operates a single store has dominated the retailing structure. The importance of this ownership class is indicated by the fact that such stores have comprised 86 to 90 per cent of total retail establishments enumerated in the various Censuses of Business from 1929 to 1958 Even though "typical" independent merchants operate smaller stores than their chain competitors, they dominate in total sales volume.

Over the same period, sales of single-unit independents have amounted to about 66 to 70 per cent of sales of all retail establishments. With only limited exceptions, single-unit independents are relatively small, family-type enterprises that operate solely or almost altogether on the retail level. In view of the visual prominence of chain retailers, as reflected by conspicuousness in shopping centers and advertising media, the persistence of the independent is indeed remarkable.

Chains or Multiunit Retailers

The major competitor of the independent is the chain. Multiunit or chain stores comprise about 10 per cent of all retail establishments counted in the Census of Business. Prior to World War II, the proportion of chain retail stores was somewhat higher, the decline being accounted for by the operation of larger scale establishments.

Relatively, sales volume of chain organizations has been fairly stable in the long run, amounting to about 30 to 34 per cent of total retail trade, with some increase in competitive position in more recent years. About one-third of the total business of chains is done by fairly small multiunit organizations (ten stores or less) whose sympathies and outlook are in most respects more closely akin to the independent than to the large chain system. All but a small part of multiunit stores are owned by *retailers,* as opposed to manufacturers and other ownership classes.

Manufacturer-Owned Stores

In certain lines of trade, independent and chain retailers compete with manufacturers who have integrated their operations forward in the distribution channel by the use of their own retail outlets. Several reasons account for this practice. First, some manufacturers have opened stores in the belief that complete control over the entire marketing channel constitutes their most profitable alternative. This motive accounts for the presence of various well-known, manufacturer owned chains in the men's clothing, shoe, candy, and millinery lines of trade. Second, some manufacturer-owned stores are used to supplement other forms of distribution.

Three of the best-known tire manufacturers operate company-owned retail outlets, but in no case do these constitute the company's sole outlets for tires and related automotive and household products. Such locations are usually established only in communities where there is an expectation of an unusually large volume of sales or where suitable independent outlets are not available. Third, a limited number of manufacturer-owned stores serve as experimental stations for testing product innovations or for developing merchandising methods or techniques that may be adapted for use by regular retailers. Finally, some manufacturers utilize their own retail establishments at factory locations in order to dispose of off-selected, rejected, or "stale" merchandise that is not salable through regular channels.

Expansion of retailing activities by manufacturers is limited by two major principles. First, manufacturer-owned stores are feasible only for well-financed companies that produce a relatively full line of related products, or products which are of relatively high unit value. In the absence of this condition, adequate sales volume cannot be obtained in a single retail establishment.

As a corollary of this principle it has become apparent that successful manufacturer-owned stores usually function as merchant middlemen to some extent. Leading stores owned by men's clothing and tire manufacturers sell many items which are purchased from outside sources. Such goods are bought to round out the merchandise line, thus increasing sales volume per establishment and enhancing the efficiency of operation.

Second, many manufacturers who might prefer to develop some retail outlets are restrained by independent wholesalers and retailers, who object to such ventures as introducing unfair methods of competition. On certain occasions, the animosity of retailers has been so vociferous that attempts have been made to prohibit by legislation the operation of retail stores by manufacturers. Integration in marketing channels is now widely accepted, so that such public restrictions appear highly improbable. Fear of incurring "ill will" of regular outlets remains sufficiently strong, however, that it deters many manufacturers from engaging in retailing.

It is probable that the total of manufacturers' sales distributed through their owned retail stores does not exceed 2 per cent of the total of all manufacturers' sales distributed through all channels. To the extent that manufacturers make supplementary purchases from other sources, their retailing activities differ little from those of other multiunit retailers, except with respect to the major merchandise line of their own manufacture.

Farmer-Owned Stores

Another ownership class consists of farmers, some of whom maintain roadside establishments or leased facilities in public retail markets. The character of such establishments often results in a misleading impression that they involve, principally or entirely, direct farmer-to-consumer marketing. It is practically impossible for farmers to operate a *regular* retail establishment *on a continuing basis* solely by the sale of their own produce. When an investment is made in physical facilities or when market space is leased, it is almost always necessary for the farmer to buy many items from other farmers and from regular wholesale sources.

Experience has revealed that the typical farmer cannot afford to devote time and energy to retailing and expect the same returns that are afforded to him by concentrating on agricultural production and marketing his output through regular wholesale trade channels. Genuine direct retailing of farm produce is confined largely to seasonal and sporadic efforts. There is, for example, a considerable volume of roadside marketing during the home canning season for fresh farm produce. There is also evidence that farmers are most likely to resort to retailing as a desperation measure when prices are low or declining rapidly. So long as wholesale prices are adequate to cover the costs of agricultural production and afford the farmer a fair living, he is not likely to engage in the complex of activities necessary for satisfactory retailing.

Government-Owned Stores

In a socialist commonwealth the government would own and operate business organizations for the benefit of the state. In the United States, however, the organization of practically all productive facilities reflects the democratic ideal of private competitive enterprise. Nevertheless, there are exceptional circumstances in which governmental units engage in retailing. Certain state governments maintain liquor stores: While such stores constitute an important source of government income, that cannot be considered as the motivating factor.

The state has the alternative of levying excise taxes of any reasonable amount and could probably obtain the same or greater revenue on alcoholic beverages distributed through orthodox retail channels. State operation must then be viewed primarily as a device to effect social control of the distribution of alcoholic beverages.

Another form of government stores consists of commissaries, post exchanges, and similar establishments often used in connection with military installations, for the purpose of providing a special type of "fringe benefit" to employees on military bases. It is estimated that all classes of government operated stores account for only about 1 per cent of total retail sales volume.

Consumer Cooperatives

A consumer cooperative is a marketing organization owned and operated for the mutual benefit of consumerowners, who have voluntarily associated themselves for the purpose. Such an organization is an attempt to substitute joint or cooperative efforts of consumers for those of private enterprise. Properly speaking, *consumer* cooperation does not embrace cooperative dealings in industrial or business goods, such as farm supplies or equipment. There are, however, many farm cooperative associations that also handle consumer goods, and thus serve the farmers' interests as individual consumers, although such organizations are primarily concerned with the advancement of the interest of farmers as owners and operators of profit-making agricultural enterprises.

The modern consumer cooperative movement dates from 1844 when a group of poverty-stricken English weavers opened a crude store in Rochdale. Out of their experience a set of basic principles was developed and these have governed most consumer cooperatives throughout the world. These so-called "Rochdale principles" highlight the character of consumer cooperation and distinguish it from retailing as carried on by private business organizations. In brief, they are as follows:

- *Membership is open to all* adult persons, without regard to political or religious affiliations or social status;
- *Democratic control* is achieved by providing all members with one vote, regardless of amount of capital stock owned;
- *Limited interest is paid* on capital investment in accordance with the view that capital is to be regarded as the servant, not the master, of the organization;
- *Sales are made at prevailing market prices* to accumulate a surplus to be distributed in lump sums to patrons;
- Services are limited, as exemplified by the policy of *selling only for cash*;
- Any surplus accruing from the spread between prevailing market prices and cost of merchandise and store operation is paid to members in proportion to their volume of purchases as *patronage dividends*;
- Consumer cooperatives are supposed to adhere to a policy of *religious and political neutrality*; and
- Certain percentages of earnings are usually set aside for purposes of *education* in order that alleged benefits and ideals can be spread among nonmembers, thus expanding the scope of operations and influence.

While such "principles" have been widely observed, some cooperative organizations have found it expedient to depart from them. For example, some have tried to attract a wider membership by selling at unusually low prices, offering some types of credit service, and others have worked actively for political candidates who favour consumer cooperation and by stimulating legislation favorable to the cooperative programme.

In certain European countries, consumer cooperation has achieved notable success, especially in England, Scotland, Wales, Sweden, Norway, Finland, Denmark, Switzerland, and Holland. By way of contrast, in the United States *strictly consumer* cooperative establishments (i.e., excluding the operations of those primarily engaged in selling feed, farm supplies, and petroleum products for farm business use) account for only a small fraction of 1 per cent of total retail sales volume.

Considerable controversy about consumer cooperatives has resulted from the fact that "earnings" or "savings" distributed as patronage refunds are not treated as profits for purposes of income taxation. This, it is often alleged, gives the cooperative an unfair advantage compared to private enterprises that pay income taxes on all profits.

Consumer cooperatives, on the other hand, have obtained judicial support for the view that patronage dividends are a refund of purchase price rather than profits, and they point out that they comply with income tax laws, the same as any other business, on profits paid to shareholders as a return on capital investment and on all other profits not distributed on the basis of patronage. In any event, the tax advantage is a relatively minor one which gives this type of organization little or no pricing advantage, even though it may operate to increase the amount of annual patronage refund accumulated on a member's total purchases.

In the light of more than a century of experience with consumer cooperation, some explanation must be offered for the negligible part of this ownership group in the United States. For one thing, cooperatives in Europe achieved notable success in a competitive environment characterized by small, inefficient, tradition-bound, retail shops.

In the United States, their success has been limited because consumers have had the opportunity to patronize chains and other limited-service retailers who have succeeded in attaining all types of economies sought by cooperatives. Second, in most European countries, the population has been more homogeneous in terms of heritage, social status, and religious affiliations, which has been conducive to cooperative effort. In our country, the population of urban areas usually reflects a variety of occupations, social interests, and cultural values. This has made it difficult to assemble large groups of people who are favorably inclined to the cooperative movement.

Third, under economic conditions favorable for the masses, the American consumer has had a higher level of real income, has felt much less need to "pinch pennies," and has preferred to shop in a wide variety of stores which afford him an exceedingly wide range of choice of novel and unusual merchandise as well as basic necessities. Indeed, the consumer cooperatives which have achieved most notable success in this country have tended to be the ones which have sought to serve their owner-patrons by having better or superior stores rather than by emphasis upon savings or economy alone.

When due consideration is given to the efficiency of our mass distribution retailing organizations and other circumstances that have limited cooperative development, it appears certain that consumer cooperatives will not become a significant competitive factor in our retail trade structure.

Consumer cooperatives are, nevertheless, of considerable and continuing marketing interest due to various factors, including the following: distinctive ownership arrangement; idealistic objectives including operation for the economic benefit of patrons; rather substantial concentration in one line of trade, food stores; and conspicuous success in some localities.

Extent and Nature of the Line of Goods Handled

Classification of stores on the basis of the extent and nature of the line of goods handled is useful because size, location, and, to a degree, merchandising methods are greatly affected by this factor. Three broad classes of stores are discernible:

- General merchandise stores,
- Single-line stores, and
- Specialty stores.

In distinguishing stores on this basis, the terms "variety" and "assortment" may be employed to advantage. As used in retailing *variety* implies generically different kinds of goods. Variety may be present in a related line of merchandise such as foods and is indicated by such diverse products as bread, canned tomatoes, frozen peas, cheese, and so on. It may also exist without any natural relationship among items, as in the variety store where one may find candy, toilet articles, stationery, toys, hardware, apparel, and so on. *Assortment*, on the other hand, relates to the range of choice among substitutable characteristics of a given type of article. A millinery store or department may be said to have broad or extensive assortments if a woman can choose the most suitable hat for a given purpose or use from many styles, colors, materials, and prices of hats.

General Merchandise Stores

General merchandise stores handles such an extensive variety of goods that they cannot be classified into some kind of business grouping designated by the name of a principal type of commodity. Stores within this broad group are of several distinct types, including general stores, department stores, dry goods stores, and variety stores. *General stores* are found chiefly in areas of scattered and isolated population, often as the only retail outlet in a small town or at some rural location. Such stores are usually small and non departmentized. Among the principal commodities commonly sold are groceries, hardware, dry goods, notions, toilet goods, staple lines of apparel and furnishings. A gasoline pump and very limited automobile service facilities are often a part of such businesses. The general, store was once a very significant type of outlet but has greatly declined in importance due to population growth, urbanization, and increases in automobile use and highway improvements which have made larger shopping districts more accessible to rural residents.

Department stores are usually large urban retail institutions that handle a wide variety of lines, such as women's ready-to-wear and accessories, men's and boys' clothing, piece goods, small wares, and home furnishings. Merchandise is segregated into separate departments for purposes of promotion, service, accounting, and control. Because department stores normally serve a large trading area, they are usually located in downtown areas or in major secondary shopping districts of large cities. The distinguishing feature of department stores is *variety* of shopping goods offerings, organized departmentally. When the department store is operated on a sufficiently large scale, individual departments are as large as or larger than ordinary specialty stores and are characterized by breadth of assortment as well as variety.

Dry goods stores are similar to department stores in terms of merchandise handled, although home furnishings are often absent. They are classified separately because they do not meet certain department store classification criteria, including sale of all required merchandise lines, large scale operation, or departmental organization. As the name implies, *variety stores* handle many different kinds of merchandise, mostly of low unit value. They were the first important type of institution to emphasize self-service methods of retailing.

Operations are characterized by giving merchandise maximum open display, rather than by providing active personal selling assistance by salespeople. The role of the salesperson is that of maintaining the stock in order and handling the transaction for the consumer. These stores are still popularly known by their historical connotation, "5 and 10 cent stores," even though this term is no longer descriptive due to extension of price lines and greater emphasis on shopping goods. Originally, they were essentially convenience goods stores. They are generally situated at points of heavy concentrations of consumer traffic, and most of them are units of chain organizations.

Single-Line Stores

An extensive variety of one line of merchandise that is *related in sale or use* is the basis for classification as a single-line store. Such stores are usually designated in terms of the principal line of goods, such as groceries, drugs, hardware, men's clothing, furniture, or jewelry. In a men's clothing store, for example, a consumer expects to find all kinds of men's apparel including hosiery, shoes, underwear, shirts, neckware, suits, coats, and hats. Large assortments of any one of these kinds of merchandise are found only in fairly large clothing stores. Thus it may be said that the basis for the single-line store is related variety; wide assortments are dependent upon a scale of operation that permits an extensive inventory investment.

When single-line stores operate on a very large scale, they are usually departmentized. This is especially true in the supermarket and chain drugstore fields, as well as in the furniture and apparel trades. Stores handling men's, women's, or family apparel and organized on a departmental basis are commonly known as "departmentized specialty stores." This gives rise to some confusion because the word "specialty" in this case is used to distinguish such stores from regular department stores rather than to denote the type of limited variety characterizing small specialty stores which are described in the following section. Historically, single-line stores tended to replace general stores as small communities grew in size. While their variety of merchandise is ordinarily much more limited than in stores of the general merchandise group, it is much more extensive than in the case of specialty stores.

Specialty Stores

This term refers to stores which handle an extremely limited variety of goods. In some trades, practically all establishments are of this highly specialized character. Examples include automobile dealers, gasoline service stations, florists, and book stores.

In other instances the specialty store handles only part of a line of goods customarily sold by single-line stores. Single-line grocery stores compete with specialty stores such as baked-goods establishments, dairy stores, and meat markets. In the clothing field single-line stores divide the market with specialty stores such as shoe stores, millinery shops, lingerie establishments, maternity dress shops, and furriers. Because specialty stores confine their offerings to a narrow range of items, they have more extensive assortments than single-line stores of comparable, size.

A men's shoe store, for example, is a highly specialized operation in which the consumer expects to find a wide range of styles, colors, and prices in his size. The operation of a specialty store should not be confused with the sale of specialty goods. The term "specialty" when used to designate a store implies limited variety of goods. These may be convenience goods as illustrated by cigar stands, they may be shopping goods such as apparel items, or they may be specialty goods such as automobiles, vacuum cleaners, or collectors' items as, for example, rare postage stamps.

Specialty stores often have relatively simple buying problems in that most or all merchandise is drawn from one or few suppliers in the same trade. They have a competitive advantage over single-line stores in terms of assortments, but have a more limited opportunity for related, item selling. Specialty stores, for the most part, operate in well-established shopping districts.

Kind of Business Groupings

Single-line and specialty stores are not separately classified in Census tabulations, and it would probably be impossible to provide quantitative information about each of these two classes. For purposes of business use it is more desirable to classify both single-line and specialty stores within kind-of-business classifications. With the exception of the general merchandise group, all stores included in this table may be considered as single line or specialty. It is easy to distinguish certain single-line operations, such as grocery stores, from specialty establishments like meat markets or candy stores. In other cases, such distinctions are not possible. One women's dress shop may handle a large variety of apparel, and be classified as a women's clothing store; another may specialize to the extent of selling only cotton dresses within a narrow price range, but still be grouped in the same classification.

Classification by Location

Classification of stores according to location indicates the extent to which retail trade is concentrated or dispersed, and it is indicative of consumer buying habits. Stores are found in:

- Rural buying centers;
- Small cities or towns, in their downtown areas or in neighborhood locations; and
- Urban areas in a wide variety of specific types of locations.

The distribution of retail establishments and sales volume corresponds rather closely with the distribution of population and disposable personal income among the largest metropolitan areas, other metropolitan areas, and the remainder of the country. Somewhat fewer establishments are to be found in the largest metropolitan areas than would be expected on the basis of population and income, due to the location of many stores of unusually large size in such areas.

Sales volume is greater in the largest areas than would be expected on the basis of population, because of a tendency of major shopping goods stores to draw trade beyond the boundaries of the metropolitan area; it is less, however, than would be expected on the basis of income distribution, owing to a tendency for families of unusually high incomes (and with relatively low propensity to consume) to be concentrated in the largest population areas. The local character of retailing is well illustrated by the fact that outside of the 189 major metropolitan areas are to be found 43.0 per cent of the retail establishments, 32.7 per cent of the sales volume, 38.2 per cent of the population, and 30.3 per cent of the disposable personal income.

Retail trade has tended to become more localized than was formerly the case. Since 1929 the proportion of the total population residing in metropolitan areas has increased substantially, but the proportion of retail sales accounted for by such areas has remained constant. As a result, per capita retail sales in nonmetropolitan areas have risen faster than in metropolitan areas, and nonmetropolitan areas have become relatively more important as trade centers than would be expected on the basis of their population importance.

Among the plausible explanations for this situation are the following conditions:

- Changes in food purchasing patterns, reflecting increasing purchases of food store products for home use by farm families, and diminishing importance of home production for home use;
- Growing importance of brands as standards of value and increasing widespread distribution of most branded items of merchandise;
- Changes in consumer tastes and shopping habits which have tended to increase the number of items purchased on a local, or convenience, basis; and
- General decline of the attractiveness of shopping in the central retail districts of major cities.

The local nature of retailing is also demonstrated by the dispersion of sales volume within metropolitan areas. Between 1954 and 1959 the proportion of retail trade transacted within the main city of the ten largest metropolitan areas declined from 61.0 to 54.8 per cent while the proportion of total sales in the remainder of such areas (consisting primarily of suburban communities which accounted for most of the population growth of the period) increased from 39.0 to 45.2 per cent..

MAIL ORDER AND CATALOG RETAILING

The number of firms operating exclusively on a mail order basis is relatively small, but this method of operation is sufficiently widespread to justify detailed consideration. Moreover, it represents a distinctive way of doing business and illustrates the effect of changing conditions upon retailing institutions.

Types of Organizations

Four distinct types of organizations sell by mail. The most important are the general merchandise mail order houses which sell a great variety of consumer and farmer goods, carrying more items than are sold by any department store. Such companies are primarily retail institutions. They purchase the majority of their goods from manufacturers, although the two biggest companies in this field Sears, Roebuck & Company and Montgomery Ward & Company both control the manufacturing of many private brand items.

A second type consists of specialty retailers. Kinds of business in which specialty mail order operations by retailers is of some signficance include books, home furnishings, apparel and apparel accessories, food, and automotive accessories.

Manufacturers who sell by mail constitute the third type of mail order institution. Some such producers have found that their particular products can be sold directly to the consumer by mail without the use of wholesalers or retailers. The fourth type of mail order retailing is carried on by certain department and other large stores which accept orders by mail. Primarily confined to orders for merchandise currently advertised, this type of selling is a supplement to the receipt of orders over the telephone.

History of Mail Order Retailing

Mail order selling arose in a number of ways. Montgomery Ward & Company was founded in 1872 by a former clerk in Chicago who had also worked as a traveling salesman. The Patrons of Husbandry (the Grange) had established a number of cooperative stores and needed a wholesale connection. Mr. Ward saw the opportunity and started the business which still bears his name. The Grange stores were not generally successful so Mr. Ward's business was expanded into a mail order house to take advantage of good will among former members of the cooperative stores.

Sears, Roebuck & Company, the largest mail order firm, grew out of the efforts of Mr. Sears, a small-town station agent in Minnesota, to sell watches which had been shipped to his station on approval but rejected. The success of this venture led to a watch and jewelry mail order house in Minneapolis which was later moved to Chicago. The present large scale enterprise has grown from this small part..

Other general mail order houses had varied beginnings. Many have expanded from ordinary retail stores. Others started as specialty mail order houses and gradually expanded until they handled a more general line of merchandise.

Probably the most important reason for the success of the mail order houses in the early stages of their development is to be found in the failure of country merchants to adjust to changing conditions. In the post— Civil War period the country general store was a dominant institution. Throughout the West and South, farmers and small-town residents raised their standards of living after the period of reconstruction. Cash farm income became larger and farmers became interested in the kinds of things bought by city people. Rural and small-town merchants, however, did not appreciate such changes and continued to stock only staple merchandise which had sold well for many years. Even if such merchants had realized the significance of environmental change, the limitations of their small, local markets would have made it impossible for them to rival the assortments of the evolving mail order institution.

Another factor contributing to the development of mail order retailing was the growth of rail transportation. This made it possible to place orders by mail and to deliver merchandise to scattered areas at reasonable cost and at relatively certain dates.

The spectacular and consistent development of mail order retailing began, however, with the establishment of rural free delivery service. Farmers as a class began to subscribe for city daily papers. They were thus reached by style news and by information on various changing methods of life which before had come to their attention only indirectly.

Later, the moving pictures and the rotogravure supplements of the newspapers exercised their effect in creating demand for many articles not previously included in the rural standard of living. Mail order retailing offered an opportunity for the purchase of these goods. Developments in catalog making made it possible to advertise goods effectively and to supply realistic photographs. Establishment of the parcel post system in 1913 made it possible to ship small packages more economically. Another factor in the growth of mail order houses was the recognition that this method of selling could take advantage of the economies of large-scale retailing.

The larger mail order companies engaged in programs of diversification as the country became more urbanized and opened many retail establishments of the department store type. Such stores now account for the majority of the business of both Sears' and Ward's, but mail order or catalog retailing continues to be a very large segment of their total sales volume.

Present Status of Mail Order Establishments

In 1958 there were 2,550 retail mail order establishments, of which 1,502 had paid employees and 1,048 were small units operated exclusively by proprietors and family members. Aggregate sales volume of these establishments amounted to $20 billions, or about 1 per cent of the sales of all retail establishments. There has been practically no change in the relative sales volume importance of mail order establishments over the period 1929-58.

While the 2,550 mail order establishments operated in many lines of trade, more than 75 per cent of their sales was reported by only 35 large establishments handling a complete line of department store merchandise. More than one-half of these establishments are operated by two companies—Sears' and Ward's—thus indicating high concentration in this field.

Competitive Position of General Catalog Houses

The general merchandise mail order organizations have, in the main, the advantages and disadvantages of other large-scale retail enterprises. Due to the peculiar nature of their business, certain special conditions affect their competitive situation.

Advantages

As compared with single-line and general stores in the rural districts, mail order houses offer a more complete and varied line of merchandise. Their location in the larger cities gives a certain amount of prestige to their merchandise, especially in style goods. Prices, at least for many articles, are somewhat lower than those charged for corresponding articles in the rural communities. Buying from a catalog is perhaps quicker and easier for rural people than going to stores in somewhat distant cities, and such shopping can be done at any time of day or evening that is most convenient. Convenience, moreover, is a strong appeal among urban customers who patronize catalog order offices or telephone order facilities maintained by leading mail order companies in large cities. Absence of pressure to buy, avoidance of the confusion of crowded stores, informative statements concerning products, guaranties, and a liberal returned-goods policy are other attractions. Because sales are made in all sections of the country and to different classes of consumers, sales are not greatly affected by local industrial depressions, as are those of local merchants.

Some general advantages enjoyed by all mail order vendors grow out of certain operating economies. Warehouses are located in parts of the city where rent is much lower than that which must be paid by the ordinary retailer. Expensive fixtures are unnecessary, for only equipment of the warehouse type is required. It is unnecessary to employ retail salespeople, for the catalog descriptions plus the reputation of the firm and price appeals effect sales. Hence, employees of the clerical and shipping department type are used and their work is scheduled to permit an efficient utilization of time—something difficult to accomplish in retail stores which must be staffed in accordance with daily and hourly variations in consumer traffic.

Disadvantages

Selling by catalogs is limited by the impossibility of examining merchandise in advance of purchase. For shoes, gloves, or clothing, it may be difficult for the buyer to secure the right articles without trying them on for size and fit. Many consumers hesitate to order products where size, colour, style, or texture are significant in choice making.

An important limitation is inflexibility of the merchandising programme. Semi-annual catalogs published by Sears' and Ward's comprise between 1,000 and 2,000 pages. Plans must be made well in advance of the season as to the detailed composition of the line of goods and the manner in which they are to be featured and illustrated. More important, prices must be determined months before catalogs are distributed, and the firm usually must live with its pricing decisions throughout the catalog season.

While the catalogs contain statements that prices are subject to change without notice, and even though special sale catalogs are issued, the companies do not have the pricing flexibility of other forms of retailing. They cannot mark down individual items of merchandise as the rate of sale becomes too slow or as costs decline; neither can they raise prices on individual items as demand increases or as wholesale costs rise. New items can be added or dropped only when new catalogs are prepared.

Dynamic Adjustments in Catalog Retailing

The inception and period of rapid early development of mail order retailing was associated with the concept of a new merchandising service to the non urban population. In modern times, with contemporary conditions of communication, transportation, and urbanization, it is indeed remarkable that catalog retailing has been able to hold a stable share of total retail sales, thus growing at the same rate as all of retailing. This is attributed to certain dynamic, and in some cases distinctive, methods and policies adopted by the general catalog houses—in large measure for the purpose of capitalizing upon their advantages, minimizing their limitations, and adjusting to changing consumer preferences.

Sales promotion activities are efficiently organized. Mailing lists are prepared with care and efforts are made to keep them up to date. Careful tests are made of the success of different types of copy and appeals. Experienced copy writers know the language and the appeals which are most useful in reaching their clientele.

In order to overcome the reluctance of buyers to purchase articles which they cannot see before the order is placed, mail order houses give a very liberal guaranty, covering as a rule both quality and price. If the purchaser is dissatisfied with the commodity, it may be returned at the expense of the seller, and the purchase price is promptly refunded.

The general catalog houses have a special brand problem. To attract business, as they do in part, on a price-appeal basis, they must purchase from suppliers at lowest prices. For this reason such houses do not generally carry very many nationally advertised, branded articles. They prefer to sell unbranded commodities or those which carry their own brand. It is usually necessary to brand the specialties which they sell, in order to identify them and give them a certain distinction. Hence it is common for catalog houses to purchase such articles as vacuum sweepers, gasoline engines, washing machines, farm implements, cosmetics and drugs from suppliers who manufacture to the specifications of the catalog firm and who attach to the goods the private brand of the mail order company.

In order to reach a larger number of potential customers, the major firms have opened a large number of catalog order offices which are located in storerooms in hundreds of small cities and in many suburban shopping centers of large cities. No merchandise is available for sale over the counter in these establishments, but selected items and swatch and sample books are displayed for examination.

Employees assist customers to make out and transmit orders. Many such order offices have teletype communication with a regional warehouse which services the area. Orders received prior to a certain time each day can be delivered to the customer's home on the following day in most cities, thus rivaling the speed of delivery service available from local stores. Similar catalog departments are also found in the regular retail stores operated by mail order companies. In the typical Sears' store, the catalog order desk is usually the largest sales volume department.

Some catalog companies have expanded their customer contact points by establishing order stations in retail establishments operated by other companies. Certain small-town and cross-roads stores have displayed the general merchandise catalogs of some companies for a number of years, and accept and process orders on a commission basis. More recently some variety chains and supermarket organizations have made similar arrangements with mail order firms. For example, in 1960, Ward's established catalog order stations in certain New York state supermarkets of Loblaw, Inc., thus giving Ward's sales outlets in areas where it had no retail stores, and providing the Loblaw organization with a 100,000 item increase in its offering of nonfood merchandise lines.

Another feature is the operation of telephone order offices. While confined to larger cities in which there is a considerable potential volume of daily business, this development is one of increasing significance, accounting in 1960 for more than 30 per cent of all catalog sales volume at Sears'. The catalog customer can sit in her home, order by number from the catalog, have her order dispatched by teletype as explained above in connection with catalog order offices, and receive next-day delivery in many large cities.

As a consequence of such innovations, the historic *mail order business* has evolved into a more modern conception of *general catalog retailing*, characterized by efforts to bring to the consumer wanted merchandise at various points of sales contact, using means of communication and delivery which are appropriate to contemporary conditions.

Catalog Selling by Store Retailers and Manufacturers

Mail order selling is used to some extent by specialty retailers and by certain manufacturers who sell direct to the consumer. It is also used in the direct marketing of some farm products with a special appeal, such as Smoked Virginia Hams, smoked turkeys, and gift packages of fruit.

Such sellers usually do not have elaborate catalogs, but secure orders by advertising in newspapers and magazines, on radio and television broadcasts, and by direct mail addressed to the homes of consumers. Goods so ordered are shipped by parcel post, express, truck, or ordinary freight.

This type of selling brings many kinds of goods to the attention of a broad market. Items so sold are often of a novel or unusual character and are not available in local stores, especially in smaller communities. Some merchandise is sold direct to consumers by manufacturers who stress a price appeal. While specialty mail order retailing is relatively expensive, since it usually involves substantial advertising and handling and shipping costs, many consumers are nevertheless influenced by an appeal which suggests that they save money by purchasing direct rather than from a retail store.

Appeals of "lower prices," "greater values," or "substantial savings," have been used by most of the major book and record club companies that have a membership which is contacted by mail. Such savings are customarily offered in terms of "free" or "bonus" books, awarded when the member actually purchases a predetermined number of books at regular prices, in accordance with a membership agreement. Bonuses offered in this manner are largely due to low purchase prices negotiated with publishers when contracting for large numbers of copies and not to economies of selling and distributing to individual consumers on a mail order basis.

Manufacturers and retailers who sell a narrow line of goods by the mail order method are subject to most of the disadvantages enumerated above in connection with general catalog houses. In addition, they usually lack the prestige enjoyed by a large nationally known organization. Hence, such selling is relatively unimportant, and there are no reasons to believe that it will ever be of much significance in other than a very narrow range of merchandise items.

Catalog selling is also an important form of supplementary promotional effort among many regular *store retailers,* especially large department stores and departmentized specialty stores, who have a ready-made mailing list consisting of their regular charge account customers. This is especially significant for the promotion of gift merchandise during the Christmas shopping season.

LARGE-SCALE RETAILING

The antithesis of the small-scale retailer is illustrated by a variety of specific kinds of stores—the metropolitan department store, large departmentized stores in the apparel and home furnishings trades, mail order companies, large supermarkets and discount houses, and multiunit or chain organizations of many kinds. Each of these types has its unique problems and advantages, but all of them have attributes in common, to the extent that they arise out of scale of operation or size of enterprise. One of the most important advantages of scale is the elaborate *division of labour* that results from specialization in effort. Size permits employment of experts for executive positions. Skilled buyers, advertising managers, accountants, statisticians, and personnel directors are all at the command of such big businesses. Large firms can usually afford *extensive departmentization.* By carefully classifying merchandise and creating departments for the sale of particular lines of merchandise or for more specific appeal to differentiated groups of customers, management enjoys not only advantages of specialization on the part of buyers and salespeople but is also facilitated in discovery of profitable and unprofitable classes of goods and in a more accurate measurement of the efficiency of department or store managers.

A most important competitive advantage is *large buying power.* Since purchases are large and hence important to suppliers, large-scale retailers can often circumvent the wholesaler in an economical manner and, by so doing, can obtain the most favorable prices. Not only are large discounts from list prices secured when big quantities are purchased, but other concessions, such as advertising allowances, exclusive rights for distribution, or free goods, may also be obtained. While manufacturers' freedom to quote more favorable prices to large buyers has been somewhat limited by legislation, particularly the Robinson-Patman Act, large-scale retailers remain in a position to purchase on much more favorable terms than their smaller rivals on purely economic grounds. Further buying advantages are realized through ability to employ experts to perform this function.

The *financial strength* of large institutions often attracts investors and facilitates the acquisition of capital for expansion. Size is an advantage in making banking connections which may enable the borrower to secure loans on favorable terms. Large financial resources make it possible to take advantage of cash discounts offered by sellers and to attract vendors who may be led to offer especially favorable terms of sale.

Large retailers have the ability to *command the most favorable locations.* Many leases in retailing involve rental payments calculated as a per cent of sales volume. In such cases, the large firm, with a demonstrated capacity to generate substantial volume, is generally a preferred tenant. Shopping centre developers prefer to obtain leases from large, financially strong companies because such leases can be used as security in obtaining loans from banks, insurance companies, and other sources of capital for shopping centre construction.

Many large-scale retailers achieve operating economies or derive additional income from the *integration of other business activities* with retail merchandising. Many chains, department stores, and mail order companies have established their own warehouses which are operated on an efficient scale and in which are performed the distributive functions of the regular wholesaler, with the exception of personal selling activities which are largely eliminated between these two levels in the channel of distribution.

Outright ownership or control of manufacturing plants is not uncommon among large organizations in the apparel, general merchandise, and food trades. Some retailing corporations have subsidiary companies which perform essentially a banking service by financing accounts receivables for the parent organizations. Real estate developments, particularly of the planned shopping centre type, are also integrated into the operation of some department store groups and food chains, usually by means of separately incorporated subsidiaries.

The *prestige* which results, in part at least, from the great size of the leading chain, department store, and mail order companies is a distinct advantage in attracting patronage. The reputation of such firms is well established, either because of a long history in a given location or the publicity associated with their operations on a widespread geographic basis. This prestige, when accompanied with integration, is particularly suitable for the promotion of private brands of merchandise. All forms of large-scale retailing benefit from a certain amount of *risk distribution.* Customers are drawn from large areas or many different lines are sold. The organization can usually assimilate severe losses in some departments or operating units, without greatly impairing the profitmaking possibilities of the entire organization. Finally, *experimentation and research* represent types of activity which may prove most effective in increasing efficiency and which, while practical for the large retailer, may be too expensive to be undertaken by his smaller competitors.

Inherent Disadvantages

The unfavorable factors incident to large-scale retailing are less numerous than the advantages and for that reason may be stated much more briefly. This should not, however, lead to an underestimation of their importance, because it is these disadvantages that contribute a great deal toward explaining the significance of small-scale operation in our retailing structure. Furthermore, each of the various forms of large-scale retailing has some disadvantages that are peculiar to it, but which are not discussed at this point.

A major weakness of large companies lies in the *absence of close personal contact between the owners or general managers and the consuming public.* Most consumers meet only the rank and file of subordinate employees, rarely the owners or major executives. While the self-interest of routine workers, together with their training and supervision, may produce some measure of efficiency, hired managers usually function with less effectiveness than do the more able owners of small businesses with their sharpened personal interest in customers.

Another disadvantage consists of *high overhead costs arising out of the complex organization structures* of large-scale enterprises. Some advantages of specialization are offset by lack of close contact between top management and subordinates and may have unfavorable effects upon efficiency. Larger concerns ordinarily have a much greater proportion of nonselling employees than smaller retail organizations.

Much nonselling labour results from the need for costly methods of recording and checking the activities of the various divisions and maintaining the minute supervision necessary to fix responsibility, check performance, and minimize waste.

Legal Limitations

Belief in small business as a manifestation of the American way of life has had an important bearing upon the history of trade legislation. Numerous enactments have been designed to curb some of the buying power and other advantages of large organizations and to provide, thereby, legal methods of balancing the competitive situation between the large and the small. Noteworthy are the Robinson-Patman Act, and fair trade and unfair trade practices legislation designed to curb uneconomic price-cutting tactics.

The Robinson-Patman Act.

It is important to note briefly how such legislation operates to limit large organizations. The Robinson-Patman Act, a federal law enacted in 1936, represents an attempt to curb certain uneconomic advantages of large retailers, which they enjoyed merely because of large size and great purchasing power. Numerous instances are on record in which large-scale buyers have more or less compelled manufacturers to sell to them at prices much lower than paid by wholesalers who supply small independent merchants. Supporters of this legislation contend that such manufacturers must then charge wholesalers or independent retailers a higher than normal price to compensate for abnormally low prices given to large-scale buyers.

To prevent unjustifiable differences in prices, the Act makes it unlawful for sellers to discriminate in price between different buyers (of the same type or class) on goods of like grade and quality where the effect of such discrimination may be substantially to lessen competition, to tend to create a monopoly, to injure, destroy, or prevent competition. In substance, the law provides that *only those price discriminations are allowed which are justified by differences in cost to the vendor* or when done *in good faith to meet the lower price of a competitor.*

Thus, in many instances large retailers are deprived of the sizable discounts and other price concessions which they once enjoyed. In some cases, however, a manufacturer may show that his economies in selling to large buyers are greater than the discounts given, but in general the effect has been to reduce the buying advantage of the large firms.

Because of their great importance to resources, large retailers have been able to secure substantial advertising allowances. Numerous manufacturers follow a policy of advertising cooperatively with their retail outlets, with part of the cost paid by the manufacturers.

This established practice usually works to the benefit of both parties and is above criticism. Objections arise not from the nature of the practice but from its abuse in the form of unjustified discrimination. Chains and large department stores were able to secure substantial advertising allowances from many companies which did not grant such allowances to small independents. In essence, such discrimination amounts to a subsidization of the big retailer's advertising programme at the expense of independents who are not able to obtain comparable discounts.

A second major provision of the Act attempted to prevent this kind of discrimination by *prohibiting advertising and all other forms of sales promotional or service allowances, unless they are made available on proportionally equal terms to all customers.* It is perfectly legal for a manufacturer to give a large buyer an advertising allowance amounting, for example, to 3 per cent of such buyer's purchases, but it cannot do this *legally* without making the same percentage allowance available to all customers. Another practice curbed by the Act pertains to brokerage fees. Numerous manufacturers cannot support their own sales force and hence employ brokers who also serve other manufacturers. In performing the selling function for the manufacturer, the broker renders a valuable service for which he is entitled to reasonable compensation. Many large chains and department store buying offices set up subsidiary purchasing companies which were, in effect, *dummy* brokerage offices. Retailers required manufacturers to sell through these subsidiaries and grant to them the usual brokerage fee.

In such an instance, the dummy brokerage office is not a representative of the seller, but rather an agent of the purchaser. As a purchasing company seeking out sources of supply, it would be logical to expect that it should be compensated by the buyer rather than the seller. When an organization owned by a buyer obtains a brokerage fee from a seller whom it does not serve, this merely amounts to an unjustified price discrimination, because other purchasers must pay the manufacturer's factory price with perhaps a brokerage fee *added* rather than *deducted.*

A third major provision of the Robinson-Patman Act was designed to *prohibit sellers of merchandise from paying brokerage fees to other than their own agents.* A broker may only collect a commission or fee when he acts as a bona fide third party, rather than as an employee of the buyer, for services rendered to the principal who pays the fee.

These provisions do not curb any *economic* advantages of large-scale retailers. To the extent that a seller can deal with a large buyer at lower costs of marketing than encountered when dealing with small independents, he can give a lower price. The large retailer can still obtain advertising allowances, but only if the allowances are made available to all of the vendor's customers on proportionally equal terms.

It cannot obtain brokerage fees for itself, but this does not place it at a disadvantage with respect to small merchants. The effect of the Robinson-Patman Act has been substantially that of restricting *power* advantages of giant retailers, that is, benefits that they once enjoyed to a high degree because of ability to secure concessions by coercion. It does not penalize them through curbing any natural advantages they enjoy *because of ability to perform marketing functions in a more efficient and economical manner.*

State Pricing Legislation

In many states, laws have been enacted which limit pricing freedom, thereby restricting the price appeal and price-cutting tactics of some merchants, primarily in the large-scale classification. Other laws place restrictions on price discrimination in *intrastate commerce.*

The best known of these are the so-called *fair trade* laws. The first such law was enacted in California in 1931, for the purpose of putting a floor under the resale prices of the branded items of manufacturers that chose to operate under this type of law. Eventually, 45 states passed similar laws, and they were legalized in interstate commerce originally by the Miller-Tydings Act of 1937 and later also by the McGuire Act of 1952.

These laws became highly controversial in the 1950's. Constitutionality was challenged in the court systems of most states, and judicial opinion was approximately equally divided regarding the constitutionality of such laws, either in entirety or in regard to some major provision. In 1961 some 26 states still had fully operative fair trade laws with respect to nonsigners, as explained below.

Fair trade laws permit the manufacturer of a branded item to set the minimum, or in some cases the actual, price which must be observed by retailers in reselling such merchandise. To establish a resale price under the state laws, a manufacturer must ordinarily obtain a contract with one retailer who agrees to maintain the resale price. In most states, the price is then binding on all other retailers as soon as they are notified of the agreement. Fair trade legislation has been described by opponents as "handicap competition."

It has been compared with a cross-country race in which handicaps are placed on the swiftest, to assure equality of opportunity for retail contestants of varying strengths vying for consumer acceptance in the market place. Protagonists, on the other hand, attribute to it all the qualities that make for healthy competitive business enterprise.

Regardless of the intent, these laws have been widely utilized in only a few lines of trade. Although effectiveness has been limited, they have enabled some small merchants to compete on more nearly equal terms, in sale of fair-traded items, with price-cutting competitors.

While fair trade laws are only permissive, that is, they merely allow a brand owner to operate under them if he so elects, there are so-called *unfair trade practices acts* which are mandatory. Some 31 states have enacted such legislation and it was still operative in 1961 in 27 states where constitutionality has been upheld or uncontested.

These laws directly prohibit sales below cost, or sales below cost plus some designated per cent of markup. Also, some 26 states have laws prohibiting "sales below cost" of specifically designated products (e.g., cigarettes, liquors and malt beverages, dairy products) which are commonly used as "leaders" by price-cutting stores.

About one-half of the states have specific *price discrimination laws* which are in essence state Robinson-Patman Acts. They prohibit price discrimination such as is forbidden in the federal law but apply, of course, only to transactions in intrastate commerce.

The net effect of the federal and state trade legislation has been to curb buying advantages incident to mass purchasing power and to render it more difficult for large retailers to engage in price-cutting practices designed to make consumers believe they have tremendous operating advantages over independent merchants. Large organizations, however, have not been the only price cutters. This practice has been important among some small independent merchants, and the laws apply to them with equal force. Because of limited buying power, somewhat higher operating costs, and less emphasis upon price appeal among independents as a class, the laws are to be regarded primarily as limitations to large-scale operations.

FITURE OF E- RETAILING

CONSUMER BUYING DECISION PROCESS

A potential e-consumers buying decision process will follow the established stages of need recognition, information search, information evaluation, purchase decision and post-purchase behaviour.

Need Recognition

An e-retail website is a combination of the traditional store display window, information desk, stocked display shelving, mood lighting/sound, promotional material that shout out specials, and the time-honoured *barker/ spruiker* used to stimulate shopping interest. Such an e-retail site ought to elicit a need recogni tion response from any visitor to the site.

A new or returning visitor should be treated to a combination of the four basic marketing elements - *price* (e.g. specials, discounts, interest free periods), *product* (e.g. new lines, clearance items, seasonal products, fashion and fad limited ranges), *promotion* (e.g. sales, seasonal specials, select shopper campaigns) and *distribution* (e.g. free delivery, lay-away, home installation) that accentuate the visitor's own need identification.

Technology within the website, for example cookie files, captures data about the visitor's responses and what information was accessed. Such information then enables e-retailers to improve the rapport with the online customer by tailoring the site content to consumer demand. One positive application from such data collection is the inclusion of customer loyalty programs that encourage return visitation to the e-retailer site and increased purchases.

Information Search

Improved telecommunications technology and general population access to the Internet have transformed user availability to customization of, and digestion of, large information volumes. Unlike the bricks and mortar retailer, an e-retail site has the facilities to make available such large volumes of information in a customized format to meet the immediate and potential queries of site visitors following the need recognition stage.

Without personal embarrassment or the self-consciousness of asking a stranger (e.g. a shopkeeper) what may be an obvious or foolish product-related question, the e-retail site visitor can access online product brochures, price comparisons, frequently asked questions (FAQs), suggested product applications, cleaning and repair information, and an efficient search engine technology, as well as asking for specialized information via the e-retailer's e-mail system.

Information Evaluation

When seeking to evaluate the collected information on products and services, the potential shopper will often turn to the experiences and advice of family, friends and persons who have already experienced use of such merchandise.

Also, e-retailing gives the user added facilities to access evaluative experts and previous users of the merchandise in question to aid in the digestion and customization of all this information.

Many consumer groups act as such reference experts through the testing and personal evaluations of retailed products and then make these findings available to others. Experienced e-retailers encourage interactions between previous, current and future shoppers by way of:

- Online discussion groups.
- Suggesting site visitors rate the available merchandise.
- Suggesting site visitors express comments about this merchandise and the service exchange experiences.

Monitoring of the online discussions and visitor comments endows the retailer with invaluable knowledge regarding merchandise features and limitations that may be incorporated into promotional materials. To conclude, apart from all the benefits mentioned above, the e-retailer gains all this free information that would normally require expensive market research.

Purchase Decision

After a visitor to an e-retailer site has determined the merchandise to be appropriate for their needs, it is still not a certainty that this visitor will finalize a purchase. Commonly, an online customer nominates particular merchandise from an e-retail website and places those items in the online *shopping cart* (also known as a *shopping trolley*) for the checkout, but later the customer discontinues the purchase process and leaves the e-retailer's site. This action of discontinuing an online purchase is termed 'abandoned cart syndrome;

- A lower level of education.
- Higher frequency of Web purchases.
- Greater concern of online data risk and fraud.
- Greater frequency of website service problems.
- The use of shopping as a facility to see family and friends.
- High levels of concern about online retailers' tracking data.
- Younger buying groups.

- Shopping causing little arousal.
- Higher frequency of browsing for a later purchase.
- Higher fashion consciousness.
- Higher frequency of Web search for product information.

Although the e-retailer cannot yet duplicate the human interactions possible in a physical store setting, e-retailers may still empower customers in an attempt to reduce the incidence of online cart abandonment. One positive step to improve the e-retailer's customer interactions is streamlining the order process by:

- Making improvements in the e-retailer's site navigation.
- Incorporation of help links and interactive facilities to stimulate the shopper's arousal and fashion consciousness.
- Supplying the relevant merchandise information as needed.
- Greater use of online help facilities and screen prompts.
- Establishing chat rooms and customer discussion opportunities to share experience with family, friends and new acquaintances.
- Improved guarantees (including deliveries, data security, 30-day trials).
- Offline contact details (phone number, fax number, street address).

Post-purchase Behaviour

The key to a retailer's survival and success whether offline or online is to generate repeat purchase behaviour. For a customer to return to a retailer that customer needs to have confidence in the retailer, but e-retailer confidence is often difficult to establish in light of online issues that have caused customers to make complaints and/or never return to the e-retailer. According to Cho *et al.* (2002), the online issues that often alienate customers and lead to complaints are the failure to meet customer *expectations* in relation to:

Merchandise offerings.

The e-retailer's store-front technology (this includes, but is not limited to, the website) that integrates:

- Usability of the technology;
- The technology failing to carry out a function.

The e-retailer's information sources (the policies).

Payment/settlement issues;

- Agreed conditions (including delivery timing).

To reduce the chance of customer expectations being unfulfilled, e-retailers will compensate for the lack of a face-to-face exchange by making available more information details than would otherwise be considered in a bricks and mortar environment. Dealing with each of the Cho *et al.* (2002) points, we suggest the following responses:

Merchandise offerings:

- Define all dimensions of the size options, colour variations, and accessories provided. One suggestion is to include the supply of actual colour swatches to reduce the colour errors often attributed to variations on computer colour monitors.

The e-retailer's store-front technology (this includes, but is not limited to the website):

- Provide sufficient technology to cope with peak buying periods such as St Valentine's Day and Mother's Day.
- Keep redundant backup to take over when systems fail.
- Offer facilities to store (file) partial orders for future use should the customer be interrupted and/or wish to continue the shopping process in the near future.
- Provide improved access facilities for the disabled/impaired computer user. Facilities may consist of:
  - Selectable larger display fonts;
  - Voice recognition commands;
  - Spoken responses embedded in the web pages;
  - Written descriptions of displayed images (these can be read out to the non-sighted user even if they can't see the picture).
- Alerts given by the e-retailer's site to advise users:
  - Pending specials;
  - Replenishment of merchandise that was out of stock;
  - Arrival of special orders.
- Such alerts can reach the user through e-mail, phone short message service (SMS), automated faxing or other communications technologies.

The e-retailer's information sources (the policies):

- Information is to be detailed (even exhaustive), accurate and timely (not noticeably out of date).
- Information is to be easy to find on the e-retailer site.
- Links to relevant or 'just interesting' sites shall establish the e-retail not only as an appropriate purchasing site but as a point of reference or portal for future enquiries in this area; thereby achieving a great milestone: being bookmarked as a favourite site in the user's Web browsing software.
- A continued customer relationship should be maintained after a purchase by:
  - Continued updates on the relevant and near-relevant issues by e-mail or newsgroup (for example, a customer purchases an electric grill and then receives a monthly recipe; the e-retailer keeps the contact and the customer's satisfaction in the purchase is supported);
  - Space may also be sold to sponsors seeking to promote their products.

Payment/settlement issues:

- Not all customers want to reveal their personal details and movements to online parties. To aid these potential customers, e-retailers can now provide alternatives for the customer in the shopping cycle to minimize risk.
  In Australia, a purchaser using the Wishlist retailer (www.wishlist.com.au) may opt to have their online purchases delivered to a participating BP petrol service station rather than to their home address. In this way the customer picks up the merchandise at a time that suits and conceals their personal address details while still gaining the advantages of shopping online.
- Most courier organizations (i.e. DHL and FedEx) used by e-retailers have facilities for the purchaser to trace and track the merchandise while it is in transit. The e-retailer receives proof the item is 'on its way' and the client achieves the peace of mind of 'seeing' where the item is any time they go online.

Index